This book may be

Famous Soviet Spies

THE KREMLIN'S SECRET WEAPON

Famous Soviet Spies

THE KREMLIN'S SECRET WEAPON

Books by
U.S.News & World Report

Joseph Newman—Directing Editor

A division of U.S.News & World Report, Inc.
Washington, D. C.

Permissions

Contents

Appendix V

Illustrations

Photographs

11

Charts

Maps

Acknowledgments

The editors express their appreciation to *Dewitt Copp* for his help in researching and writing the text of this book.

Judy Lowy edited the text and supervised the preparation of the manuscript.

A word of appreciation is also due to officials in the Federal Bureau of Investigation and the Subcommittee to Investigate the Administration of the Internal Security Act of the Committee on the Judiciary, United States Senate, and to the many archivists and librarians who helped in collecting the material for the manuscript.

Introduction

Throughout history all nations have resorted to espionage in an attempt to learn the military and political secrets of their enemies or potential enemies. We find an early intelligence operation described in the Bible. The Lord told Moses to send agents to "spy out the land of Canaan." Moses directed his spies to "see the land, what it is; and the people that dwelleth therein, whether they be strong or weak, few or many." In the fifth century B. C., Sun Tzu, a Chinese philosopher, wrote that "foreknowledge is the reason the enlightened prince and the wise general conquer the enemy whenever they move. What is called 'foreknowledge' cannot be elicited from spirits, nor from gods, nor by analogy with past events, nor from calculations. It must be obtained from men who know the enemy situation. Hence the use of spies. . . ."

Thus there is nothing surprising about the fact that Russians engage in espionage. They spy on us, and we spy on them. That having been said and recognized, the difference between the Soviet Union and other countries in their practice of espionage is so great that it can be ignored only at the peril of the free countries of the world. The difference lies in the objectives, the scope, and the techniques of espionage operations.

Generally speaking, with some exceptions, the espionage objective of the United States and its allies is defensive—to learn of any aggressive plans being prepared by their enemies and, if possible, to thwart them. The objective of the Soviet Union is also defensive, but it is much more than that. It is offensive. And the scope of this offensive character of Soviet espionage extends to every country because it is intimately related to the declared Soviet aim of creating a Communist world over which the Kremlin would preside. In pursuing this aim, the Kremlin feels justified in expanding the conventional defensive scope of its espionage operations to the point where they become subversive operations. The intention is not only to weaken an enemy but also to undermine his government and to ripen his country for a Communist takeover. To the extent that it is political and ideological, Soviet espionage represents a threat to every country.

And the threat of Soviet intervention applies to Communist as well as non-Communist countries. Immediately after World War II, when Tito established a Communist state in Yugoslavia, Stalin began dispatching an increasing number of agents to Belgrade for the purpose of infiltrating every branch of the new government. Tito soon realized that his rule was being undermined. He could choose between being nibbled to death by an army of Soviet spies and gambling on survival by expelling the spies and facing the danger of direct Soviet military intervention. He took the latter course and won his gamble.

In more recent years, Dubcek was less fortunate in Czechoslovakia. When Soviet agents failed to hold the Czech leader in line, the Kremlin sent its tanks into Czechoslovakia and installed a new government there. This provided the occasion for proclaiming the so-called "Brezhnev doctrine." The essence of this doctrine is that Moscow has the right to enter any country which it considers to be a threat to its leadership of the international Communist community.

Above all other countries, Communist China today feels menaced by this Soviet doctrine. And there appears to be ground for its fears. The flight and demise of Lin Piao, heir apparent to Mao Tse-tung, have been related to a Soviet conspiracy to overthrow Mao's government and to install one subservient to Moscow.

The concluding chapter of this book relates the attempts by Soviet agents to organize subversive movements which would overthrow existing governments and install Soviet satellite regimes in Mexico and Bolivia. These occurred as recently as 1971 and 1972, when the Kremlin presumably was moving toward "friendlier relations" with the United States. The Bolivian foreign minister, commenting on the attempted Soviet coup, said that Moscow had offered his country peace and trade on the one hand, while supporting guerrilla warfare on the other.

This dual policy is particularly disturbing to those countries which would like to believe that "Communist" and "capitalist" states can coexist peacefully and even achieve long-term cordial relations. The recent experience of Britain raises serious doubts as to whether the Soviet regime, as structured at present, is capable of freeing itself from its dual policy of seeking to undermine a country while establishing friendly relations with it.

On December 3, 1970, British Foreign Secretary Alec Douglas-Home sent a personal letter to his opposite number in Moscow, Foreign Minister Andrei Gromyko, pointing out that Soviet espionage in Britain had reached such proportions as to endanger their mutual efforts to establish closer relations between Britain and the Soviet Union. He appealed to Gromyko to do something about this situation. Gromyko did not reply. However, at a meeting with a British official in Moscow, Gromyko complained that British interference with the activities of Soviet agents in the United Kingdom was hampering "creation of a favorable atmosphere for the development of Anglo-Soviet relations."

On August 4, 1971, in another letter to Gromyko, Sir Alec rejected the suggestion that "Her Majesty's Government should allow these intelligence agents of yours to conduct their activities in the United Kingdom unhampered lest Anglo-Soviet relations should suffer." He again called on Gromyko to terminate rampant Soviet espionage operations in Britain. This letter, too, was ignored by Gromyko. The following month the British government announced the expulsion of 105 Soviet diplomats and representatives operating as spies in the United Kingdom—the largest single mass expulsion of Soviet spies in recent history.

At a time when President Nixon and his aides are seeking better relations with the Soviet Union, the unanswered letters of Sir Alec have special meaning for the American people. The question arises as to whether the Soviet price for friendlier relations is to include a free hand for Soviet agents to operate in the United States. In that event, under the favorable conditions of "friendly relations," the Russians might look forward to even greater successes than those achieved by the famous espionage operations described in this book.

Youngsters of school age may never have heard such names as Richard Sorge, the greatest spy of the twentieth century; Igor Gouzenko, the defector whose revelations contributed to the exposure of Klaus Fuchs, Allen Nunn May, Bruno Pontecorvo, the Rosenbergs, and others who stole atomic secrets for the Soviet Union; Bogdan Stashynsky, the assassin who revealed the terror tactics employed by the KGB; and Rudolph Abel, who became known as the "Master Spy." Their elders have only the vaguest recollection of these agents. The following chapters should help inform the uninformed and refresh the memories of those who may have forgotten the skill of the Soviet Union in the art of espionage and the danger it represents to the United States, whatever the state of our relations with the Soviet Union.

CHAPTER ONE

GRU and KGB
The Eyes and Ears of the Soviet State

In Russia, the tradition of a powerful secret police goes back to the Czars, who depended for survival on the Okhrana (the secret police). The present-day leaders of the Soviet Union owe their existence in large part to the secret intelligence services.

In their rise to power, the revolutionaries in Russia had developed intelligence techniques to an unprecedented degree. From days of the prerevolutionary underground on, the Communist leaders were the world's most astute and professional spies. Secrecy was their way of life; conspiracy was as necessary to them as the air they breathed; espionage was an essential weapon to be used in advancing world communism.

In the early twenties, before organization caught up with fervor, there were six different organs of the Soviet government operating separate espionage networks in foreign countries. The People's Commissariat for War, under Leon Trotsky, established an intelligence agency of its own; the Foreign Office, under Chicherin and Litvinov, gathered secret information from its representatives abroad; the Third International (Comintern), whose membership was made up of Communist parties all over the world, had a global network of underground cells which collected information; the Central Committee of the Communist Party of the Soviet Union set up secret espionage organizations; the People's Commissariat for Foreign Trade passed on information through its trade legations; and the

Cheka organized intelligence operations in the capitals of the world.

By the mid-twenties, however, two organizations were carrying on most of the espionage operations: the Intelligence Department of the General Staff of the Army and the Foreign Department of the Secret Police. Today these organizations, one military and one civilian, direct all Soviet espionage. They are called the GRU and the KGB.

Soviet Military Intelligence was organized by Leon Trotsky in 1918 as a bureau of the General Staff of the Red Army. It became known as the GRU—*Glavnoye Razvedyvatelnoye Upravlenie*—the Chief Intelligence Directorate of the General Staff, also referred to as the Fourth Bureau. The GRU operates under the supervision of the Central Committee of the Communist party of the Soviet Union. Its primary missions are strategic intelligence, operational intelligence, and battle intelligence. There are six major divisions within the GRU. The first four deal with espionage on a global scale, the fifth is responsible for diversion and sabotage operations, and the sixth controls intelligence along the Soviet Union's borders. There is also an information directorate which processes, evaluates, and passes on the intelligence received.

In 1940, the Soviet navy established its own much smaller intelligence branch.

Soviet State Security, the secret police intelligence agency established in 1921 under the direction of Felix Dzerzhinski, was an outgrowth of the Cheka. The name stands for "Extraordinary Commission Against Counterrevolution and Sabotage." Created in December, 1917, as a security organization with executive powers, the Cheka was a terroristic police force. In its militant effort to "fight counterrevolution," its assigned task, the Cheka ruthlessly liquidated all civilians accused of "bourgeois origins." In 1921, the Cheka established a foreign arm, since by that time White Russian *emigrés* had fled to Western Europe. In 1922, the Cheka was reorganized into the GPU—the State Political Administration. In 1924, the GPU became the OGPU, which was made a department of the NKVD (the People's Commissariat for Internal Affairs) in 1934.

Over the next twenty years, the names of the intelligence organizations changed several times. The NKVD was divided into two ministries: the Ministry of State Security and the Ministry of Internal Affairs. Later, the two ministries were reconsolidated. After the execution of its chief, Lavrenti Beria, the Ministry of State Security was set up as a separate organization called the Committee for State Security—*Komitat Gosudarstvennoi Bezopastnosti*—or KGB. Since May 19, 1967, the director of the KGB has been Yuri A. Andropov.

Yuri V. Andropov, chief of Russia's KGB espionage system (extreme right, top row), sits directly behind Leonid Brezhnev, top Soviet leader, at a Kremlin meeting being addressed by V. Grishin, first secretary of the Moscow Communist Party.

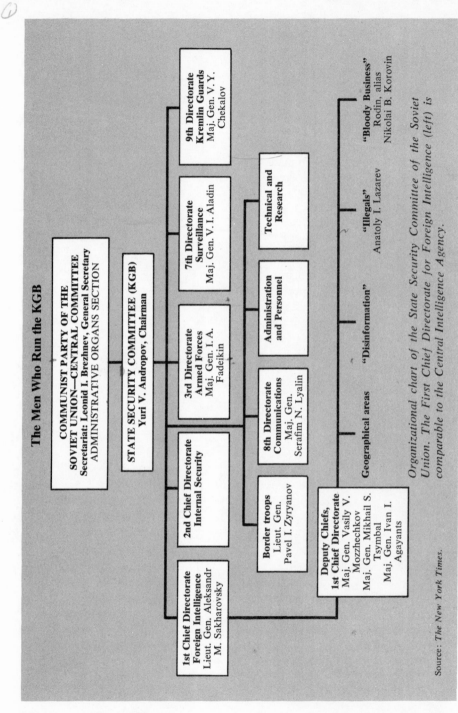

Organizational chart of the State Security Committee of the Soviet Union. The First Chief Directorate for Foreign Intelligence (left) is comparable to the Central Intelligence Agency.

Source: *The New York Times.*

Originally, the GRU was slated to be the principal intelligence agency of the Soviet Union. However, the KGB's dual role of internal as well as external spying has made it far more powerful than the GRU. Former CIA Director Allen Dulles called the KGB the "eyes and ears of the Soviet state abroad as well as at home." He went on to describe it as "a multi-purpose, clandestine arm of power that can in the last analysis carry out almost any act that the Soviet leadership assigns to it. It is more than a secret police organization, more than an intelligence and counterintelligence organization. It is an instrument for subversion, manipulation, and violence, for secret intervention in the affairs of other countries. It is an aggressive arm of Soviet ambitions in the Cold War. If the Soviets send astronauts to the moon, I expect that a KGB officer will accompany them." [1]

Although all countries have been targets of Soviet espionage, the Kremlin has, at various times, focused on one country or another as the *glavni vrag*—the main enemy. In the beginning, Soviet efforts were directed against Poland and Roumania; later France became the main target. In the period before World War II, Japan was the *glavni vrag,* followed by Germany. In 1943, the United States became the main enemy.

Since the end of World War II, public disclosures in almost every non-Communist country have proved the continuing scope of Soviet espionage by both GRU and KGB. The recent exposures of 105 Soviet agents in Great Britain and 39 in Belgium gave some indication of the numbers involved. Estimates vary as to the number of KGB and GRU agents engaged in espionage outside the Soviet Union, but 250,000 would be a fair approximation. The annual KGB budget is estimated by Western Intelligence to run around $2 billion. [2] This figure covers the cost of maintaining spies on the ground, but does not include expenditures for the electronic satellites in the air.

The USSR also utilizes the intelligence departments of its East European satellites. The FBI estimates that between 70 and 80 percent of all Soviet and Soviet bloc personnel assigned to missions in the United States are engaged in some form of intelligence activity. As of February 1, 1972, there were 1,166 such personnel.

The activities of some of these Soviet agents are described in the following chapters. They present a comprehensive view of the massive intelligence operations conducted by the Soviet Union in different parts of the world.

CHAPTER TWO

The Journalist
Richard Sorge –The Spy Who Tricked Hitler

Although few could perceive it at the time, 1933 was the year the world turned a corner and set a course toward war.

In Germany, Hitler was installed as chancellor on January 30, 1933; by the end of the year Germany had walked out of the League of Nations and the October Disarmament Conference.

Japan had left the League early in the year, refusing to accept continuing criticism of its occupation of Manchuria in 1931 and its attack on Shanghai in 1932.

Between an aggressive Germany in the West and a militant Japan in the East lay the Soviet Union. In 1933, Soviet fears were focused on Japan. The long-standing antagonism between the two countries had been fueled by the Japanese move into Manchuria, which Stalin viewed as a threat to the Russian sphere of influence.

Thus, in 1933, the leaders of the Soviet Union believed that the future of their country was tied to actions in the Far East, and they were extremely anxious to know the plans and intentions of a Japan that appeared to be aggressively on the move.

* * * * *

Four of the five came to Japan under orders, traveling by different routes, arriving at different times. The fifth was already there, unaware of the part he would play.

Of the four, Branko de Voukelitch, the Yugoslav, arrived first, on February 11, 1933. As a special correspondent for the French pictorial magazine *La Vue* and the Yugoslav daily *Politica,* his cover as a newsman and photographer was secure. To further assure it, he brought his stolid Danish wife, Edith, and their small son, Paul.

Slight, scholarly looking, balding, Branko de Voukelitch possessed charm and intelligence. Because of his military bearing the Japanese took him for a German, and he settled in their midst—a twenty-nine-year-old journalist whose loyalty to the Soviet Union was unquestioning.

In his student days, Voukelitch had been involved in the Communist movement in Yugoslavia. Later, he had joined the Communist party in France. He had contributed articles to the Comintern publication *Inprecorr.* But he had never been a spy, and it was only after considerable persuasion by a woman he knew as Baltic Olga, who was an officer in the covert section of the Comintern, that he agreed to accept the job.

His mission, Olga told him, was to report events as a journalist and to analyze them as a Marxist. He was instructed to move into the Bunka Apartments in the Hong-ku section of Tokyo and to establish his cover as a journalist, while waiting to be contacted by a man named Schmidt. Before his departure in late December, 1932, Voukelitch was supplied with a small sum of money and given the code name of Gigolo. Believing that he was working for the Comintern, he remained totally unaware that his espionage assignment had been mapped out by the Soviet Army's Fourth Bureau (GRU), then under the command of General Jan K. Berzin.

At that time, GRU was still *the* official Soviet espionage agency. The first chief of GRU, Berzin, was an astute organizer and a keen tactician who had risen swiftly through Red Army ranks. Prematurely gray, he was nicknamed *Starik,* which means old man.

On a day in January, 1933, Berzin welcomed home one of his agents who had recently returned from three years of operation out of Shanghai. The agent had headed a very successful ring, reporting on Chinese internal affairs as well as on Sino-Japanese relations. To some in his *apparat,* he had been known as Johnson, an American newspaperman, while to the Chinese authorities and others he had been Schmidt, a German journalist. Berzin and his colleagues knew him as Dr. Richard Sorge, a top Soviet spy.

Thirty-eight at the time of his reunion with Jan Berzin, Sorge, with his arresting manner and compelling face, was a romantic, attractive figure. Broad-shouldered, tall, with a thick mop of light brown hair, he moved gracefully, although with a slight limp, which was a result of wounds suffered in World War I. He was a consummate actor. Men liked him and women found him irresistible. A hard drinker and an adventurer, he was, at the same time, a student and an intellectual. Possessed by a ferocious drive to know as much as possible about any given area of operation, he read and wrote voluminously. When Berzin asked him at their meeting what he wanted to do next, he said, "I want to finish a book I've been doing on Chinese agriculture."

He was born on October 4, 1895, near Baku in Russia. His mother was Russian, his father a German engineer, and his grandfather had been, at one time, a close associate of Karl Marx. The Sorges moved to Berlin before the outbreak of World War I, and Richard enjoyed a comfortable, middle-class childhood.

World War I completely changed Sorge's life. Wounded three times in the trenches, he became disillusioned with a society which had plunged him into the nightmare of war. He turned to Marxism. The success of the Soviet Revolution excited him so much that by January, 1918, when he was released from the army, he was sure that a German revolution would start within a year. Although the attempt to organize a revolution in Germany was unsuccessful, Sorge became a dedicated worker in its behalf. He had earned his doctorate in philosophy at the University of Hamburg, and he put his knowledge, skill, and enthusiasm to work in a variety of ways: teaching Marxism, writing pamphlets, organizing coal miners in Aachen and working with them in the pits, and, when the Communist party was outlawed, going underground and continuing his work.

In 1924, when a ranking deputation of Soviets representing the Comintern visited Germany clandestinely, Sorge handled their security. They were so impressed with his perception, bearing, and organizational ability that they invited him to come to the Comintern headquarters. Sorge accepted the offer and went to Moscow, where he began his intelligence career. He studied, wrote articles for *Inprecorr*, became a member of the Soviet Union Communist party, and undertook covert operations for the Comintern in Scandinavia and England. In 1929, under instructions, he dissociated himself from the Comintern and transferred to General Berzin's command. Shortly afterward, he began espionage operations in Shanghai.

On this day in January, 1933, having concluded an extremely successful mission, Sorge was back in Moscow at Berzin's request. After required meetings with members of the Central Committee, the

Richard Sorge, chief of Soviet spy ring in Japan.

Commissariat of Foreign Affairs, and the GPU, he had been summoned by *Starik*. They were old friends and often met for long talks at Sorge's hotel, or at the General's *dacha* (country villa). Now, with Berzin's deputy, General Semyon Petrovich Uritsky, present, the meeting began.

"Ika," Berzin said, using Sorge's nickname, "we're assigning you to a new post." He smiled. "Where would you like to go?"

"Oh, somewhere in Asia, North China, or Manchuria, I suppose." And then, with mock seriousness, Sorge added, "or maybe I could do something in Japan."

Berzin nodded. Sorge was unaware that Japan was the site the Central Committee and the Fourth Bureau had planned for his next mission. A few days later, Berzin informed him that he was assigned to Japan to explore the possibility of setting up an espionage operation in Tokyo.

As Sorge put it: "One would have to discover whether it was possible for me and my collaborators to enter Japan legally, whether it would be possible for us to contact Japanese and foreigners in Japan, what would be the technical capabilities of W/T (wireless transmission) or other means of communication, and finally whether it would be feasible to collect information on Japanese policy toward the Soviet Union."

It was agreed that Sorge would have two years to learn whether he and his ring could succeed in mounting an espionage operation against the Japanese government. In this endeavor, they would stay clear of any contact with the Japanese Communist party, leftist groups, or the Russian Embassy. Their legitimacy in their professions must be firmly established. Communication with the Fourth Bureau was to be maintained through couriers, who would signal their arrival by radio transmission.

Sorge asked that Max Klausen, a fellow German with whom he had worked in Shanghai, be assigned as his radio operator. Klausen was a bluff, heavy-set major in the GRU. Sorge asked for him, not because of his beliefs—he lacked strong Communist convictions—but because of his extraordinary abilities as a radio technician. However, at the time, he was unavailable because he was engaged in China, building radio sets and sending messages for agents in Shanghai, Canton, Harbin, and Mukden.

Miyagi Yotoku, the fourth member of the Sorge ring recruited by Moscow, was a fluent Japanese-English translator. The plan was to encode all communications in English, so if intercepted and decoded, they would not reveal whether the source was Japanese, Russian, or German.

The detailed plans for the establishment of the operation were formulated by Sorge, Berzin, and others in the Fourth Bureau during the first four months of 1933. However, judging from the date of Olga's approach to Voukelitch—October, 1932—the original decision to undertake the mission had been arrived at before Sorge was contacted.

In preparation for the operation, Sorge engaged in a series of background briefings with selected Soviet experts and officials, some of whom had served in Japan. For his cover, he planned to operate as a German newspaper correspondent. To firmly establish himself in this role, he realized that his mission must begin, not in Tokyo, but in Berlin. There he would attempt to obtain press accreditation from several newspapers, as well as a German passport in his own name.

Nineteen thirty-three was a dangerous year in which to embark on an espionage operation in Berlin. Most German Communists who had not fled the country were in concentration camps, in hiding, or dead. The new Nazi government was determined to wipe out all enemies of the state, and its storm troopers were going about the task with vengeful determination. Certainly, in the police records of half a dozen major German cities under Gestapo control at this time, there were thick files on Dr. Richard Sorge.

However, as Sorge saw it, risking his life in Berlin was a gamble worth taking if it would insure his arrival with a secure cover in Tokyo. Before setting out for Germany, he studied national socialism, and memorized passages from *Mein Kampf*. Then, taking the code name of Ramsey, he headed for Berlin, leaving behind his common-law wife, Katerina. Previously he had been married to a German woman, Christiane. Even after they were divorced, he would visit Christiane in Berlin. Wherever he went, Richard Sorge was never far from a woman or a bottle.

In May, 1933, Berlin was a city permeated by fear and tension on the one side and fanatical enthusiasm on the other. In March, the Reichstag had been set on fire and the Communists throughout Germany blamed for it. On the night of the fire, nearly five thousand Communist and Socialist leaders had been arrested. On April 1, Hitler had announced a national boycott against the Jews. And so, when Sorge arrived a month later, terror had engulfed many residents of the city. At the other extreme were those Berliners who were full of explosive zeal for the new order and were anxious to climb on the Nazi bandwagon. In obtaining what he needed without being discovered, Sorge knew he must move with extreme caution.

First, he went about getting press accreditation. He had little difficulty in securing Far Eastern assignments since he was already known in German journalistic circles as an expert on Far Eastern affairs, and he brought with him letters of introduction from correspondents in China. In short order, Sorge was established as the senior Tokyo correspondent for the prestigious *Frankfurter Zeitung* and was accepted as a correspondent for two other Berlin newspapers: the *Tägliche Rundschau* and the *Börsen Zeitung.* The influential Dutch newspaper, the *Algemeen Handelsblad,* also agreed to accept articles from him.

Through the power of his personality, Sorge obtained an impressive group of letters of introduction to people connected with the German Embassy in Tokyo. The chief writer for the *Tägliche Rundschau,* Dr. Zeller, gave Sorge a letter of introduction to Lieutenant Colonel Eugen Ott, then an assistant military attaché posted in Nagoya, Japan. Next, Sorge approached the editor of a leading Nazi theoretical journal, *Geopolitik.* The editor, Dr. Vowinckel, was impressed with the journalist's enthusiasm for the new order. He passed him on to the publisher, Karl Haushofer, and they both provided Sorge with letters of introduction to members of the German Embassy staff in Tokyo and to the Japanese ambassador in Washington.

Obtaining the necessary press credentials was one thing; securing a passport in his own name was quite another. Again, Sorge was successful. He reported to the police on June 1 and submitted his application for a passport together with several letters of recommendation from highly regarded Germans, including two reliable Nazi party members. The country was in a state of flux, the Nazis were just coming into power, and German efficiency was not at its best. Sorge acquired a completely legal passport.

His next step, application for Nazi party membership, was a bold move. Usually, the party thoroughly investigated every applicant. Here, too, Sorge's impressive recommendations effectively deterred a close examination of his background. However, time passed and he did not receive his party acceptance notice. Sorge was growing restless; Berlin was not a city in which a spy should linger. On June 9, he sent a secret message to Berzin: "The situation is not very attractive for me here, and I will be glad when I can disappear from this place."

On July 3, he signaled the Fourth Bureau: "With things livening up in these parts, interest in my person can become much more intensive."

Only twice during his two-month stay did Sorge break his cover. The first time he stepped out of his role was when he held a covert meeting with a German, Bruno Bernhardt, who was to be his wireless operator in Tokyo.

"I hope it's not as bad in Tokyo as it is here," Bruno complained to Sorge.

"There is one way to find out. You are traveling with your wife."

"Yes, she is anxious to leave as soon as possible."

"Everything is in order then?"

"Nearly, but I think I'm being watched."

And with a final admonition to "cheer up," Sorge left his assistant. He was dismayed by Bernhardt's nervousness. Sorge's evaluation of his fellow man was seldom wrong. The wireless operator seemed to him unreliable, timid.

His second secret meeting took place in June. In a small café, he made contact with another Russian agent, who also was on his way to a Far Eastern post. The Russian knew Sorge under his code name of Ramsey. They discussed what Sorge later described as "certain operational questions."

It was not until late July that Sorge received his passport and felt free to leave. He had not yet obtained his membership card in the Nazi party, but he knew that he had pushed his luck far enough. The card could be sent to him in Tokyo. Carrying impressive letters of introduction, press credentials, and a legal passport, Sorge knew that his cover was secure.

His course was west via Cherbourg to New York City. At the Lincoln Hotel in New York, he made contact with a Comintern agent, receiving information on another contact to be made in Chicago. Before meeting his next contact, he took a side trip to Washington, D. C. There he paid a call on Ambassador Debuchi at the Japanese Embassy, presenting a letter of introduction from the publisher of *Geopolitik*. In return, Sorge received from the ambassador a letter to the director of the Information Department of the Foreign Ministry in Tokyo.

His next stop was at the World's Fair in Chicago, where he met a Soviet agent who worked for the *Washington Post*. This reporter informed Sorge that the Japanese member of the ring would be coming to ·Tokyo from California. They set up the method of contact to be used.

After that, there were no more meetings, no more contacts, until Sorge reached Japan on September 6, 1933, after a long voyage by ship from Vancouver. It had taken the GRU nine months to put the leader of the ring in place.

The fourth member, Miyagi Yotoku, was yet to arrive. Like Voukelitch, Miyagi had no training as an espionage agent, and he traveled to Japan without any idea that he was going to become one.

Born in Okinawa, Miyagi was sixteen years old when he learned that he had tuberculosis. His father, a farmer, had immigrated to California, and Miyagi decided to follow him, hoping to study painting. Growing up in California, Miyagi developed into a fine artist. He also developed a smoldering hatred of capitalists and what he considered to be their inhuman oppression of Oriental people. He became a Marxist, helped to organize a study group, and in 1931 he joined the Communist party of the United States. In 1927, Miyagi married a Japanese girl, and in 1932 he and his wife rented an apartment in West Los Angeles. Here, they became friendly with another party member, their landlady, Mrs. Kitabayashi.

In late 1932, Miyagi was approached by Comintern agents who asked him to return to Japan on a special mission for the Comintern. At first, he resisted the idea. He was earning his living as an artist, and he had no desire to go to Japan. He was told his stay would be brief. After vacillating for almost a year, Miyagi departed reluctantly. Expecting to return shortly to the United States, he left his wife and most of his belongings behind.

Miyagi had been instructed carefully on how to make contact in Tokyo. Daily he was to scan the *Japan Advertiser,* an English language American-owned newspaper, and look for an advertisement for a *Ukiyoye* print. He was to answer the ad as soon as it appeared and bring with him a U.S. one-dollar bill. He was told that his contact would also carry a dollar bill. The bills would bear consecutive numbers so that the two men could identify each other.

Observant and adaptable, Miyagi possessed the sharp eye for detail so necessary to the artist, and to the spy. His motivations for joining the Communist cause were primarily personal, rather than theoretical. He was against repression of Orientals, which he equated in his mind with being against capitalism. With his arrival in Tokyo in October, the ring, as conceived in Moscow, had assembled. To form it, General Berzin had utilized GRU and Comintern agents in Shanghai, Berlin, Paris, New York, Chicago, and Los Angeles.

The Imperial Hotel in downtown Tokyo was a noted gathering place in the thirties for the Western traveler as well as for Western residents of the city. With its shopping arcade and American bar it was—although staffed by unobtrusive Japanese—an occidental oasis in an oriental world.

In its well-populated lobby, on a day in October, Richard Sorge met again with Bernhardt, his Moscow-trained wireless operator. Their conversation was brief. Sorge spoke first:

"You are settled?"

"Yes. In Yokohama. I have an export business."

"Are you ready to start exporting to the home office?"

"No. Not yet. . . . It—it's not easy. There are so many interested in my business."

"If the business is to succeed, you will want to start making preparations at once. There may be someone who can assist at the Bunka Apartments. I'll give you his name. You can call on him."

Later that same day Bernhardt paid a visit to the apartments. The man who answered the knock looked haggard.

"Do you know Johnson?" Bernhardt asked, standing in the doorway.

"Yes, I know him."

"I myself am not Schmidt, but I was sent by him."

And that was all. Before Branko de Voukelitch could respond, Bernhardt, nervous and perspiring, turned and walked away.

The next day, Voukelitch again received a caller. This time it was Sorge. Sorge looked him over and began the conversation.

"You are not well."

"It's nothing, but I would get better faster if I had some money."

"You are broke?"

Voukelitch smiled wanly. "Exactly. I wasn't given enough money when I left, and it is very expensive here."

"We'll take care of that, and I think it would be better if you moved into a house. How does the press work go?"

"Very slowly."

Sorge nodded. "We'll try to improve that, too. Meet me for lunch tomorrow at the German Club."

Sorge was disheartened. After a month in Japan, he had made contact with two of his ring members. And who were they? A radio operator who had not even begun to build a transmitter, and a fellow journalist who was sick, broke, and obviously not getting around.

Sorge, on the other hand, had been working hard. Already, he was well received at the German Embassy and a great social success in German circles in Tokyo. His journalistic reputation, the introductions he brought with him, and his magnetic personality had gained him many highly placed acquaintances. Among his friends was Lieutenant Colonel Eugen Ott, then the assistant military attaché at the embassy.

Sorge made a trip to Nagoya to meet Ott, presenting him with the letter from Dr. Zeller of the *Tägliche Rundschau*. About Sorge's age, Ott was anti-Nazi and had been transferred to Japan by influential friends in the army in order to keep him out of danger. Zeller's letter, together with their shared background as soldiers in the German Army in World War I, sparked a friendly relationship between the two. It was a friendship that was to change the course of history.

As for the Japanese, Sorge's letter from Ambassador Debuchi had gained him entry to Amau Eiji, director of the Information Department of the Ministry of Foreign Affairs. Amau, in turn, introduced Sorge to a number of Japanese correspondents and invited him to attend his weekly press conference. Sorge also made himself known to the foreign press corps, particularly to his colleagues at the DNB, the official German News Agency. In newspaper circles, he was generally regarded as a quiet, unassuming, intelligent reporter.

But in spite of Sorge's initial success, the dangers of his position were soon impressed upon him. One of the journalists he met at the German Embassy was a Japanese, Mitsukado Aritomi. Mitsukado was friendly, smiling, and gracious. He suggested a less expensive hotel than the one where Sorge was staying and invited him to dine. As Sorge noted, dryly, "He was exceedingly eager to cultivate my friendship."

Realizing that Mitsukado was a counterintelligence agent for the police, Sorge set to work to convince the Japanese that he was a bona fide German correspondent and nothing more. When Mitsukado introduced him to a "former Socialist" who spoke to him in Russian, Sorge pretended not to understand the language. The ruse was successful, and a short time later, Mitsukado drifted away. But police surveillance, either by the *Tokko* (the Special Higher Police) or the *Kempei* (the Military Police), was a fact of life in Tokyo that all foreigners came to expect.

This surveillance was one manifestation of the tension that characterized the Japanese political scene at this time. Japan was in turmoil. In 1932, the prime minister had been murdered by naval officers. In July, 1933, a plot to assassinate the entire cabinet had been exposed at the last minute.

The country was split into two factions: the group in power, the *Kodo-ha* (the Imperial Way), whose leaders foresaw war with the Soviet Union by 1935; and their opponents, the *Tosei-ha* (the Control Faction), made up of young, fiercely nationalistic officers who believed the army should take over the government and break down the power of the large capitalistic combines which controlled the Diet. Both sides were completely opposed to international communism, with the result that all through 1933 the police carried out mass arrests of suspected party members and their sympathizers.

The most important mission assigned to Sorge was, as he later wrote, "to observe most closely Japan's policy toward the USSR . . .

*Ozaki Hotsumi,
key Japanese member of the ring.*

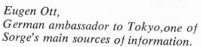

*Eugen Ott,
German ambassador to Tokyo, one of
Sorge's main sources of information.*

*Max Klausen,
radio operator, who transmitted
secrets from Tokyo to Moscow.*

and at the same time, to give very careful study to the question of whether or not Japan was planning to attack the USSR."

High on the list of Sorge's instructions were orders to find out the plans for the reorganization and expansion of Japanese army and air units. Sorge wrote that this "entailed the obtaining of very broad military intelligence, because the Japanese military, in order to justify their increased budget demands, were pointing to the Soviet Union as Japan's principal enemy."

On the foreign policy level, Sorge was ordered to watch relations between Tokyo and Berlin. Also of interest to Russia was Japan's China policy and the role of the Japanese military in influencing foreign affairs. As the power of the Japanese navy began to increase, Sorge tried to learn what naval leaders believed and wanted.

For an outsider to surmount the barriers erected by Japanese bureaucracy and obtain secret information was almost impossible. It was a feat Richard Sorge was to achieve, however, by becoming the confidant of the very officials whose secrets he was stealing.

But first, he had to forge his espionage chain. In mid-December, 1933, Sorge made contact with Miyagi. Unlike Voukelitch, the Japanese artist had adjusted to life in Tokyo. He had friends, his paintings sold, and he was earning a living. As soon as Voukelitch placed the signal in the *Japan Advertiser,* Miyagi replied by mail, setting up a meeting at the newspaper office.

Voukelitch asked Miyagi to pay a visit to the Ueno Art Gallery at a specified time. At the gallery, late in December, Sorge met the third member of his ring. The conversation at the first meeting between the master spy and the recruit was limited to general topics. By the fifth meeting, Sorge informed Miyagi that his assignment was espionage. However, it was some time before Miyagi agreed to join Sorge's group. He was finally won over because, as he was to say in retrospect: "I realized the historical importance of the mission, since we were helping to avoid war between Japan and Russia . . . although I knew well what I was doing was illegal and that in wartime I would be hanged."

Sorge devoted his first months in Japan to learning, assimilating, and developing an understanding of this strange, paradoxical country. The spy who drank and sang with his Nazi friends in the bars of Berlin and Tokyo applied the same enthusiasm to scholarly research. He built a library of one thousand books on Japan, studying and digesting works on topics ranging from Japanese economic and political problems to Japanese history and art. It was the diligence of Sorge, the student, that was largely responsible for the success of Sorge, the spy. And it was this scholarly Sorge who wrote: "Had I lived under peaceful conditions and in a peaceful environment of political development, I should perhaps have been a scholar—certainly not an espionage agent."

Throughout this early period of study, penetration, and groundwork, Sorge was settling in. He and Voukelitch rented homes in different suburbs. Sorge's house at 30 Nagasaka-cho, Azabu, was a ramshackle two-story cottage in a small garden. It became the scene of raucous parties for his hard-drinking press and embassy associates.

In the house where the Voukelitch family lived, Sorge instructed Bernhardt to build a second transmitter. Voukelitch also installed a darkroom to process and prepare all documents and reports stolen by the ring. Voukelitch now began to make himself known to Western press and embassy contacts, as well as to the Japanese newsmen at the Domei News Agency.

By the spring of 1934, Sorge had become firmly entrenched in German Embassy circles. His friend, Ott, had been transferred to Tokyo, and he had two new drinking partners: Captain Paul Wenneker, a naval attaché at the German Embassy, and Prince Albrecht von Urach, correspondent for the *Volkischer Beobachter*. Wenneker had no knowledge of the Japanese political scene and relied on Sorge for information and interpretation; Urach admired Sorge's writing and enjoyed his company. All three were bachelors, and their nightly carousing in the bars, cafés, and hotels of Tokyo soon became a favorite topic of gossip for the German community.

In this same period, the new German ambassador, Herbert von Dirksen, arrived in Tokyo. He had previously been ambassador to the USSR. Sorge was sure that Dirksen's primary aim was to steer Japan on a course hostile to the Soviet Union and he paid particular attention to obtaining information on Dirksen's views.

By this time, Sorge was living the peculiar double life of the spy. To his friends and fellow newsmen, he was a brilliant, gifted journalist and a hard-drinking playboy; to the members of his ring and Soviet Intelligence, he was a conscientious, dedicated agent, working hard to obtain avenues of information.

In a message to Moscow, Sorge said slyly, "I think I'm beginning to lead them all by the nose."

At this juncture, he was suddenly confronted by a genuine war scare. A stalemate had been reached in the talks between Japan and the Soviet Union on the future of the Russian-controlled Chinese Eastern Railway, which cut across northern Manchuria. Japan wanted the line, and at this time it seemed as if the Japanese Kwantung Army would take over the railway. The war scare died down, but although Miyagi and other sources were able to supply some information on the crisis, Sorge realized that he needed expert advice on Japanese policies in China. He decided to enlarge his *apparat* by enlisting Ozaki Hotsumi.

Born on Taiwan in 1901, the son of a newspaperman, Ozaki began to take a serious interest in Marxism while a student at Tokyo Imperial University. Shortly after joining the staff of the *Asahi Shimbun* in 1925, he was assigned to China. There he was swept up in the fervor of the Chinese revolutionary movement. Through association with Chinese Communists, he became very close to Agnes Smedley, a well-known left-wing American journalist. Miss Smedley introduced Ozaki to Sorge. Sorge called Ozaki "my first and most important associate" during his China days. The Japanese newsman was a great help to Sorge in gathering information on China and its Nationalist government.

Like Sorge, Ozaki was an intellectual and an idealist. He was not a member of any Communist party; neither did he know that through Sorge he was passing on information to Soviet Intelligence. He believed that he was working for the Marxist cause. Plump, outgoing, and friendly, Ozaki masked his true feelings skillfully. His writings were admired; his opinions sought after. In choosing Ozaki for the ring, Sorge made what one historian called "one of the luckiest choices in the history of espionage."

Sorge knew that Ozaki was on the staff of the *Asahi* in Osaka. Ordering Miyagi to arrange the meeting, Sorge planned a rendezvous with his former associate at Nara Deer Park. From their China days, Ozaki knew Sorge under the name of Johnson, and he would continue to call him by that name for several more years.

Johnson had one principal question: would Ozaki be willing to resume their former relationship, giving Johnson his opinion and information on Japanese political, economic, and military affairs?

In the pastoral scene where sightseers walked and fed the deer, Ozaki Hotsumi readily agreed to aid his friend, Johnson-san.

To Sorge, Ozaki was an important addition to his sources. He was also pleased with Miyagi, who was busy cultivating contacts in the lower military echelons and building his own ring of informants. Voukelitch had a firm cover as a newsman. The only weak link was Bernhardt. Sorge's mind was made up; Bernhardt would have to go.

Bernhardt was afraid to transmit the messages Sorge gave him because, as he said, "I felt the frequent sending and receiving of messages would be tantamount to inviting discovery by the police." As a result, almost all the reports were being passed on to couriers through meetings arranged principally in Shanghai.

"He was forever drinking," Sorge said, although Sorge, of all men, might have been expected to make excuses for a man who liked the bottle. But Bernhardt was not doing his job. Sorge went on, "in many cases he neglected to send out information. A man engaged in espionage must show some courage; he was extremely timid and did not send half the messages I gave him."

By the beginning of 1935, arrangements had been made for the Bernhardts to return to Moscow within the year.

Bad luck for the ring, but, at the same time, some good luck, too. Ozaki was transferred from Osaka to the Tokyo office of the *Asahi*. The newspaper had established a research organization to study Chinese affairs, and Ozaki, considered an authority on the subject, was assigned to the study group. Such research would entail meetings with senior officials in the Japanese government, and this would greatly enlarge the range of Sorge's contacts. Sorge and his new recruit began meeting on a regular basis at carefully selected *geisha* houses, where they could be assured of privacy.

Soon after Ozaki's transfer, Sorge left for Moscow. It was time to report in person, time to consider the future of the mission. In June, 1935, he sailed for the United States. In New York, he was supplied with a forged passport, giving him an Austrian identity to cover his travels to the Soviet Union.

At the Cafe Brevoort on Fifth Avenue, he met his old *apparatchik* comrade, Hede Massing. They had known each other in Berlin in the twenties. Seeing Sorge for the first time in six years, she described him as follows:

> Ika . . . whom I had first known as a quiet and scholarly comrade, had undergone a considerable change of personality . . . he had been transformed into a boisterous hard-drinking man. Little of the charm of the idealistic scholar was left, though he was still startlingly good looking. His cold blue eyes . . . had retained their quality of looking amused for no reason at all; his hair was still thick and brown, but his cheeks and the heavy sensuous mouth were sagging. His nose was thinner. It was a very different man from the one who had taken me to dinner in Berlin in 1929.

Sorge arrived in Moscow in July, 1935, to find that after fifteen years as chief of the Fourth Bureau, General Jan Berzin had been replaced by his deputy, General Semyon Uritsky.

To Uritsky, Sorge presented the pile of documentary microfilmed information he had brought from Tokyo. One report, prepared by Miyagi, gave a breakdown of the internal power structure of the Japanese army. Even more valuable was Sorge's verbal report;

he assured the general that he could carry out the original mission as assigned. What he needed, above all, was a competent radio operator, so that information could be relayed to the Moscow Center swiftly. He also asked for permission to strengthen his position in the German Embassy by whatever method he chose. One method, he told Uritsky, was "to exchange information of minor importance for information of major importance—in other words, to use a sprat to catch a mackerel."

Permission was granted. Permission was also granted to enlist Max Klausen, who at that time was in disgrace with his Fourth Bureau superiors. Recalled to Moscow from Mukden in August, 1933, Klausen had refused to accompany the female agent sent to travel with him, but returned, instead with his common-law wife, Anna Wallenius, a pretty Finnish widow whom he had met in Shanghai.

Anna was not only unaware of Klausen's espionage activities, she was also a strong anti-Communist. But, above all, she loved shaggy Max, a rotund, rough-and-ready fellow who was devoted to her.

Shortly after their arrival in Moscow, the Fourth Bureau punished the couple by banishing them to the Volga-German Republic, where Max was employed as a repairman in a motor tractor station. At first, they had a difficult time trying to eke out a living on a tractor repairman's wage. But Max's ability was soon recognized. His supervisor put him to work installing wireless sets in farms and on tractors, thus establishing a two-way farm-to-tractor intercommunication system. His pay increased, and so, when a telegram came from the Fourth Bureau, summoning him back to Moscow, he ignored it. He paid no attention to the second telegram, either. The third wire, however, was signed by Marshal Voroshilov and delivered personally by a stern party official. It ordered Max to return to Moscow immediately. Max left.

Back in Moscow, without Anna, he met with Sorge and other GRU officers and agreed to join the ring. His code name would be Fritz; his cover that of a German businessman. Anna, he was told, would be permitted to join him in Tokyo once he was established.

In August, 1935, Sorge left for Japan. A month later, Max was on his way, leaving a tearful and frightened Anna behind. By prearrangement, the two men met again in late November at the Blue Ribbon bar in Tokyo. Nearly six years of operations lay ahead.

Early one morning in May, Max Klausen and Branko de Voukelitch, dressed in hiking clothes, each carrying a bulging knapsack
and walking stick, boarded a train in the Tokyo suburb of Shinjuku.
Packed inside their knapsacks were three transmission transformers,
a radio receiver, and assorted parts of the bulky sending set that
Bernhardt had constructed at Voukelitch's home. The two hikers
had decided to get rid of the equipment. The house of a foreigner
could be searched at any time, and the set was conspicuous and difficult to conceal. It was a dangerous attempt, since trains always had
police on board and inspection was a frightening possibility. The two
spent an uncomfortable journey, nervously making small talk and
trying to appear nonchalant.

After a change of trains and a taxi ride, they arrived at their
destination, a hotel on Lake Yamanaka. As they entered, the bellboys
came forward to relieve them of their packs.

"Sir, what are you carrying?" one of them asked, hefting the
heavy load.

Klausen paled and was unable to answer, but Voukelitch replied
airily, "Oh, we brought along a half a dozen bottles of beer."

"We have plenty of beer, here," came the response.

The original plan had been to dump the incriminating equipment in the lake that night, but once they were alone in their room,
the spies decided to act at once. Bellboys were supposed to report
anything they considered suspicious to the police, and many hotel
employees were police agents. Klausen and Voukelitch rented a boat
at the lake. Far from the shore, they consigned Bernhardt's handi-
work to the depths.

In Klausen's words, "We returned to Tokyo relieved of a heavy
burden, indeed."

Later, when Klausen told Sorge what they had done, Sorge
snapped, "You should have gotten rid of it in Tokyo instead of going
so far away." Spying in an enemy capital, at a time when the political
atmosphere was thick with tension and unrest, he fully recognized
the urgent need for each member of the ring to avoid taking unnecessary risks. In the game they were playing, the rules never varied: a
move by one player was a move for the whole ring; a risk taken by
one player endangered the lives of all.

Some indication of the danger which constantly overshadowed
Sorge's daily life was revealed in his confession: "My maid and laun-
dry man were frequently questioned by the police. I was constantly
watched by policemen even at the Imperial Hotel. A Japanese translator employed by the German Embassy was questioned about me by
the police. I was watched by either plainclothes men or *Kempei*,

even at restaurants. My house had been searched and my briefcase examined during my absence on a trip to China."

The first task was to set up efficient communications. Sorge assigned Klausen to build a radio set. After purchasing the parts in various shops along the Ginza, the radio operator soon assembled an amazingly efficient set, small enough to be packed into a briefcase and moved from place to place. He could prepare the equipment for sending in less than ten minutes and dismantle it in less than five. Sending sites were located in heavily populated areas to make it difficult for Japanese monitoring stations to zero in on the source of transmission. Further, to cut down on interference and facilitate transmission, all sending was carried out from the second floor of wooden houses.

The first sending site, which was used on and off until the middle of 1938, was the home of a highly regarded economic and financial reporter, Gunther Stein. Later, Klausen was to describe the German-born Stein as a member of the ring, while Sorge called him a "sympathizer."

Stein did not know that Sorge was an agent working for the Fourth Bureau. However, motivated by a strong hatred of the Nazis and a belief that only the international Communist party was able to fight fascism, he was of considerable service to the ring. Stein acted as a courier, supplied information to Sorge, knew the identity of several of the ring's members, and bore the code name of Gustav.

During the period in which Klausen sent coded transmissions from Stein's home, Sorge continued to use courier contacts in Shanghai and Hong Kong as his principal means of passing on information and receiving funds. The contacts were arranged via radio. Although careful means of identification were worked out—dress, passwords such as "greetings from Gustav"—a courier carrying rolls of incriminating microfilm was in a dangerously vulnerable position. Max found this out on his second trip to Shanghai.

He was going to Shanghai, not only to make contact with a courier, but also to see Anna, who had finally been permitted to leave Russia to join him. He had just made himself comfortable in a second-class compartment on the train to Nagasaki, where he would board ship for Shanghai, when a plainclothes policeman entered. In his trouser pocket, Klausen was carrying a bundle of microfilm; the two suitcases on the overhead rack contained further incriminating evidence.

Afraid that the police had ordered his arrest, Max forced a weak smile and quickly produced his business card, bearing the imprint, "Klausen Company."

The policeman took the card, carefully studying it as if it might reveal some hidden meaning.

"What is your business?" he asked.

"I manufacture and sell printing presses for industrial blueprints," Max answered, and he embarked on an explanation of the operation.

"And where do you do that?" the policeman interrupted.

"My plant is near Shimbashi station. I employ fourteen workers, all Japanese."

"What is your nationality?"

"Oh, I'm German."

"And where do you live?"

As Max later described the encounter: "He asked me various questions with a grave bearing—where had I come from—where was I going—but about thirty minutes later he left the train at one of the stations without examining my baggage. I had escaped by the skin of my teeth. After I boarded the boat, I was constantly on guard lest the roving patrol had been contacted. The film never left my pocket, and I was prepared to toss it overboard if necessary."

Once in Shanghai, Max's spirits rose. Anna was waiting, and before the two returned to Tokyo they were formally married. Through Sorge's insistence, Anna, too, became a courier.

In 1936, the fruits of careful advance preparation ripened; the Sorge ring began to operate with masterly efficiency. The information obtained by the ring was of great value to the Soviet government, and Klausen skillfully transmitted the messages.

In February, there was a brief, but violent, mutiny within the Japanese armed forces. The insurgents, about fourteen hundred in all, seized the principal government buildings and assassinated a number of prominent officials. Two days after the armed outbreak, the rebels surrendered. All foreign embassies were extremely anxious to understand the underlying causes of the stillborn coup d'état and its implications for the future.

Through Ozaki and Miyagi, Sorge had the answer swiftly, and he gave it not only to Moscow, but to Berlin and *Geopolitik* as well.

Explaining the affair, he said: "To Dirksen, Ott, and Wenneker I stressed again and again the social aspects of the February 26 Incident, telling them that I understood the social problems facing Japan. As a result the embassy staff turned their attention to this side of the Incident, and they tried to collect as much material as possible about it. . . . My espionage ring, of course, amassed a great deal of material on the whole affair. In fact, I came to learn a lot from various sides. So my opinion easily colored the view taken by the embassy; and both Dirksen and Ott tried to draw even closer to me. This was why I was asked to write a report on the Incident for Berlin."

As to the significance of the February 26 Incident: the *Kodo-ha* group was finished, and the *Tosei-ha* was now in control. "There were two ways in which the Japanese government could handle the aftermath of the affair," Sorge said. "They could either introduce social reform . . . or they could adopt the policy of permanent expansion."

Sorge accurately forecast that Japan would adopt the second course, and that this expansion would be directed towards China.

Sorge's report to Berlin on the incident also cemented his ties with the German Embassy, earning him a position as unofficial secretary. He was given his own room at the embassy, which enabled him to photograph the official documents that came into his hands. This was, as Sorge realized, "really dangerous work," but he added, "If I was unable to take this kind of chance—namely borrowing the actual document—I waited until the papers were transferred to the archives, and then I could borrow them at my leisure. I did my photographing not only in my room, but elsewhere in the embassy, if I happened to be in a hurry."

Another significant coup for the ring that year was Sorge's penetration into the secret negotiations between the German and Japanese governments over the Anti-Comintern Pact. The operation began with a private meeting between Eugen Ott and Sorge.

"I tell you this in strictest confidence, Ika."

"Of course."

"The ambassador and I have learned through a friend on the Japanese Army General Staff that secret negotiations are going on in Berlin between General Oshima, and von Ribbentrop, and Admiral Canaris.[1] We don't know what it means, but we'd like to find out, so I'm going to send a telegram to Army Headquarters, and I want you to help me encode it. Because of the need for absolute secrecy, I don't want to use the help of anyone here. We'll do it at my home."

The telegram brought no response, and Dirksen told Ott to try again, but to be sure to do the encoding only with Sorge. The second query brought a reply, advising Ott to get his information from the Japanese General Staff, which put the matter back where it had started originally.

A few months later, Dr. Frederick Wilhelm Hack, a German businessman acting as von Ribbentrop's special agent, came to Tokyo to explore the possibilities of a German-Japanese alliance against the Soviet Union. Hack confided the reason for his visit to both Ott and Sorge, warning that the need for secrecy was absolute: "We know that Soviet agents have been watching the homes of Herr Ribbentrop, General Oshima, and Admiral Canaris. It is for that reason that I have been acting as a go-between. We do not want the Russians to get word of this."

Sorge solemnly vowed to remain silent and promptly passed on the information to the director of the Fourth Bureau.

The Anti-Comintern Pact was announced on November 25, 1936. Its public clauses amounted to no more than a pledge of mutual cooperation against Comintern actions. Its secret provision was weak as well, simply stating that in case of attack or threatened attack by the Soviet Union against either of the partners, they would consult each other. Through Sorge, Moscow knew the details of the pact, open and secret, long before the public announcement.

While Sorge's influence at the German Embassy was growing, both Ozaki and Voukelitch were also advancing to high positions.

In the summer of 1936, Ozaki was selected to be one of Japan's principal representatives to the Institute of Pacific Relations conclave held at Yosemite National Park in California. The Institute, founded in 1925, with headquarters in New York City, was an important international organization composed of a dozen national councils representing Pacific nations. To its members, IPR passed on information covering a broad range of political, economic, and social matters affecting peoples of the Pacific area. IPR's primary aim was to influence public opinion to accept its policies. Covertly, the organization was heavily infiltrated by Communists and their sympathizers. As a member of the Japanese delegation to the IPR conference, Ozaki was recognized as a spokesman for Japan's China policy and an important adviser to the Japanese government.

As for Voukelitch, he, too, had gone up in the world, becoming the number two man in the Tokyo bureau of Havas, the official French news agency. The Havas bureau chief was a knowledgeable and highly regarded newsman, Robert Guillain. Through him, Voukelitch gained entry into the inner circle of the French Embassy and a wide range of contacts with Domei, the Japanese news agency.

Voukelitch and journalists representing American news agencies and newspapers had their offices in the Domei Press Building. The newsmen liked his friendly manner and shared his open dislike of the Nazis. Soon, he became "Voukey" to his press colleagues.

Of his work, Sorge later commented: "While I found my newspaper work irksome because intelligence was my real job, de Voukelitch spent more and more effort on his reporting and repeated to me everything he heard with no sense of discrimination. He left all evaluation to me."

The accuracy of one of Sorge's evaluations—his analysis of the implications of the February Incident of 1936—was soon demonstrated to Berlin and Moscow. In July, 1937, Japan attacked China. Von Dirksen and Ott asked Sorge his opinion on what the result of the attack would be. In giving his appraisal, Sorge had the benefit of Ozaki's first-hand knowledge. In June, Ozaki had been appointed a member of a high-level, policy-planning brain trust which advised the new prime minister, Prince Fumimaro Konoye. Weaving together Ozaki's analyses and Miyagi's nuts-and-bolts military information, Sorge produced his own evaluation.

"Dirksen and Ott were very optimistic," he said, "claiming that the Kuomingtang were extremely weak. But I maintained that hostilities would last for a long time, that the strength of the Kuomingtang could not be underestimated."

"Neither Dirksen nor Ott agreed with me. But the course of events turned out as I forecast. So Dirksen and Ott had to admit that I had been right and my stock in the embassy rose accordingly."

It was shortly after the outbreak of the Sino-Japanese War that Max Klausen made a careless mistake which put the *apparat* in grave jeopardy. As he related it, "I had taken a taxi from my neighborhood as usual to radio some messages to Moscow, and upon my arrival at Voukelitch's home, I discovered that a large wallet I had put in my left trousers pocket was gone! I darted outside but the taxi had disappeared. The wallet had in it 230 yen in Japanese currency, my driver's license with photo attached, and Sorge's English text of a financial report that we were to send to Moscow. It was to be photographed at Voukelitch's home."

Klausen was beside himself. "I didn't know what to do! I told Voukelitch I had lost my wallet and a large sum of money."

Because Voukelitch was talkative and might tell Sorge, Max did not reveal the real seriousness of the loss. Instead he spent a sleepless night, trying to decide what to do. The next morning, he coolly walked into the police station and reported his loss. The wallet was never recovered, but for weeks Klausen lived in constant fear.

Soon after this incident, Klausen had another terrifying encounter. One night a policeman, appearing out of nowhere, loomed out of the darkness and stopped the taxi which had just picked him up at Voukelitch's home.

"Who are you, sir?"

"I—I'm Herr Klausen."

"Where have you been?"

"I'm on my way home from the German Club. I live in Ryudo Cho. Here, perhaps my card will help."

"What are you carrying in that bag there?"

"Business papers. Would you like to see them?"

The policeman told the driver to move on and turned away. The black bag Klausen held in his shaking hands contained the radio. Max sat in the taxi, mopping his face. The perspiration on his brow had nothing to do with the temperature.

In 1938, the pace of onrushing events throughout the world quickened, bringing the prospect of global war very close. For two years there had been civil war in Spain. Now there was war in China, and full-scale war between Japan and the Soviet Union appeared imminent. It was a productive period for the members of the Sorge ring, but for a time their operations were endangered by an accident which narrowly missed taking the life of their leader and exposing his espionage activities.

At the end of April, von Dirksen was made German ambassador to England and Eugen Ott became German ambassador to Japan. Sorge, as Ott's close friend and confidential adviser, became, for all intents and purposes, the number two man in the German Embassy. Knowing Ika was planning a trip to Hong Kong, Ott asked him if he would mind acting as an official courier. Mind? Of course not, anything to oblige a friend. So Sorge went off to Manila and Hong Kong to make contact with Soviet agents, carrying official German pouches which were stuffed with microfilm and assorted reports for Moscow.

On the evening of May 13, Sorge celebrated his return to Tokyo with fellow newsman Prince Urach. After they had closed up one of his favorite haunts, the bar at the Reingold restaurant, Sorge suggested that they proceed to the Imperial. He had a friend there who kept a well-stocked bar in his room. An excellent idea, Urach agreed, and they made the journey on Sorge's motorcycle. A bottle of whiskey later, Sorge suggested that they now ride to his house for a nightcap or two. Urach had already had several more than enough for the road and declined, "No thanks, Ika. Time for bed."

Nothing daunted, Sorge set off on his bike at full throttle. He delighted in speed, delighted in gambling with his life openly on a motorcycle, just as he gambled with it secretly in espionage work day in and day out. He played for high stakes, but this time he nearly lost. Turning off a main thoroughfare, he went roaring up a narrow incline beside the wall of the American Embassy, zoomed straight ahead when he should have turned, and slammed full tilt into the wall.

It was three o'clock in the morning, but the sound of the crash was heard by the police at the embassy gate. They rushed to the scene. Badly injured, his teeth smashed and his jaw fractured, Sorge exhibited his enormous willpower by refusing to lose consciousness. In his pockets were incriminating reports and a large amount of U.S. currency. He could barely speak, but he managed to mumble to the police to notify Prince Urach at the Imperial. Urach and Dr. Stedfeld were summoned. The latter gave him first aid, while Sorge whispered to Urach, "Tell Klausen! Tell Klausen to come at once! Get Klausen! Get him!"

Klausen, awakened by a messenger, rushed to St. Luke's Hospital, where Sorge had been taken. In spite of his condition, the injured spy refused to let the Japanese attendants give him an anesthetic, and when Klausen arrived, Sorge still possessed the strength to order the hospital aides out of the room.

Then, as Max described it: "He handed over the English reports and American currency and, as if relieved at last, fainted. From the hospital I went straight to his house to remove all papers relating to our intelligence activities, even taking his diary. A short while later, Weiss of the DNB (German News Agency) came to the house to seal all his property so that nobody would touch it. I shuddered when I thought of how our secret work would have been exposed had Weiss arrived before I did. I was also worried because it was unnatural for an outsider like myself to appear instead of a representative of the German Embassy or the Japanese police."

When Sorge left the hospital, he convalesced at the Otts' home, where Frau Ott looked after him. A gentle and artistic woman, Rena Ott had a calming effect on Sorge. But there was no real rest in store for the "battered knight bandit," as Sorge described himself.

In June, 1938, G. S. Lyushkov, a general in the GPU, defected from the Soviet Far East Army and crossed over into Manchuria, handing himself over to the Japanese Kwantung Army. He brought with him vitally important details of Soviet military strength in the Far East. The Japanese forwarded the information to Major Scholl, a German assistant military attaché. Scholl and Sorge had served in the same unit during the war, and Scholl trusted Sorge implicitly. He informed Sorge of the defection, adding that the Japanese Embassy was asking Berlin to send a specialist in Soviet affairs to interrogate Lyushkov.

The general proved to be a gold mine of information for Tokyo. He brought word of Red Army demoralization over the purging of such military commanders as Marshall Tukhachevsky. If the Japanese attacked Siberia, he maintained, Soviet forces would collapse. He gave full details of the number of divisions facing the Japanese and similar information on Soviet forces in the Ukraine. Sorge promptly transmitted the details of Lyushkov's statements to Moscow. Thanks to Sorge, Moscow knew the Japanese army's exact estimate of Soviet military strength in Siberia.

However, Sorge saw at once the peril in which Lyushkov's information placed the Soviet Union. As he commented later, "One consequence of Lyushkov's report was a danger of a joint Japanese-German military action against the Soviet Union." About a month after Lyushkov defected, this danger was increased by a clash between Japanese and Soviet troops on the borders of Korea, Manchukuo, and Soviet Far Eastern territory. A fierce battle developed over the ownership of a commanding ridge at Changkufeng. Moscow was genuinely alarmed. How could Sorge help?

In five years, the *apparat* had weathered many storms, but this was its first critical test. The response of the Sorge ring was swift and accurate. Ozaki, as a cabinet consultant, knew the government did not plan an invasion. Miyagi, through his military contacts, was able to report that no major troop movements were underway, and Sorge, after listening to Ott and others at the German Embassy, knew the location and strength of Japanese units in the contested area. From Voukelitch's house, Klausen tapped out the information to the director of the Fourth Bureau.

In late July, even before the fighting had stopped, it was evident that Sorge's reports had been believed by the Soviet Union. In Moscow, the Japanese ambassador was informed that the only way hostilities could cease was to return to the status quo as of July 29, 1938. Japan agreed, and on August 11, the clash was over. The battle of Changkufeng had been bloody and costly for Japan and the Soviet Union, but it was a personal triumph for Richard Sorge.

At about the time the guns stopped firing, Admiral Canaris's Soviet expert, Colonel Greiling, arrived in Tokyo to interrogate Lyushkov. Sorge notified "Wiesbaden," the code name for the receiving point to which Klausen transmitted his messages.

Moscow was upset and radioed Sorge: "Do everything possible and use every available means to get copies of documents to be received by Canaris's special envoy from Japanese army or copies of documents received personally by envoy from Lyushkov. . . ."

Sorge's method for getting the information was simple. From Scholl, he borrowed the 100-page document detailing the interview. Sorge brought it to his room at the embassy, took out his Leica, and the results were passed on to a courier.

However, Sorge continued to worry about the effect of Lyushkov's information on the Japanese and German governments. He recognized that Stalin's purges were devastating the Red Army, and he was afraid that the defector's statement that the Soviet Union was on the verge of disintegration might generate a plan for a joint German-Japanese attack against the USSR. Sorge brought his powers of persuasion to bear on Ott in the hope that he could dispel acceptance of Lyushkov's picture of increasing Russian weakness. "Eugen," Sorge argued, "you can't judge Russia's internal situation from statements made by a man like this. His remarks are just the kind of thing you find in anti-Nazi books written by German refugees. Don't you often find them predicting imminent collapse in Berlin?"

Sorge may have convinced Ott and others at the embassy that Lyushkov's revelations were not to be taken seriously, but militant officers in the Japanese army were anxious to put the information to the test. In May, 1939, at the village of Nomonhan, the Japanese initiated a probing attack. The fighting quickly spread along the borders of Manchukuo and Outer Mongolia.

Again, Moscow panicked and radioed Sorge: was this the opening gun for an all-out war?

Again, Sorge responded: *Nyet!*

And again, it was Ozaki and Miyagi who came through with the essential hard information. The Konoye government was not seeking all-out war; the army was simply testing. Voukelitch also made a solid contribution to the ring's response. Invited with other journalists to observe the fighting, he was able to inform Sorge that Japanese commanders in the field viewed the fighting as local and were using the battles to test the quality of their equipment. Through previous intelligence, Sorge had passed on to Moscow detailed reports on this equipment and the numerical strength of the armies using it. As a result, Soviet forces, under the command of Marshal G. K. Zhukov, mounted a successful counterattack which drove the Japanese back across the border.

The Soviet attack was launched on August 20, 1939. Three days later, the world trembled under the impact of the announcement of the Hitler-Stalin Pact. A week later, Nazi Germany attacked Poland from the west; on September 16, Soviet armies struck from the east. Stalin sent Hitler a telegram stating, "The friendship of the peoples of Germany and the Soviet Union, cemented by blood, has every reason to be lasting and firm." After the Soviet victory at Nomonhan, the fighting on the Mongolian border was stilled by the roar of the opening guns of World War II. .

The war in Europe had a direct effect upon the operations of the ring. The Japanese, always suspicious that all foreigners were spies, tightened security, and Sorge notified the Fourth Bureau that the method of dispatching information by courier had become too risky. As a result, in 1939, Klausen sent sixty separate transmissions to "Wiesbaden," containing nearly twenty-five thousand words. The following year the figure rose to nearly thirty thousand. In 1940, a new method of sending information was instituted.

Klausen was instructed by the Moscow Center "to receive funds from and maintain liaison with, a comrade in Tokyo. He will send you two tickets for the Imperial Theater. The man seated next to you will be the comrade."

Thus began a method of exchange—rolls of microfilm for funds —that took place in theaters, in restaurants, and even in Klausen's home and office. Klausen's principal contact was the second secretary and consul of the Soviet Embassy in Tokyo, Viktor Sergevitch Zaitsev, who doubled as a GRU officer. (In 1947, Zaitsev served as press attaché at the Soviet Embassy in Washington.)

At the outset of the operation, Sorge had instituted ground rules to guard the security of his ring. Meetings were always arranged well in advance. Since he and Max were members of the German Club, there was nothing suspicious about their getting together, but Klausen varied his means of travel and his routes for all meetings to avoid the chance of being stopped by the police. He knew that when Sorge's gate lamp was lighted, he should stay away. In spite of the precautions he employed, Klausen frequently found himself in dangerous situations. Transporting his wireless set from point to point, he needed cool nerves and quick thinking. On one occasion when he was transmitting, a repairman on the roof tried to peer in at him. Max stood up, placing his back to the window. Another time a police inspector called when he was tapping out an urgent message to "Wiesbaden." Anna greeted the inspector, while her husband hurriedly locked the door to the radio room and came downstairs to receive his guest.

As fellow newsmen, Sorge and Voukelitch also could meet without raising undue suspicion. They got together at a number of popular German restaurants, a dingy bar on the Ginza called the Fledermaus, and at each other's homes. In meeting with Ozaki and Miyagi, Sorge had to exercise much greater care, and meetings were kept to a minimum.

Only Sorge himself was aware of the identity of all the members of the ring. As the radio operator, Klausen knew the code names of all the principal members, but even he did not learn Ozaki's real identity until 1941, and he never knew Miyagi's true name. Ozaki never met Voukelitch, saw Klausen once, and did not know his name, either.

When the Konoye government fell after eighteen months in power, Ozaki remained an important member of a special advisory group called "the Breakfast Club." Through his contacts in the club, he secured a position as consultant to the Investigation Department of the South Manchurian Railroad. His new job provided Ozaki with an opportunity to be of great help to Sorge. Because of the importance of the railroad, Ozaki had carte blanche to vital classified information on all aspects of Japanese policy, as well as to the plans of the Japanese military, including the movements of the Kwantung Army.

Although Anna Klausen and Edith Voukelitch were not actual members of the *apparat,* Sorge made use of both as couriers. Anna's reluctance to cooperate was tempered in part by her love for her husband and in part by her fondness for shopping in Shanghai and Hong Kong. But her political views remained unchanged; she disliked everything about communism. Edith, dull and stolid, simply did as she was told. In 1938, she and Branko separated when he fell in love with a Japanese woman, Yamasaki Yoshiko.

After the Voukelitches separated, Sorge was worried that Edith's bitterness toward her husband might lead to exposure of the ring. He asked for and received permission from Moscow to finance her departure from Japan. Voukelitch wanted her to take their son and return to Russia. Anna talked her out of it, saying it was no place for anyone to live. Edith selected Australia, and during the summer of 1941, she departed, to the relief of Branko and Sorge.

As for Sorge's personal life, the long list of his mistresses includes the names of wives of officials at the German Embassy, as well as that of Yamasaki Yoshiko (in the period before she married Voukelitch). Had Voukelitch learned of Sorge's affair with Yoshiko, he might have become furious, because he was deeply in love with the Japanese woman. But if Sorge was a careful spy, he was also a careful Don Juan, and his subordinate never discovered the truth.

In spite of his amatory roving, Sorge did have a permanent mistress to whom he was generous and kind. Her name was Miyake Hanako and he met her in 1935 while celebrating his fortieth birthday at the Rheingold, where she was working as a waitress. She had a good voice, and Sorge encouraged her aspirations to become a singer by arranging for voice lessons for her. Hanako came to regard herself as Sorge's common-law wife and remained completely loyal and devoted to him. She never knew that he was a Communist spy.

But, of course, Sorge *was* a spy, a hard-working spy, whose cover was beginning to be threatened. Ott wanted him to take an official post in the German Embassy and grew annoyed when he persistently refused the offer. Sorge did so because he knew that if he accepted, the Gestapo would instigate a thorough review of his background.

To placate Ott, he agreed to become an unofficial press adviser with an office in the chancery. Daily, he arrived at 6:00 A.M., sorted out the news cabled from Berlin, and prepared releases for embassy members, the Japanese press, and the German community.

Soon, Sorge's fears were realized; Berlin began to suspect that he might be a Soviet agent.

Wilhelm von Ritgen, an editor in the Nazi party's Reich Press Department, had been receiving reports from Sorge which impressed him. He brought them to the attention of higher officials, and German Intelligence became interested. Ritgen was instructed to request Sorge to start sending information on the Soviet Union and China, as well as Japan. Everything he turned in would be closely monitored and checked against other sources, the assumption being that if he were a spy, at some point he would trip himself up by sending false information.

German Intelligence also had another more direct way to maintain surveillance over Sorge's activities. Colonel Josef Meisinger, a colonel in the Gestapo, had just been dispatched to the embassy in Tokyo to supervise German security in Japan.

Meisinger's record of brutality in Poland had earned him the nickname, "the Butcher of Warsaw." [2] He was given a full briefing on Sorge and told to investigate his activities. However, when the colonel arrived on the scene in the summer of 1940, Sorge quickly became his drinking partner. Any suspicions Meisinger might have harbored disappeared in a haze of cigar smoke and *sake*. In addition, Sorge was too clever to send von Ritgen false information, and soon German Intelligence issued a favorable report.

In September, 1940, the Japanese joined with Germany and Italy in the Tripartite Pact. The agreement was aimed against Great Britain and the United States, particularly the latter. The alliance committed Japan and Germany to go to war against the United States should one or the other be attacked by her. Through Sorge, Moscow knew the provisions of the pact before they were made public. Six months later, however, largely through the efforts of Japanese Foreign Minister Matsuoka (who had just held secret talks with Hitler) and the insistence of Stalin, Japan signed a neutrality pact with Russia.

Sorge, for once, was taken completely by surprise by the news, as was Ott. But while the ambassador was dismayed by the pact, Sorge was overjoyed. However, he knew full well the unpredictable nature of the Japanese military clique, and even though Konoye was again prime minister, Sorge was not convinced that Russia was safe from Japanese attack. Ozaki agreed, and both felt that should Hitler move against Russia, the pact would be meaningless. It was this last grave threat that now occupied all of Sorge's attention. As early as March, 1941, he had passed on to the Fourth Bureau microfilms of telegrams exchanged by von Ribbentrop and Ott, giving mid-June as the possible date of such an attack.

In May, Colonel Ritter von Niedermayer arrived from Berlin with a letter of introduction to Sorge from von Dirksen. He further supported Sorge's fear that plans were going forward to launch an invasion, but it was Sorge's old friend, Colonel Scholl, on his way to a new post in Bangkok, who finally gave him the specific details: "The attack will begin by June 20. There may be two or three days delay. Preparations are complete. 170-190 German divisions are massed on the Eastern frontier. There will be no ultimatum or declaration of war."

It was a clear, hard warning, a clarion call to arms, but Stalin refused to accept it, even though he had received the same warning from an agent in Prague and from the British government.

On May 15, Sorge radioed Moscow that Hitler would invade Russia on June 22. On June 22, exactly as Sorge had predicted, the attack took place.

Sorge's reaction to the German invasion offers a rare insight into his feelings.

"On that day," Hanako said, "he wept as though his heart would break."

"Why are you so upset?" she asked.

"Because I am lonely. I have no real friends."

"But surely you have Ambassador Ott and other good German friends."

"No, no! They are not my friends." [3]

After the attack, Moscow had only one question for Sorge to answer: would Japan strike her northern neighbor in the back?

In the hectic and dramatic days leading up to and following Hitler's invasion of Russia, the ring members began to show the strain of their long, arduous years of undercover operations. Klausen had been under continuous stress because of his wife's hatred of communism. In 1940, he had suffered a serious heart attack, and his attitude toward the Fourth Bureau began to sour. When Moscow demanded that he finance the *apparat* out of the profits from his increasingly successful blueprint business, he became furious. Morose and withdrawn, he grew slack in his work, developing a reluctance to transmit frequently or at length.

Voukelitch had become similarly disenchanted. A father again by his Japanese wife, Yoshiko, he was anxious to break from the ring completely. His wife knew nothing of his spying. He was a respected journalist with a position he enjoyed at the French Havas News Agency. He began to avoid Sorge, often failing to show up at pre-arranged meetings.

Sorge's most frequent contacts were with Miyagi, who had built up a ring of seven agents located in or around the military. Miyagi's information on Japanese military strength was so sensitive that in 1941 Sorge was able to send to Moscow the details of Japanese battle plans in all areas. But with the relentless tightening of security and the constant rounding up of suspected Communists, Miyagi saw the end coming. Fatalistically, he went his appointed rounds, feeling a sense of impending doom.

Ozaki's principal doubts at the time concerned not so much his own survival as that of the Soviet Union. If caught, he assumed his high position would protect him. His motivations were idealistic; he saw himself as a patriot, trying to prevent Japan from engaging in war, particularly war against the Soviet Union. He believed he was seeking the brotherhood of man.

Sorge was weary. He wanted, needed, a rest. He was not dis-illusioned with communism, but news of Stalin's blood purges had given rise to searching doubts. Berzin was a victim, Uritsky, too. The length of the list seemed endless. Hitler's attack had brought its own special anguish. "Why didn't Stalin listen to me!" he raged, when the news came.

Also there were the long years of constant trickery and deceit. The Otts looked upon him as a deep and trusted friend, as did many others he had deceived. Beneath the hard crust of the ideologue, beneath the cold manipulator, lay the inner man, sorely troubled. "Eternally a stranger, fleeing from himself," Sorge once confessed. The arrogance, the conceit, the driving ego had sustained him in the grueling game of outwitting his adversaries, but he could not hide the cost; it was there, reflected in his face. His broad forehead was ridged with furrows, and twin lines slashed down from his nose like scars. His face had become a tragic mask from a Japanese Kabuki play.

On July 2, 1941, a fateful Imperial Conference, with the em-peror present, mapped out Japanese strategy for the future. Nego-tiations with the United States—principally over the U.S. insistence that Japan withdraw from China—were still pending. The members of the conference decided that if these negotiations failed, Japanese forces would strike south into Indochina and the Dutch East Indies.

However, Ozaki reported to Sorge that Japan: "would prepare for an emergency in the *north or the south* by carrying out a general mobilization which would make possible the dispatch of troops in either direction."

Through Ott and his embassy staff, Berlin worked overtime to try to bring pressure to bear for a northern attack, but although the Japanese firmly believed Stalin's days were numbered, they did not appear anxious to strike at this time.

A few days after the conference, Ozaki informed Sorge that an expeditionary force would be sent to Saigon. Moscow found this reassuring, but was alarmed by Miyagi's intelligence that winter clothing was being issued to some of the newly mobilized units.

The mobilization, which was supposed to be completed by August 15, called for 1,300,000 men, and was to be carried out in three phases. Sorge and Ozaki were, as Sorge described it, "tormented by the fear that the Japanese government would accept this grand scale mobilization as a fait accompli and the mobilization itself might lead to war with the Soviet Union."

Ott did not believe that Japan would attack Russia, and even though in early August Sorge had signaled Moscow of heavy troop reinforcements in Korea and Manchuria, the issue remained in doubt. The Japanese government was being swayed, on the one hand by German victories on the eastern front, and on the other, by the possible outcome of their negotiations with the United States.

On July 24, Japanese forces moved into Indochina. On July 26, the United States froze Japanese assets abroad and instituted a trade embargo against her.

Moscow continued to press for an answer. Sorge's only source of information on the question was Ozaki. Finally, in late August of 1941, following a conference of the Japanese High Command in Tokyo, Ozaki came up with the answer the Fourth Bureau was seeking so desperately.

Klausen tapped out the most important communication of the ring's career:

"The Conference decided not to declare war this year, repeat— decided not to declare war this year against the Soviet Union . . ."

No attack!

Historians continue to debate whether Sorge's "no attack" message changed the course of history. Many believe that it did, pointing out that between the time Moscow received Sorge's assurances and mid-December, when the Wehrmacht advance was stopped, more than 250,000 of Russia's Far Eastern forces were shifted from the Siberian front to stem the German tide. These troops were to join in the defense of Moscow by the early part of December. Some military experts are convinced that the reinforcements from the Far East saved the Soviet regime from defeat and thereby contributed to the collapse of Nazi Germany.

Sorge and his subordinates had fulfilled the major purpose of their mission, but more questions came crackling in from the Kremlin. Now the focus was on relations between Japan and the United States. Would there be war between the two?

On October 4, 1941, Sorge gave his reply:

> According to information obtained from various Japanese official sources, if no satisfactory reply is received from the U.S. to Japan's request for negotiations by the 15 or 16 of this month, there will be a general resignation or a drastic reorganization of the Japanese government. In either event there will be war with the U.S. this month or next month. The sole hope of the Japanese authorities is that Ambassador Grew will present some sort of 11th hour proposal through which negotiations can be opened. . . .
>
> With respect to the Soviet Union, top-ranking elements are generally agreed that if Germany wins Japan can take over her gains in the Far East in the future and that therefore it is unnecessary for Japan to fight Russia. They feel that if Germany proves unable to destroy the Soviet government and force it out of Moscow, Japan should bide her time until next spring. In any event, the American issue and the question of the advance to the south are far more important than the northern problem.

It was the last message the ring was to send.

For some time, the Japanese had been sure that they had a spy ring in their midst. As early as 1938, the Japanese Home Ministry of the Special Higher Police was picking up both Klausen's transmissions to "Wiesbaden" and "Wiesbaden's" coded replies. A year later, the Japanese navy reported that it had detected coded transmissions for which there was no explanation. By 1940, the Japanese were convinced that the ring existed. However, they could not pinpoint it. Klausen shifted the transmission from one heavily populated district to another, so that it was almost impossible to get a fix on his location at any given time. Further, the Japanese detection equipment was inadequate. Knowing that a spy ring was operating in the heart of Tokyo, but finding themselves totally unable to trace its coded footprints to their source, infuriated the Japanese.

The key to Klausen's enciphered messages was two volumes of the *German Statistical Year Book for 1934-35*. All wireless transmission between Klausen and "Wiesbaden" was coded from it and went out in groups of numbers. It was a code the Japanese never broke.

Because of their obsessive fear of spies, the Japanese automatically kept a close watch on foreigners, and by 1940 the *Tokko* and the *Kempei*—whose lack of cooperation with each other made for duplication and inefficiency—had Sorge under close surveillance.

The *Kempei*'s suspicions had been stimulated by Colonel Meisinger. On Meisinger's arrival in Tokyo to take charge of German security, he had admitted to his opposite number in the *Kempei* that Sorge was under suspicion. Although Meisinger's attitude toward Sorge changed swiftly, the *Kempei*'s did not. They posted an agent in a house directly across the street from Sorge's residence to watch his movements.

The *Tokko* also regarded Ozaki with suspicion, not as a possible spy, but as the author of liberal books and articles. As for Klausen and Voukelitch, they were no more suspect than any other foreigners.

So, during the years between 1938 and 1941, the Japanese were slowly, imperceptibly weaving their net. However, in the end, it was neither wireless transmission nor surveillance that was to enable them to pull in the big catch. Instead, it was a combination of the *Tokko*'s constant and patient trolling for local Communists and some clues supplied by a very small, insignificant fish.

Ito Ritsu was known by Japanese security to be a Comintern member. Previously arrested, he was picked up again in November, 1939. The *Tokko* knew that there was a close Comintern association between U.S. and Japanese members of the party. They questioned Ito on these links. At the time of his arrest, he was suffering from tuberculosis and afraid of what a long prison term would do to his health. That, coupled with Japanese interrogation methods, led him to talk. Among other U.S. Japanese party members, he mentioned Mrs. Kitabayashi, Miyagi's former landlady in Los Angeles. She had returned to Japan in 1936 and was living quietly with her husband in the countryside. For a year after Ito's confession, the Kitabayashis were watched by the *Tokko*, who found nothing suspicious in their actions. Then, on September 28, 1941, on the strength of information provided by Ito Ritsu's common-law wife, Mrs. Kitabayashi and her husband were picked up and brought to Tokyo for questioning.

Miyagi had visited his old landlady once or twice a year, mainly out of kindness, although occasionally she did offer him inconsequential information. After her arrest, she mentioned Miyagi's name to her interrogator, assuming that the police knew him. They had never heard of him.

On October 11, a loud knock thudded on Miyagi's door. He

answered it, and the police marched in. They had come to arrest him as a Communist suspect. On searching his house, they were dumbfounded to find confidential government documents that had been translated into English, including a secret memorandum from the offices of the South Manchurian Railway.

Roughly, the police bundled him off to the second floor of the Tsukiji police station where serious questioning began. The interrogation was brutal and unceasing and Miyagi's health was weak, but he stoically refused to admit a thing. Finally, the interrogators broke for lunch. Miyagi waited for a chance, and when his guard turned away for a moment, he leaped up, ran for the window, and dived headfirst through it. He hoped to kill himself in the thirty-foot fall. Instead, he landed in a pile of brush, his chief questioner right beside him. Miyagi had broken a leg. The police carried him back, and the questioning continued. This time, the interrogators were successful. Miyagi's resistance was broken; he saw in his failure to commit suicide the irrevocable hand of fate. The next morning, he confessed that he was a member of a spy ring which consisted of Sorge, Voukelitch, Klausen, and Ozaki.

On October 15, the police came for Ozaki. Later he wrote: "I had had an uneasy premonition for several days and on that morning I knew that the final hour of reckoning had come. Making certain Yoko had left for school, for I was anxious that my daughter should not be present, I left the house without looking at my wife and without any farewell speech. I felt that with my arrest everything had ended, that it was all over."

On that same day, Sorge drafted a message to the Fourth Bureau, saying that the *apparat* had completed its work. He asked for recall and reassignment.

Klausen described the last meeting of the three remaining members two days after Ozaki's arrest: "Around 7:00 P.M. I went to visit Sorge, who was in bed at the time, to talk about our secret work. He was drinking with Voukelitch when I arrived and I joined the circle opening a bottle of *sake* which I had brought. The atmosphere was heavy and Sorge said gravely—as if our fate was sealed—'Neither Joe nor Otto showed up to meet us. They must have been arrested by the police.' I was gripped by a strange fear and left after ten minutes. We did not discuss what we would do if we were arrested."

Early the next morning, the three were arrested. There was nothing any of them could do. It was all over.

Sorge's guilt was obvious to the authorities before the confessions were obtained from him and his fellow ring members, from the wealth of evidence found in his second-floor den. The police searched his house and catalogued his belongings. There, in the list, was the tangible proof of espionage: cameras, copying equipment, sixteen notebooks with details of agent contacts and financing, decoding and encoding tables, reports and charts in English, and his last unsent message. It was enough to hang any spy.

Faced with the evidence, faced with the statements of confession by the others and the implication that his confession might help to mitigate their punishments, he gave in. He is reported to have burst into tears and cried out, "I am defeated! For the first time in my life I am defeated!"

The rest was epilogue: a brief, painful meeting at Sugamo Prison with Eugen Ott, whose career was now ruined; months of interrogation in preparation for the trial; the trial, and then, almost two years after his arrest, the sentencing.

On September 29, 1943, Richard Sorge and Ozaki Hotsumi were sentenced to death, Max Klausen and Branko de Voukelitch to life imprisonment, and Anna Klausen to three years. Hanako and Yoshiko were declared innocent. Miyagi was never sentenced; he died in prison in August, 1943, as a result of ill health and mistreatment. His seven subagents, as well as Ozaki's four, received long sentences, and the unwitting Mrs. Kitabayashi was sentenced to a five-year term. She died soon after her release in 1945.

Voukelitch, the man who had wanted to give up his espionage activities, also perished before the war's end. For a time he was in Sugamo Prison where his wife was allowed to visit him. Transferred in July, 1944, to the grim Abashiri Prison, located in Hokkaido, where the climate is harsh and savage, he refused to allow his wife and baby to move near him. On January 15, 1945, his wife received a wire: Voukelitch had died of pneumonia two days previously.

Sorge and Ozaki appealed the verdicts against them without success. On November 7, 1944, the twenty-seventh anniversary of the Russian Revolution, the sentences were carried out. To the very end, Sorge believed that the Kremlin, which he had served so long and so well, would come to his rescue and arrange to bring about his exchange. It was a vain hope. He and Ozaki went to their deaths silently, stoically, alone.

Of the principals, only tough, shaggy Max Klausen survived, survived after nearly being burned to death in an American air raid on Tokyo, survived weighing ninety-nine pounds. When he was released by U.S. troops in October, 1945, Anna was waiting for him. Soviet officials quickly spirited the pair by special military aircraft to Russia, where Max was placed in a hospital. After he recovered his health, he took Anna to East Berlin, where they changed their names, joined the German Communist party, and lived in quiet obscurity.

It was through the investigative work of Major General Charles A. Willoughby, at the war's end, that the story of the Sorge ring was brought to light. At the time, Willoughby was chief of intelligence under General Douglas MacArthur. After the first clue was provided by a Japanese official, Willoughby and his staff compiled a full report on the Sorge ring. The Willoughby report was released to the press in Tokyo on February 10, 1949.

Until 1964, the Soviet Union continued to assert that neither the Soviet government nor the Soviet Embassy had any connection with the Sorge case. Finally, on November 5, 1964, two days before the twentieth anniversary of Sorge's death, the country for which he had died—the country that had never so much as admitted that he had ever lived—suddenly hailed him and praised his services. Posthumously, he was awarded the Kremlin's highest accolade, the supreme decoration of Hero of the Soviet Union. A street and a tanker were named after him. The following spring, a four-kopeck stamp bearing his likeness was issued to further commemorate his deeds.

In October, 1964, the East Germans conferred a gold medal on Max and Anna Klausen. In the spring of 1965, Yoshiko and her son were invited to Moscow. There, Anastas Mikoyan, then president of the Soviet Union, presented them, in Voukelitch's memory, the Order of the Patriotic War, First Class. Some months later, Hanako visited the Soviet Union through special invitation.

Sorge had been buried in Zoshigaya Cemetery in a part of the burial ground reserved for homeless vagrants. No one took care of his grave. For two years, Hanako petitioned authorities to have him moved. At last she was successful. Today, through Hanako's efforts, Sorge's grave lies next to those of Ozaki Hotsumi and Miyagi Yotoku.

CHAPTER THREE

The Defector
Igor Gouzenko – The Spy They Wouldn't Listen To

On August 2, 1939, Albert Einstein wrote President Franklin D. Roosevelt a personal letter. He did so at the urging of two atomic physicists, Dr. Edward Teller and Dr. Leo Szilard. The pair had made a special visit to see Einstein to report that they and their colleagues, most of whom were refugees from Hitler repression, had reached a critical stage of development in their momentous search for a method to utilize the power of the atom. Now, if they were to continue, they needed funding from the U.S. government. From the evidence of their research, these scientists believed they could create a new kind of weapon, which would be the most devastating on earth. Would Einstein ask the president if there was interest?

By the time the letter reached Roosevelt, Europe was at war and Hitler and Stalin were allies. The president was interested. Funds and vital uranium ore would be made available.[1]

Of course, absolute secrecy was essential. Thus, the Manhattan Engineering District (MED) was formed as a covering agency. What went on within its confines during the war in various laboratories in the United States, Canada, and Great Britain was supposed to be a closely guarded secret. In fact, the secret was kept from the general public in the Allied nations and from Axis Intelligence, but not from Soviet Intelligence.

It is no exaggeration to say that the ink was hardly dry on Einstein's letter before the Kremlin knew of the proposal. At that time, Russian scientists, although limited by funds, had been engaged in similar research, and even during the period of the Hitler-Stalin Pact they had available to them all the pertinent scientific papers and journals published in the West. Before the war began, they had open access to the data; later, they obtained their information through the diligence of Soviet Intelligence. However, after Hitler struck in June, 1941, Russia was fighting for survival, and Soviet scientists had little chance to delve into the giant steps the MED was taking in striving to harness and control the power of the atom.

In addition, Stalin, with the same kind of blindness he had shown in failing to heed Richard Sorge's warning, for a time did not understand the importance of the work of the Manhattan Project. Thus, while Soviet agents continued to collect all the data they could on the development of the atom bomb, their reports were largely ignored until 1943. Then, in 1943, as the MED drew closer to success, the Kremlin awoke to what was at stake. In a few short years, the finest scientific minds in the world had taken the concept of nuclear fission, guided it through a maze of enormous intricacies, moved it from possibility to probability, and brought it to the threshold of certainty.

At first, Russian scientists were in no position to catch up. They had been far outdistanced in research development and technology, and they lacked the necessary uranium ore with which to experiment. However, through Soviet espionage *apparati* operating in the United States, Canada, and Great Britain, Russian scientists received technical information as well as actual samples of the type of uranium used in the atom bomb. Soviet Intelligence enabled the Soviet Union to become an atomic power at least a decade earlier than anticipated.

Some of these *apparati* were eventually exposed after the fact and many of their agents were apprehended. Many of them confessed to their spying. Some did not, and still others sought asylum behind the Iron Curtain. The exposure of these spy rings—three in the United States, several in Great Britain, and one in Canada—came not only through the efforts of Allied Counterintelligence and the FBI after 1946,[2] but also through the revelations of one man—Igor Gouzenko. He was, until his defection, a Soviet spy.

Having had the opportunity to compare the Soviet Union with the West, Gouzenko made a choice. He did so at the risk of his life.

*   *   *   *   *

In the dusk of the unseasonably hot September evening, Igor Gouzenko made his solitary way from his residence at 511 Somerset Street toward his place of business on Range Road in the city of Ottawa, Canada. He had gone through the motions of eating an early dinner. Then he had said good-by to Anna, his wife, and Andrei, his two-year-old son. He did not know whether he would be returning to them, and, if he did, into what kind of peril he might be plunging them. He knew only that he had crossed his Rubicon. Anna, from whom he drew strength, supported his decision. She was nearly six months pregnant, and he must act now while she was still able to move with reasonable speed.

Ostensibly, Gouzenko worked in Canada as a secretary and interpreter attached to Colonel Nikolai Zabotin, the military attaché at the Soviet Embassy. Actually, however, he was one of a number of such officers at the embassy whose identity and purpose was concealed under the cover of a diplomatic cloak. Gouzenko's real job was to encode and decode secret messages sent to and from the Moscow Center; he was a cipher clerk. A lieutenant in the GRU, he served as a member of an extremely successful spy ring, directed by Colonel Zabotin.

Gouzenko's fateful decision had been formulated a year ago on another September night when, after wandering the streets in the rain, he had returned home to tell his wife that word had arrived from Moscow for his recall. For the first time since their arrival in Canada, they had blurted out their mutual feelings. They wanted to stay! They wanted a new life in a free land for Andrei and for themselves. To go back to what they had left was unthinkable. But how could they remain?

At that time, in order to delay his recall, Gouzenko had suggested to Colonel Zabotin that because of his skill in English, he might continue to be of service. Surprisingly, Moscow had agreed, and during the twelve-month reprieve, Gouzenko had wrestled with the problem of devising a course of action that could make his stay permanent. This had been no easy thing to do, for life within the closed embassy community was a constant exercise in poker playing in which everyone watched everyone else.

The Secret Police agent in the embassy was Vitali Pavlov, the second secretary. He was also the NKVD chief for Canada. Pavlov ran his own spy ring, staffed by embassy personnel. The NKVD cipher clerk, Farafontov, was listed as an embassy chauffeur. To Gouzenko's knowledge, nineteen members of the embassy staff were agents either of the GRU or the NKVD. Their primary mission was to steal all secrets of military, political, and economic significance that they could lay their hands on and transmit them to Moscow.

The constant internal spying by the "neighbors," as the GRU called the NKVD, created a closed and tense atmosphere within the operation. A careless word, a thoughtless act, and one could be sent back to Moscow "for reassignment." That could mean anything from a demotion to a bullet in the head. Even within the two bodies there was jealousy and intrigue. For example, Gouzenko had witnessed an attempt by Lieutenant Colonel Motinov, the assistant military attaché, to have his superior, Zabotin, cut down. Motinov had secretly passed on derogatory information to Moscow, indicating that Zabotin had recommended for promotion a subordinate who frequently got drunk and misbehaved. Gouzenko knew that Motinov's story was false; furthermore, he admired Zabotin, a handsome, gregarious man. Still, he kept silent because inside the Soviet Embassy silence was a prerequisite to survival.

Under the circumstances, to prepare to break free took courage. But to set up an escape plan as audacious as Gouzenko's—to carry away with him documentary proof of the vast espionage network of which he was a part—took an iron resolve. One misstep and he was finished.

Gouzenko continued his walk. His footsteps thudded on the pavement. This night was the culmination of a year's planning; he was about to begin Operation Escape. Perspiring heavily, he headed for the office of the military attaché.

His replacement, Lieutenant Koulakov, whom he was breaking in on the job, was scheduled to be on night-guard duty. This was of vital importance. If Koulakov were on duty, Gouzenko would not have to check in for work until noon the next day, and the chances were excellent that he would not be reported missing until then. The work of the cipher section was top secret, and only Koulakov and Colonel Zabotin knew when Gouzenko was supposed to be at the office. Since the colonel was attending a diplomatic function at the National Film Board, it was not likely that he would show up before noon, either. It was for these reasons that Gouzenko had decided to act that night. He wanted to buy as much time as he could. In the dangerous undertaking he was about to begin, time could decide whether he lived or died.

He turned into Range Road—a short, heavy-set, blonde young man, dressed in ordinary civilian clothes. Before entering the familiar two-story house which also served as a residence for the military attaché and his wife, he paused to steady himself. He must act normal; Koulakov, like himself, was keen and observant.

Smiling pleasantly, Gouzenko entered the foyer. Koulakov was sitting at the watch desk as scheduled. They exchanged greetings.

Captain Galkin, a GRU officer who doubled as a door guard, came over to join them. "Hey, Igor," he said to Gouzenko, "How about going to a movie with me?" [3]

Here was the ruse Gouzenko needed, an excuse to leave the premises quickly without arousing any suspicions. "It really is too hot to work," he said. "Wait for me. I have something to check for the colonel."

A few minutes later, in the company of Galkin and several other staff members, Gouzenko strolled to the theater. As soon as they arrived, he commented ruefully, "Damn it, I've already seen the show!" He told his companions he would take a streetcar and go downtown to another movie.

Then he was alone again, hurrying toward the trolley stop. Once he was sure Galkin and the others were in the theater, he continued walking, heading toward Charlotte Street and the embassy. Now the real ordeal was to begin. For a month, ever since he had learned that his departure was set for early October, he had been carefully selecting the documents he planned to steal. He wanted proof of the scope of Soviet espionage in Canada as performed by a single *apparat*. Zabotin had once remarked that here, in a country of 13 million people, there were nine *apparati* at work in direct contact with Moscow. Gouzenko knew that he could not prove the existence of the other eight, but he could certainly prove the existence of the one to which he was attached.

In discussing his decision with Anna, he had wondered if the Canadians would accept the warning. Those he had met seemed to consider all Russians allies. How had Motinov described Canadians and Americans? "They are trusting children." [4] And Zabotin had replied, "They can't seem to get it in their heads that today we are friends, but tomorrow we might be enemies."

Anna had felt that the information in the documents would convince anyone. She was sure that if he took this dangerous chance, he would earn the right for them to live in this country they had come to admire so much. They both knew that if he were caught, she, Andrei, and their unborn child would be in grave danger, too, unless she could secure asylum. To buy her protection from the West in case he failed to escape, Gouzenko had previously stolen three secret documents: two telegrams from the Moscow Center asking for information on the atom bomb, and a report on the reelection to the Canadian Parliament of Fred Rose, one of the two key Canadians in the spy ring. Gouzenko had managed to remove the papers from the files, replacing them with copies. He had put the documents in his

Igor Gouzenko, wearing a hood to conceal his identity, tells late columnist Drew Pearson about his defection from Soviet spy ring in Canada.

pockets, walked out of the embassy, and brought them home to Anna.

Fair-haired, blue-eyed Anna was a young woman whose courage equaled her husband's. Once he began to have second thoughts, she firmly overrode his doubts, saying "I will not hear of you changing your mind. This is your chance to do something big for this country and for yourself, and most of all for Andrei and the new baby. Anything I might have to suffer here would be preferable to what we must all certainly face if we return to Moscow."

Anna had put the incriminating papers on a pantry shelf, next to a box of matches, in case it was necessary to burn them. As an added precaution, they decided to lock their apartment door and only open it to each other when either of them used a coded knock.

Now, Gouzenko approached the door of the embassy. The building was a drafty, unattractive fortress. Never had the blocky, three-storied edifice looked so forbidding. Gouzenko remembered that Zabotin had recently complimented him on always remaining calm. He steeled himself to appear cool and collected as he walked up the steps, nodding to the guard.

In the front hall, Gouzenko routinely signed the duty register, glancing toward the reception room. For a moment he could not move—there sat Vitali Pavlov, the sharp-witted, eagle-eyed chief of the NKVD in Canada. Forcing himself to act naturally, Gouzenko walked past the reception room to the stairs. Beneath the banister there was a concealed bell. He pressed it and started up the stairs, still not sure whether the secret policeman had spotted him.

The bell had sent a signal alerting the man on duty in the embassy's secret cipher wing on the second floor. Entrance to the wing was through a steel door hidden behind a velvet curtain at the end of a hallway. Pulling the curtain aside, Gouzenko put his face in front of a small opening so that the man within could see who he was. The door was unbarred. Gouzenko entered and was greeted by Ryazanov, a cipher clerk like himself when he was not serving as a commercial attaché. Ryazanov opened a second heavy steel door which led to a carpeted corridor with six small rooms, three on each side. The military cipher office where Gouzenko worked was on the right; across from it was the washroom. Next to Gouzenko's office was the commercial cipher office where Ryazanov did his coding; across from it was the NKVD cipher room. Facing each other at the end of the hall were two incinerator rooms.

Gouzenko was relieved to find that only Ryazanov was present. After commenting on the unseasonable weather, Ryazanov asked Gouzenko whether he was planning to work late. No, Gouzenko

How a Soviet Spy Ring Is Set Up

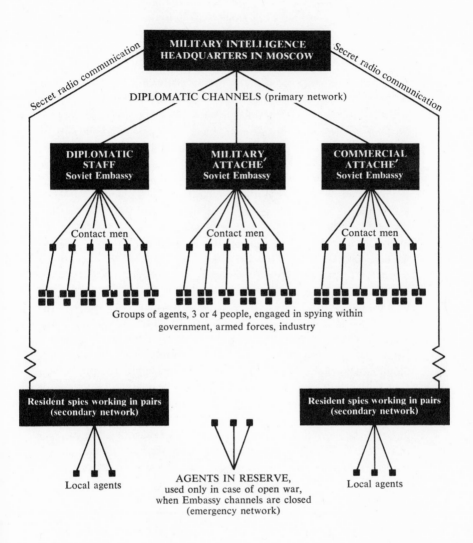

Organizational chart of a Soviet apparat, *as described by Igor Gouzenko.*

Source: *U.S.News & World Report.*

answered, there was a movie he wanted to see. He had just a couple of telegrams to do, and then he was going to catch a show downtown.

Ryazanov returned to his office and Gouzenko entered his, closing the door behind him. During the work day, Ouspensky, who was chief of the secret cipher branch, kept a radio going full blast to prevent the employees working in one room from overhearing what went on in the next. Now, it was quiet.

Gouzenko moved swiftly, forcing himself to concentrate on nothing but the task ahead. For a month he had been carefully selecting documents that would prove to the Canadians not only the scope of the *apparat,* but also the identity of its Canadian, British, and Russian members. He had marked these documents by turning down their corners. That afternoon he had taken many of the marked documents out of the files. After placing them in Zabotin's special cipher pouch, he had locked the pouch in his desk. Now, he quickly extracted the rest of the marked documents from the files. In all— although he did not stop to count them—there were 109 pieces of evidence. Somehow he managed to distribute the entire collection around his body beneath his shirt. Then he set to work encoding the telegrams he had told Ryazanov he was working on.

When the encoding was finished, Gouzenko took the telegrams to Ryazanov for transmission to Moscow. Nervously, he watched the other cipher clerk to detect any reaction to his sudden bulkiness. There was none. Gouzenko stepped into the men's room to wash his hands and check his appearance in the mirror. Then, giving his bulging shirt a final tuck, he walked to the door.

Once clear of the cipher wing, he approached the long flight of stairs, hoping desperately that he would not have to run the gauntlet past Pavlov below. He forced himself to walk slowly. Undue movement would make him crackle like a newspaper, or a small document might slip down past his belt and drop out from his trouser leg. Perspiration dripped down his face, onto his body. He was afraid to reach for a handkerchief. Approaching the yawning entrance of the reception room, he forced himself to look straight ahead. He entered the room. Out of the corner of his eye, he saw that it was empty, except for the guard. His legs felt weak. He signed out, told the guard good night, and walked down the steps, inhaling deeply and walking at a steady pace.

When he and Anna had discussed to whom he would turn over evidence of Soviet spying, they had decided a newspaper was best. Through the press, they reasoned, the story would reach everyone.

As a cipher clerk, Igor Gouzenko sat in the catbird seat of the *apparat.* For obvious reasons involving protection and security, there are few spies who are informed about more than a small part of the whole operation in which they are involved. However, through Gouzenko flowed the two-way traffic between the control in Moscow and operations in Ottawa. Because of his unique position, he was able to see the ring's workings with a clarity that he intended all to share. The 109 documents he had purloined were pieces of a puzzle. When that puzzle was assembled, it would tell a story that encompassed years of Soviet espionage. Gouzenko's revelations would shake officialdom, not only in Ottawa, but in Washington and London as well.

Here is a brief summary of the operations of Soviet espionage in Canada as reconstructed from the documents Gouzenko obtained:

Until 1942, Canada and the Soviet Union did not have diplomatic relations, therefore Soviet Intelligence lacked an official base in Canada to use as a cover for mounting large-scale operations. Moreover, until the war, the Kremlin had no real military interest in the Dominion. However, during the thirties, two factors had swelled the ranks of the Communist party in Canada, as in the United States: the Popular Front, in which Communists joined with socialists and liberals in opposing Hitler, and the depression. And, in the same period, Russia had placed two spies in the Ottawa-Toronto-Montreal area. Canadian authorities knew them as Sam Carr and Fred Rose.

Both men were born in 1906 of Russian parents; Carr in the Ukraine, and Rose in Poland. They had emigrated to Canada in the mid-twenties. Both had openly espoused the Communist cause and had become leaders of Canada's Communist party. Secretly, Carr (born Schmil Kogan) and Rose (born Fred Rosenberg) had begun working for Soviet Intelligence around 1930 after visiting Moscow and training at the Lenin Institute. Until 1942, a large part of their espionage work in Canada involved reporting to Moscow on party members who had deviated from the Stalinist line.

Carr and Rose also organized special study cells in which half a dozen neophytes of similar political orientation, guided by a professional party worker, gathered together to examine and discuss Marxist theoretical works. The members of these groups were carefully screened, and their biographical and character descriptions were placed in the Comintern file in Moscow. They were to serve as recruits for the intelligence apparatus that was mounted in 1942.

Shortly after the Hitler-Stalin Pact and the outlawing of the Communist party in Canada, Carr, Rose, and the top officials in the party went into hiding. In September, 1942, they turned themselves in to the authorities, maintaining that their previous criticisms of the war effort, voiced and written during the Hitler-Stalin alliance, had been in error. Now, they asserted, they considered the war "a just war," and they wanted to join the fight against Hitler. They promised to abstain from any further Communist party agitation; "to carefully observe and obey the laws of Canada and such rules and regulations as may specially be prescribed"; and "to strictly abstain from taking up arms against and from doing any acts of hostility toward the government of this country. . . ."

Carr and Rose were released in early October. Before the month was over, they were engaged in espionage for the Soviet Union.

The first official agency the Russian government established in Canada was a trade mission. Attached to it as a factory inspector was Major Sokolov of the GRU. Under the cover name of Davie, his assignment was to start building an *apparat*. After a Soviet Legation was set up in Toronto, Sokolov's work was directed by Serge M. Kudriavtzev, who had the code name of Leon and the official title of first secretary.[5]

Sokolov's first major contact was Rose, and Kudriavtzev's was Carr, but because Rose and Carr were assigned to the "neighbors" (NKVD), and this was to be a GRU *apparat,* it was necessary to have them reassigned. In order to do so, Sokolov, who had no radio or code facilities, had to travel to New York City where he called on Pavel Mikhailov. Mikhailov, serving as a vice consul at the Soviet Legation, was also a military intelligence officer. Sokolov asked him to signal Moscow to make the change. Moscow agreed, and Rose and Carr went to work for the GRU. By 1943, with their aid, Sokolov and Kudriavtzev had put together a small, but potentially productive, spy ring, with agents operating in Ottawa, Toronto, and Montreal.

In June of 1943, Colonel Nikolai Zabotin arrived on the scene to take command. He brought with him as his cipher clerk, Lieutenant Igor Gouzenko. Gouzenko had gone through a long period of special training and an investigation in depth by the NKVD. In his youth, he had joined the Young Communist League and as a result of top scholastic grades he was admitted to the Moscow Architectural Institute. It was here that he met Anna, who was also a student. When World War II broke out, he was transferred to the Military Engineering Academy and subsequently to the Red Army Intelligence Administration. Trained as a cipher specialist, he was assigned to Soviet Intelligence headquarters at 19 Znamesky Street in Moscow where, in the course of a year, he encoded and decoded messages to and from espionage rings all over the world.

Gouzenko was assigned to Canada in 1943. He described the Soviet spy network at that time as including "thousands, yes, thousands of agents in the United States, thousands in Great Britain and many other thousands spread elsewhere."

The twenty-four-year-old Gouzenko met his superior, Colonel Zabotin, for the first time when he reported for his departure flight to Canada. In the beginning, he admired the handsome officer who had transferred from the artillery to intelligence to become the new military attaché. Zabotin had curly, grayish hair and a military bearing. He was well-born, well-educated, and a gifted conversationalist with an engaging personality. Using the code name of Grant, Zabotin took his orders from *Politburo* member Georgi Malenkov. Malenkov stressed that the Soviet ambassador to Canada, Georgi Zarubin, was not to know anything about the ring.

When the colonel took charge, the *apparat* consisted of two small groups which operated under the direction of Rose and Carr, plus five Russian and four Canadian contacts. One contact was Mrs. Sokolov, who carried information between her husband and Kudriavtzev. By September, 1945, Zabotin had enlarged the operation to include twenty Canadians and seventeen Russians, although the number of Russians varied according to reassignments and recalls. His plan was to greatly enlarge the size of the *apparat,* partially by increasing the representatives of his country's trade mission and partially by doubling the size of his own staff. He intended to recruit many more Canadians during the postwar period, and his objective was to have each Canadian agent handled by a Russian contact.

His agents supplied Zabotin with three categories of information: technical, economic, and political.

Technically, aside from the development of the atomic bomb during World War II, the most important military advances in the West were in radar, antisubmarine devices, explosives, and propellants. All three areas were classified top secret; in all three, Zabotin had highly placed agents. One spy, Professor Raymond Boyer of McGill University, was considered by the Canadians and the Russians to be *the* leading expert on explosives in the Western Hemisphere.

Zabotin's agents obtained the secrets of all these military advances, not only in regard to operational equipment, but also in the field of research and development.

Economic information obtained by Canadian spies included reports on confidential financial matters such as international trade agreements and commercial policies. Moscow knew the location of all significant Canadian industries, their production figures and their distribution facilities. Agents handed over to the Soviet Union detailed reports on Canadian transportation as well as development plans for the future.

Political information obtained by Zabotin for Russia focused on the confidential policies of the other Allied countries. In addition, his agents supplied Soviet spies with forged identity documents such as passports, naturalization papers, and marriage and birth certificates. Much of this material was obtained by two female agents, one of whom had been passing information to Fred Rose since 1935.

As noted, by 1944, information on the development of the atomic bomb had become the Kremlin's first priority. In due course, it became the number one item on Zabotin's shopping list.

In July, 1944, Dr. John Douglas Cockcroft, a British scientist of world fame, was made director of the atomic energy project operating in Montreal and at a special plant at Chalk River, Ontario.

When Cockcroft came to Canada, he brought with him a special, hand-picked research group selected under tight security. He appointed his trusted aide, Dr. Allan Nunn May, as chief of the Montreal laboratories. May was one of the few who knew the details of the progress being made in the various installations of the Manhattan Project. He was also a Soviet spy. Known to the Moscow Center by his code name of Alek, the scientist had long been a Communist party member.

However, it was not until the spring of 1945, some months after Zabotin had begun, without much success, to try and ferret out atomic secrets, that Moscow informed him that he had "a very valuable source" at his finger tips. "He must be handled with care," said the cable. "He is a Communist party member."

From this information it was obvious to Zabotin that Alek had worked for Moscow before coming to Canada. He assigned his assistant, Lieutenant Angelov, whose code name was Baxter, to contact the British scientist. Angelov went about his work in a simple, direct manner. He looked up May's address in the Montreal telephone book, observed the premises for a time, and after assuring himself that there were no security agents about, he knocked on the door of May's apartment.

There was nothing sinister about the man who opened the door. Bald, with a diffident, scholarly air, no one could have looked less like a spy. Angelov said in greeting, "Best regards from Michael."

His hands trembling with terror, May hurriedly escorted the Soviet agent into a room. Pulling down the blind, he told the Russian in a hoarse whisper that he was being watched by Canadian security people. Furthermore, he had no intention of spying for the Soviet Union any longer.

Angelov informed May bluntly that he did not believe him. Moscow had a job for him, and if he did not cooperate appropriate action would be taken.

May was trapped. He had betrayed his country's most sensitive

Dr. Alan Nunn May, British scientist convicted of betraying Allied atomic secrets to the Soviet Union.

military secrets. Now he was threatened with exposure. What did Mr. Baxter want him to find out?

Mr. Baxter wanted intelligence on one subject and one subject alone, namely, atomic bomb research in Canada and the United States. To seal the bargain and to help restore May's courage, Angelov presented the scientist with two bottles of Scotch and $200 in cash. May took both. He later accepted another donation of $500, but the value of what he supplied in return cannot be measured in monetary terms.

Between April and the end of September, 1945, when May returned to England, he had a number of meetings with Mr. Baxter. At one, he handed over to him a comprehensive two-part report on atomic development, from both a technical and an organizational point of view. The technical section described the process used in the construction of the bomb. The organizational section gave a breakdown of the structure of the Manhattan Engineering District and the names of all those of importance involved in it. This information was exactly what Russia wanted.

The report arrived in Moscow several months before the bomb was dropped on Hiroshima. The day after the bomb was dropped, Zabotin had Gouzenko encode the following message:

> For the Director   241.
> Facts given by Alek. (1) The test of the atomic bomb was conducted in New Mexico (with "49", "94–239") The bomb dropped on Japan was made of Uranium 235. It is known that the output of Uranium 235 amounts to 400 grams daily at the magnetic separation plant at Clinton. The output of "49" is likely two times greater. . . . The scientific research work in the field is scheduled to be published, but without the technical details. . . .[6]

The technical details, of course, were top secret, but thanks to Alek, not to Moscow. In fact, May had even delivered to Angelov samples of Uranium 235 and 233, both necessary and vital components for the construction of the bomb. The samples were considered so important that Lieutenant Colonel Motinov personally carried them to Moscow. Everyone on the military attaché's staff was understandably excited by the theft. Zabotin proclaimed, "Now that the Americans have invented it, we must steal it!"

Certainly the spy called Alek must be considered the most successful of Zabotin's agents. But Igor Gouzenko realized that the names of Alek's fellow spies would be of equal value to the West. These agents covered a broad spectrum of society. Many were scientists and government officials of proven ability, who had been unusually well-educated.

Following is a list of Zabotin's agents in Canada as disclosed by Gouzenko. Their code names are in parentheses:

Fred Rose (Debouz) was elected to the Canadian Parliament in 1943 and again in 1945 as a member of the Labor Progressive party, formed in 1942 as a front for the Canadian Communist party.

Sam Carr (Frank) was a frequent candidate for office and a political writer.

Dr. Raymond Boyer (the Professor) was an ardent, independently wealthy Communist anxious to serve Moscow. A senior worker in the Canadian National Research Council, he was a scientist of international renown.

Eric Adams (Ernest), with degrees from McGill and Harvard, held a vital position in the Industrial Development Bank and had formerly served in responsible positions on banking and currency boards. His specialty was confidential economic information.

Dr. Israel Halperin (Bacon) was engaged in important research as a professor of mathematics at Queens University, Kingston, Ontario, and as a major in the Directorate of Artillery.

Durnford Smith (Badeau) and Edward Wilfred Mazerall (Bagley) were graduates of McGill and New Brunswick. They were regarded as top men in the National Research Council of Canada.

David Gordon Lunan (Back) was a captain in the Canadian Information services and formerly editor of the magazine *Canadian Affairs*. He passed on instructions to Bacon, Badeau, and Bagley, received stolen technical secrets from them, and then turned over this information to Lieutenant Colonel Rogov, the Soviet assistant air attaché.

Dr. David Shagar (Prometheus) was a physicist in Research Enterprises, a Crown company engaged in radar and antisubmarine development. Later, as an officer in the Canadian navy, he became a highly placed official in the Directorate of Electrical Supply.

James S. Benning (Foster) was posted at the Ministry of Munitions and Supplies. As assistant to the superintendent of distribution, he handed over information on the production of everything from aircraft to cargo ships. His contact was Zheveinov (Martin), the Tass correspondent.

Harold S. Gerson (Gray), Benning's brother-in-law, held a degree in geology from McGill. Through Boyer, he obtained a position with Allied War Supplies in 1942. In 1944, he transferred to the staff of the Department of Munitions and Supply where he had access to a great deal of secret information on shells and cannons. He passed on his reports to Rose.

Frederick W. Poland (code name unknown) became an administrative intelligence officer in the Royal Canadian Air Force (RCAF). He held the rank of squadron commander. In 1944, he was placed on the Armed Forces Section of the Wartime Information Board and in May, 1945, he became executive secretary of the Interdepartmental Psychological Warfare Committee. Poland knew and associated with ten of the Canadian members of the *apparat*. He was highly regarded by Zabotin and at one point was considered to be NKVD material.

Kathleen Mary Willsher (Ellie) was a graduate of the London School of Economics. She spoke German, French, and some Russian. For many years she held high confidential positions in the Office of the High Commissioner of the United Kingdom in Ottawa. She had been a Communist party member since 1936. Because of her position during the war, she was privy to most of Canada's confidential economic policies and dealings, and, as a result, so was Moscow.

Matt Simons Nightingale (Leader) was a graduate of McGill. After working for the Bell Telephone Company, he became a squadron leader in the RCAF. In 1945, he went back to work for Bell as an engineer. Nightingale had known Fred Rose for many years. A party member, he supplied valuable information on airdrome locations throughout Canada, maps of the coasts, and, upon returning to Bell, technical details for tapping telephone conversations.

There were other Canadians in the *apparat,* but the above-named were the most prominent. Six had Russian parents, and three of the agents were women. The documents that Gouzenko selected illustrated the structural breakdown of the *apparat* and how its separate rings functioned. The use of individual contacts and of individual Soviet controllers was also explained in detail. Gouzenko's papers showed that the military attaché's office, the Soviet Embassy, the Trade Commission, and Tass, the official Soviet news agency, were all involved in the running of the controllers. Finally, Gouzenko supplied peripheral evidence of other Soviet *apparati* operating in Canada, the United States, Great Britain, and even in Switzerland.

· Thus, Gouzenko carried with him detailed proof of the stealing of Canadian secrets by the Soviet Union. On that humid evening in September, 1945, World War II had been over less than a month, but as the defector hurried away from the Soviet Embassy, bringing his purloined documents to the office of the *Ottawa Journal,* he was literally a walking encyclopedia of another kind of war.

The battle was half-won, he thought. He boarded a streetcar. But by the time he got off at the newspaper office, doubts filled his mind. He felt frightened and confused. What in the name of God had he done!

He walked up and down, struggling to calm himself, trying to make sure he had not been followed. It was dark now, and the streets were almost empty. He entered the building foyer and took the elevator to the sixth floor. There he approached the editor's office. At that moment he panicked. The door became the entrance to the embassy. Pavlov was lurking behind it! There were NKVD agents in every newspaper office!

He turned and fled. After what seemed an interminable wait, the elevator came. He walked in. Somewhere between the sixth floor and the lobby it stopped to take on passengers. One was a young woman with a familiar face.

"What are you doing here?" she asked. "Is there news breaking at the embassy?" [7]

He could not answer. What could he say? He tried to smile, but his mouth began to twitch. The elevator jerked to a halt, and the operator opened the door. Gouzenko stammered an apology to the girl as he moved past her. Once on the street, he ran, then slowed down, then ran again, fighting to overcome his sick feeling of fear. He must go home. Only there could he regain control.

Anna answered his coded knock. She stood in the doorway, her face white and frightened. When he told her what had happened, she soothed him, assuring him that the girl in the elevator must have been a journalist, not a NKVD agent.

In the quiet and seeming safety of their apartment, her support steadied him. Together, they planned his next moves. He must return to the *Journal* and try again. After all, there was still plenty of time. First, he must divest himself of the documents. He removed his shirt and peeled off the papers, which were sticking to his body. Each sheet of paper was soaked in his sweat. Anna tried to dry the documents by waving them through the air. After she concealed the papers in a plain wrapper, he left for the newspaper office.

The editor, he learned, was gone until the next day. A man seated at the city room desk glanced at the documents for a moment, stared at Gouzenko, and suggested that he go to the Royal Canadian Mounted Police or return in the morning to see the editor. From the reporter's expression, Gouzenko could see the man thought that he was crazy. Shaken by this reaction, but under tight control, Gouzenko made a quick decision. He would contact the minister of justice.

Wearily, he trudged to the Justice Building. But now the hour was late, almost midnight, and the guard on duty told him to return in the morning. Gouzenko slowly plodded home.

Neither Igor nor Anna slept that night. They talked and tried to collect their thoughts. Before daylight, he told her that she and Andrei must come with him when he left the next day. It would be dangerous for them to remain alone, and the strain would be unbearable if he was not sure that they were safe.

They left the apartment in the clear morning light. Anna carried the documents in her handbag. Gouzenko had worked out a plan in case they were trapped by the NKVD. The Soviet agents would attack him first, he reasoned, and he would try to occupy their attention while Anna and Andrei escaped. With the documents she was carrying, she would be able to bargain with the West for asylum.

At the Justice Building, Anna watched her husband try to impress on a receptionist the urgency of their visit. They must have an immediate audience with the minister, he insisted. The receptionist, although skeptical, made a telephone call. After a lengthy conversation, she escorted them to the minister's office.

A secretary met them. What was the nature of Mr. Gouzenko's business with the minister?

Gouzenko tried to explain without revealing too much. He did not dare to speak to anyone except the minister. The secretary left to telephone. The wait seemed endless, but at last the secretary returned. The minister was at his office in the Parliament Building. If they hurried, they could see him there.

The Gouzenkos' hopes rose. Igor realized that the presence of Anna and Andrei gave him a degree of credibility he would have totally lacked had he been alone. His story was hard to believe, yes, but would a man bring along his wife and child unless the danger was real?

At the Parliament Building there was still another secretary and still another telephone call, this one in French. The result was that they were asked to return to the Justice Building. The telephone rang, but the call was for the secretary. After a brief conversation, he said, "I'm sorry. The minister is unable to see you."

It was a devastating blow, but if the Gouzenkos had known what took place during their wait they might have given up altogether. The minister of justice had brought the matter to the attention of Prime Minister King. At that time, King did not wish to disturb the relations between his own government and that of the Soviet Union in any way. He was not interested in determining the authenticity of Gouzenko's documents. Instead, he suggested that the young man be told to take the papers back to the Soviet Embassy.

Anna remained calm. There was one more chance; they could try the *Ottawa Journal* again. This time Gouzenko found a sympathetic reporter, Lesley Johnstone, who wrote down his story, studied the documents, and took them into the editor's office. After a short time, she returned. With a growing feeling of hopelessness, the Gouzenkos heard the editor's answer. The newspaper was not interested; no one wanted to criticize Stalin. Miss Johnstone suggested that they protect themselves by taking out naturalization papers.

The Gouzenkos tried to follow her advice. They went back to the Justice Building, where a secretary redirected them to the crown attorney's office. The walk was long. The day had grown hot, and Anna and Andrei were becoming very tired. Andrei was crying. They arrived at the attorney's office at noon only to learn that the official in charge was out to lunch. Andrei fell asleep; they knew he had to rest. Anna suggested that a friend in the building next to their own might take care of the little boy for the afternoon. Slowly, they made their way back to Somerset Street, where the neighbor gladly took Andrei.

By this time it was almost three o'clock. Gouzenko knew that by now his absence at the embassy was raising questions. Time was running out. Once the alarm was sounded, the matter would be taken out of Zabotin's hands and placed in Pavlov's.

Was no one going to help them?

It seemed as if no one would. At the crown attorney's office, they were informed that it would take several months to process naturalization papers. In desperation, Gouzenko poured out his story to an employee in the office, Mrs. Fernande Joubarne. Alert and perceptive, Mrs. Joubarne called a newspaper and explained she had a story in her office that the whole world should know.

It was an hour before a reporter showed up. Once again, Gouzenko recited his story, translating some of the documents which dealt with the atom bomb and Sam Carr.

The reporter shook his head. A newspaper could not handle a matter of this importance, he said. He recommended that Gouzenko go to the police or to a government official. Anna broke down and wept. Exhausted, too drained of hope to make new plans, Igor took her home.

As they approached their building, Gouzenko steadied himself. Fear sharpened his senses; he felt aware of immediate danger. Anna must take the documents and run next door to get Andrei while he checked the apartment. If all was clear, he would signal her from the back balcony.

The building seemed unnaturally quiet as he went up the stairs to the fourth floor. He met no one. He listened at the apartment door. Nothing. Carefully, he entered and made sure that everything was in order. Stepping out onto the balcony, he saw Anna looking across from the friend's window. He waved for her to come home.

Later, lying on the bed, all he could see were faces, the faces of those who had listened to him and then shook their heads. They were sorry, they were all sorry, but there was nothing any of them could do to help. He tried to think, to plan. Here, in the apartment, they were terribly vulnerable. This was no sanctuary. At any moment they might have visitors sent by Pavlov. But where could they go now? To a hotel? Possibly, but he fully believed that every hotel would have its NKVD man.

He rose and glanced out the window into the gathering dusk. What he saw momentarily paralyzed him. In the park across the street were two men seated on a bench looking up at him.

Time had, indeed, run out.

Gouzenko moved away from the curtain. In the fading light and from the distance, he could not recognize the watching men, but he could see that their eyes were focused on his window. He turned, planning to call Anna, when a loud knock sounded on the door.

Anna came out of the kitchen. He signaled her to remain still. There were six more knocks. They stood frozen in place, staring at each other. Then Andrei ran across the room to his mother, his shoes clattering on the floor.

The noise shattered the silence.

"Gouzenko!" came the command, "Open up!" The demand was punctuated by a fist slamming against the door. The order was re-peated several times with an accompanying tattoo. Gouzenko recog-nized the voice; it was that of Lt. Lavrentiev, Zabotin's chauffeur.

They did nothing and made no sound. Anna held Andrei against her breast. After a pause, they heard retreating footsteps thudding down the stairs. Gouzenko went back to the front window. Across the street, the watchers were in place on their bench. He returned to the living room where Anna was sitting with Andrei on her lap. She was pale and drawn, her blue eyes large and frightened.

"I'm going to get help!" Gouzenko said. He knew his next-door neighbor, Sergeant Harold Main of the Royal Canadian Air Force, must be home by now. Gouzenko ran to the adjoining balcony, and for the first time in twenty-four hours, one of his plans worked out: Main and his wife were sitting there.

Gouzenko was brief and to the point.

"Sergeant Main, I must speak to you. Would you take care of my son if something should happen to my wife and me?"

The sergeant was not a man to be ruffled by the unexpected. He suggested that his Russian neighbor step across the railing and come inside where they could talk. Seated in Main's living room, Gouzenko explained that he and Anna expected an attempt to be made on their lives by the NKVD. As proof, he pointed to the watchers outside. The presence of the two men, still on the park bench, helped convince the sergeant that his neighbor was not crazy. They stepped out on the balcony again, and Main spotted another figure lurking in the areaway. He made up his mind promptly.

"You get your wife and son, chum," he said, "I'm going to get the police."

In the span of a single day, Igor Gouzenko had known frustration, disappointment, and fear. Now, when he returned to his apartment and found it empty with the door open, he knew terror. His wife and son were gone! Frantically, he rushed out into the hallway. He stopped—there they were, Anna and Andrei, in the apartment across the hall. They were talking to another neighbor, Mrs. Frances Elliott. Shaken, he joined them.

Anna explained to Mrs. Elliott that she was afraid they were in danger. The neighbor suggested that they spend the night in her apartment, since her husband and son were away. Mrs. Elliott and Sergeant Main shared a simple code of behavior: when a neighbor was in trouble, you helped him. To the Gouzenkos, the kindness of these ordinary people typified the Canadian way of life. Again, hope was renewed. Some day they, too, would live in a country where neighbors were free to help each other.

A short time later, they heard Sergeant Main coming up the stairs. With him were two police constables, Thomas Walsh and John McCulloch. Gouzenko had told his story, in one form or another, seven times that day. Now he repeated it to the policemen. His voice was flat and tired, his tone matter-of-fact. The NKVD would try to kill him and his family, he said. The constables listened and asked a few questions. They suggested that the light be left on in the bathroom and turned off if the NKVD men returned. The light could be seen from the street where the police would keep constant watch and come running when signaled.

"Take it easy, Mr. Gouzenko," Walsh said, smiling. "You've got nothing to worry about now. If we're needed, we'll be here in a flash. Okay?" [8]

"Okay," Gouzenko sighed. He felt that these were the first officials he had spoken to all day who knew or really cared what he was talking about. Before lying down beside Anna on the Elliott's daybed, he turned out the light and peered through the window at the park.

The men on the bench were gone. Reassured, he fell asleep.

They came for him at midnight, moving up the stairs stealthily. There were four of them, led by Pavlov. The knock on the Gouzenkos' apartment door across the hallway awoke Igor instantly.

Gouzenko slid out of bed, kneeled down, and peered through the keyhole. He saw the NKVD chief. Huddled around him were Rogov, Angelov, and Farafontov. Then he heard another door open. Sergeant Main's voice boomed out, "What do you want?"

"We want to see the Gouzenkos."

"The Gouzenkos have gone away," the sergeant answered.

The four retreated down the stairs. Gouzenko sighed in relief, but the respite was brief. In a few minutes, as soon as they were sure the sergeant was no longer there, the NKVD men came back.

Pavlov went to work on the door with a jimmy. Expertly, he forced the lock. Through the keyhole, Gouzenko watched them enter his apartment and shut the door.

Frances Elliott appeared beside him. She had turned the bathroom light off, she said, but the constables had not come in answer to her signal.

"Call the police on the telephone!" Gouzenko whispered.

In a few minutes, Walsh and McCulloch came charging up the stairs. Without bothering to knock, they pushed open the door of the Gouzenko apartment. The glare of their flashlights caught Pavlov and his subordinates in the act of ransacking the rooms. The policemen asked for an explanation. Pavlov tried to bluff them, playing the role of the offended official. Walsh was unimpressed. Coolly, he asked for identification.

In producing proof of his identity and that of his colleagues, Pavlov helped Gouzenko enormously. The NKVD men could not provide a satisfactory answer to the constables' question: why were the second secretary of the Soviet Embassy, the assistant air and military attaché, an embassy commercial counselor, and a chauffeur engaged in searching the apartment of a fellow employee in the middle of the night?

"Gouzenko is in Toronto and left papers behind for us," Pavlov explained.

McCulloch and Walsh did not attempt to hide their doubts.

Police Inspector MacDonald was next to arrive on the scene. By this time, Pavlov was beside himself. This was embassy property! He had been insulted by the constables! His diplomatic position had been trampled on! The inspector, too, remained unimpressed. If the Russians would wait, he would get further instructions. But Pavlov had finally had enough. Furious, he ordered his subordinates to leave.

The four NKVD men stalked out. No one attempted to stop them.

At that moment, Igor Gouzenko did not realize that the receding footsteps of his countrymen signaled the end of his and Anna's ordeal. He only knew that those who had come to take them had been turned away, that for the present, they were safe.

The next morning Anna and Andrei were taken to a protected house, and Igor was escorted back to the Justice Building. There he was met by constables of the Royal Canadian Mounted Police and a civilian investigator. At last, he could tell his story and others would listen. (Actually, unknown to Gouzenko, the Canadian government had begun listening on the previous day. The two men he had seen on the park bench had not been placed there by Pavlov, but by Canadian Counterintelligence.) Now, after hearing the full Gouzenko report and receiving the documents, a thorough and secret investigation was instigated.

It was so secret that by October, Zabotin, Pavlov, and others in Ottawa and Moscow began to relax. Ambassador Zarubin had sent two stiff notes to the Canadian Department of External Affairs, requesting the return of cipher clerk Igor Gouzenko and his wife on charges of robbery. There had been no response, but neither had there been any arrests or accusations. Moscow, after conferring with Zabotin, decided that Gouzenko had not talked. Soon business as usual was resumed. What Moscow did not know, however, was that Prime Minister King had traveled to Washington and London to report the case to President Truman and Prime Minister Attlee.

It was not until December that Soviet Intelligence began to pick up bits of information indicating that all was not well. Orders went out. On December 13, Colonel Nikolai Zabotin secretly slipped across the border into the United States, making his way to New York. There he boarded a Russian ship, the S.S. *Alexander Suvorov*. The *Suvorov* sailed the next night, failing to report her departure. A short time afterward, Ambassador Zarubin went back to Moscow, supposedly going home for a visit. He never returned to Canada, and a year later he was named ambassador to Great Britain.

The Canadian government waited until mid-February, 1946, to make its first public statement on the case, announcing briefly that a large espionage ring had been uncovered. The name of the country involved was not mentioned. A Royal Commission was formed to conduct an investigation. Later, its findings were made public.

The Commission's report, published in June, ran 733 pages. It told the story in full, supported by the confessions of some of the *apparat* members and by the evasive but self-incriminating answers of others. On the basis of the investigation, arrests were made and the individual Canadian members of the *apparat* brought to trial. The Russians involved had long since departed. Sam Carr managed to escape, fleeing first to Cuba and then to New York. Three years later he was picked up by the FBI and returned to Ottawa where he was tried and given a six-year prison sentence. His fellow agent, Fred Rose, had received the same penalty. After Carr's release in 1953, he left Canada and emigrated to Poland. Others in the ring received lesser sentences; six were acquitted altogether. Allan Nunn May, arrested and tried in England, was sentenced in 1946 to ten years of penal servitude. He was released on December 30, 1951.

As for Lieutenant Igor Gouzenko, with his wife, son, and new-born daughter, he began a new life in their adopted country. For the Gouzenkos' protection, they were kept from public view during the trials, given new identities afterwards, and watched over by the Royal Canadian Mounted Police. Gouzenko went on to become a success-ful writer; his first book was an account of his life in Russia and Canada. Perhaps his proudest moment came when Prime Minister King told him, "You have accomplished an historical act. The people of Canada and of the world are your debtors."

No such acclamation awaited Nikolai Zabotin when he arrived in Russia, if he ever did arrive. Only a few months before his sudden and illegal departure, he was awarded a medal for his espionage accomplishments. However, after those accomplishments were dis-closed to the public, he was made the scapegoat for the exposure of the *apparat*. It was his fault that Gouzenko had defected, not Pav-lov's. Ever-resilient, the wily Pavlov somehow escaped the debacle and popped up again in 1947 as second secretary to the Soviet Em-bassy in Washington. As for Zabotin, rumors continue to spread about his fate. One report states that when he was going home as a prisoner, he jumped ship in the middle of the Atlantic. Other stories say that he was sentenced to ten years at hard labor; that in the cellars of Lubianka prison he was killed by a bullet in the head. Whatever happened, his lot was surely not a pleasant one. According to the harsh Soviet canon, to spy and to be caught by the other side is a risk of the game, but to fail through the defection of one of your own agents and in so doing expose to the world the duplicity of your government is unforgivable.

The Assassin

Bogdan Stashynsky – The Spy Who Traded His Cloak and Dagger for a Woman

With the war's end, the flood of recruits—the "thousands of agents" —that the Soviet espionage services had enjoyed for nearly a decade was sharply diminished. The number of party members offering to serve as spies thinned out drastically as a result of several factors: exposures such as Gouzenko's, changes in political attitudes toward the Soviet Union, and changes in methods of recruitment of agents by Moscow.

Gouzenko's revelations were but the first of a number to shake the West. The Whittaker Chambers-Alger Hiss case became a *cause célèbre* which illustrated, along with the testimony of such former Soviet spies as Elizabeth Bentley and Hede Massing, how deeply Soviet espionage had penetrated into the vitals of the United States government.

The awakening of Allied security agencies, the full involvement of the FBI, the formation of the CIA, all contributed to making the Soviet effort more difficult. However, more than anything else, it was Stalin's Cold-War policy that galvanized opposition and put an end to the days of clear sailing for Soviet Intelligence. As the Cold War expanded, America's political naiveté and genuine desire for friendship hardened into enmity. At the same time, the Soviet effort intensified on a global scale. And even though the United States remained the main enemy, nowhere was this Soviet intensification more apparent than in the underground espionage conflict within war-ravaged

Germany. It was a battle for which Moscow had made prior plans.

German Communist leaders had been in exile in Russia since the early thirties. So had the leadership of other Communist parties in those countries occupied by Hitler during World War II. These exiled leaders were not idle. They planned for the day of return when they would follow the Red Army back to their homelands and, with the help of the Kremlin, put themselves in power. The fighting was still raging in Berlin when a handful of these exiles were landed on the outskirts of the city. It was they who would rule the Soviet puppet state of East Germany.

A year later, Stalin's armies still occupied all of Eastern Europe. By agreement at Potsdam, Soviet reparation teams were permitted to roam the Allied Zones of Germany to inspect German industrial and scientific installations with an eye toward the collection of indemnities. Called Technical Reparations Commissions, they were directed by Colonel Igor Tulpanov of the GRU, who had formerly operated a very successful *apparat* in the United States, using Amtorg, the Soviet trade mission, as a cover. Now, his intent was to have his inspectors learn as much as they could about Allied military installations and to recruit agents in all three zones. The Soviet teams went about their espionage work undeterred until 1949, when on September 20, the Federal Republic of Germany, headed by Dr. Konrad Adenauer, came into being. By that date, there had been three years of Kremlin-inspired civil war in Greece, the Berlin blockade was still in force, NATO had been formed, and China was about to fall to the Communists.

By then, also, Allied Intelligence services in Germany had begun to fight back. In 1947, with U.S. support, General Reinhard Gehlen, who had formerly been Hitler's chief intelligence officer on the Eastern front, was secretly set up as head of an operation with orders to continue his espionage war against the Soviets. The British and the French increased their effort as well, but British effectiveness was badly damaged by the fact that Kim Philby, then in charge of British espionage against the Soviets, was actually a Soviet agent.

As for the Soviets, after February 15, 1950, when they created the East German Ministry of State Security (MFS), more and more of their espionage operations against the Bonn government were handed over to the new bureau, although always under the overall control of Karlshorst, Soviet Security headquarters in Berlin.

In this postwar period, the new Soviet spy was seldom a man who had pledged his life to an ideological revolutionary cause. He was recruited instead from the millions of war refugees who, after losing their homelands, were willing to do anything for a price.

There were others whose price was the lives of captive loved ones.

As a result of the strained relations between East and West during the decade of the fifties, Germany became the focal point of an internecine espionage war involving thousands of agents on both sides. During World War II, nearly a million Russians, under the command of former General Andrei Vlassov, had fought on the side of the Germans against the Red Army. In spite of Hitler's inhuman policy toward them, other refugee groups from the Ukraine, the Baltic States, Poland, and Belorussia were organized by German Intelligence to fight a guerrilla war behind Russian lines. Even after the war had ended, some of these groups continued to fight. Liberated by Allied forces, some refugees managed to escape forced repatriation to Russia, reorganizing in West Germany and elsewhere in Europe to continue their fight against the Soviet Union by any means possible. And espionage was a principal means. The men in the Kremlin looked upon members of these organizations as traitors and spies. The Soviets also knew that the struggle of these refugees provided the West with a dramatic propaganda weapon. Consequently, the espionage battle between the two sides soon intensified into a fiercely contested war.

Since the formation of the Soviet state, terror tactics had been a standard operating method of control. When Stalin came to power, abduction and assassination became instruments for carrying out his policies. After the fifties, the Thirteenth Department of Soviet State Security became responsible for abduction and assassination. This division was known as the *Mokryye Dela* (the Department of Blood-Wet Affairs).[1] By the mid-fifties, this department, working in conjunction with the East German MFS, had kidnapped over six hundred individuals from West Berlin alone. Two of their major targets were members of the all-Russian National Labor Council (NTS) and the Organization of Ukrainian Nationalists (OUN).

Both organizations, militantly anti-Communist, had at first wholeheartedly cooperated with the Germans against Russia during World War II. But by 1943, they had turned against Hitler because of his treatment of their countrymen and so found themselves engaged in a fight against two enemies. After the end of World War II, NTS and OUN received considerable support from the West in their anti-Communist endeavors.

The Soviet terror campaign against these refugee groups was revealed to the world on February 18, 1954, when Nikolai Khokhlov, a Soviet agent selected to assassinate Georgi Okolovich, a key NTS leader, gave himself up to his intended victim. The order for the execution had come from the Central Committee of the CPSU and was signed by Nikita Khrushchev and Georgi Malenkov. The public airing of the case created a great deal of adverse publicity for Moscow, and Captain Khokhlov's confession to Allied Intelligence compromised a number of Soviet *apparati* operating in Austria and Germany. Georgi Okolovich remained alive, but other victims marked for liquidation in this deadly twilight war were not so fortunate.

* * * * *

On October 9, 1957, a slight young man with a thin face and light gray eyes, traveling under the name of Siegfried Dräger, flew into Munich from Berlin. He registered that evening at the Stachus Hotel, an unobtrusive guest in an unobtrusive setting. Concealed, however, in his inside coat pocket, was a strange and deadly weapon. His orders were to kill.

Like himself, his intended victim, Lev Rebet, came from the Ukraine. Five years ago, orders for Rebet's execution had been handed down at a Soviet State Security staff meeting. But the young man, whose real name was Bogdan Stashynsky, did not know that. He only knew what he was supposed to do and to whom he was supposed to do it. Twice before, in April and July, he had come to Munich specifically to watch Rebet's movements.

A heavy-set, energetic man of middle years, Rebet was a popular Ukrainian exiled political leader and the editor of the anti-Soviet newspaper, *Ukrainski Samostinik*. He had been described to Stashynsky by his KGB control as a dangerous man who, with the other Ukrainian leaders, Jaroslaw Stetzko and Stefan Bandera, was "preventing Ukrainian emigrants from returning to their native country by means of influence, threats, and acts of violence . . . an influential theoretician and ideologist of the Ukrainian emigrant organization."

On previous trips to Munich, while traveling under the name of Josef Lehmann, an employee of the Soviet Zone Bureau of German Home and Foreign Trade, Stashynsky observed that Rebet divided most of his time between two offices: No. 9 Dachauerstrasse, where the newspaper was located, and No. 8 Karlsplatz, the location of the

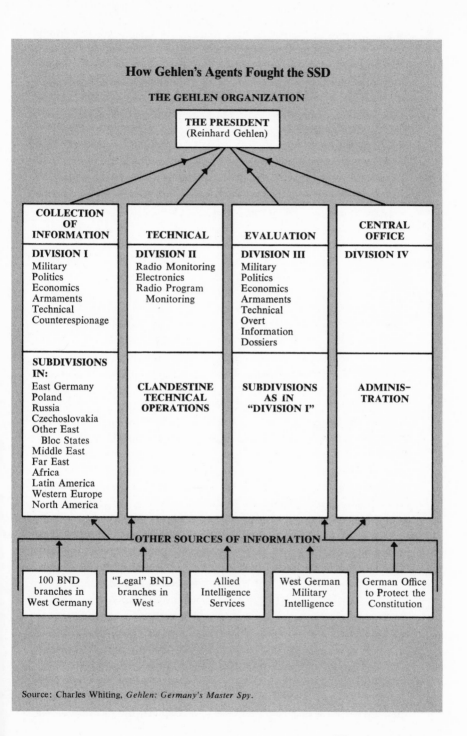

How Gehlen's Agents Fought the SSD

THE GEHLEN ORGANIZATION

THE PRESIDENT
(Reinhard Gehlen)

COLLECTION OF INFORMATION	TECHNICAL	EVALUATION	CENTRAL OFFICE
DIVISION I Military Politics Economics Armaments Technical Counterespionage	**DIVISION II** Radio Monitoring Electronics Radio Program Monitoring	**DIVISION III** Military Politics Economics Armaments Technical Overt Information Dossiers	**DIVISION IV**
SUBDIVISIONS IN: East Germany Poland Russia Czechoslovakia Other East Bloc States Middle East Far East Africa Latin America Western Europe North America	**CLANDESTINE TECHNICAL OPERATIONS**	**SUBDIVISIONS AS IN "DIVISION I"**	**ADMINIS- TRATION**

OTHER SOURCES OF INFORMATION

100 BND branches in West Germany	"Legal" BND branches in West	Allied Intelligence Services	West German Military Intelligence	German Office to Protect the Constitution

Source: Charles Whiting, *Gehlen: Germany's Master Spy.*

Organization of Ukrainian Nationalists (OUN) office. He followed Rebet constantly, riding behind him on Munich's blue trolley cars and walking behind him on the streets. On one occasion he took a photograph of the door of Rebet's apartment on Occamstrasse. Stashynsky carried out this surveillance under orders from the KGB, but he did not learn its ultimate purpose until September, 1957, when he was summoned to Karlshorst, Soviet Security headquarters in Berlin. By that date, he had been under KGB direction for seven years.

It had begun with a train ride in 1950. At the time, he was nineteen, in the fifth form of the Pedagogical College in Lvov, where he was studying to be a mathematics teacher. Once a week he would return by train to his parents' home in the small village of Borshovitsy and, when necessary, pick up a supply of food and money.

On the late summer day in question, he was out of both, and he boarded the train surreptitiously, hoping to avoid the conductor. He had no such luck. Traveling without a ticket, he was informed, was a serious criminal offense; he must report to the Transportation Police in Lemberg. Terrified, he obeyed his orders, knowing full well that the Transportation Police was an arm of the dreaded Ministry of State Security.

Stashynsky had lived in fear for many years, having grown up amid conflict and upheaval. When he had begun his schooling in 1937, the portion of the Ukraine where he lived, which had long been under Austrian rule, was governed by Poland, and Polish was the chief language taught in school. In 1939, when Hitler and Stalin divided Poland, the area fell under Russian control, and Russian took the place of Polish. Two years later, when the village was occupied by the Germans, the language was changed to German.

At that point, Stefan Bandera and his OUN brigades arrived on the scene. Supported by the Wehrmacht and directed by German Intelligence, their aim was to rally Ukrainians to the Nazi side for the purpose of forming an independent Ukrainian state. However, soon after the establishment of the new nation, Hitler gave orders to have it dissolved and its leaders jailed, as part of his savage policy toward the Slavic peoples. By 1943, many Ukrainians had become partisans fighting the Germans. When the Germans retreated westward and the Red Army moved in, OUN guerrilla bands continued to oppose the Soviet occupiers.

In 1950, there were still guerrilla bands hiding in the forests, continuing their hopeless battle. Stashynsky's family—mother, father and two older sisters—were of the Greek Orthodox faith. Their allegiance was pro-OUN and anti-Soviet. So, for more than ten years, the boy had survived in a country scarred by terror, privation, and death. Today, facing the Soviet official, the young man knew that his punishment would be severe; he appeared at the Transportation Police Department literally shaking in his boots.

The owl-faced officer who interviewed him was named Captain Sitnikovski. Not once did he mention the matter of the railroad ticket. Instead, in the first of a number of interrogations, he asked questions about the young man's family, the village where they lived, and the attitude of the people living there. At times he sounded like a political lecturer, particularly when discussing the OUN: "Their resistance is senseless! Senseless! More than that, their acts of violence against peaceful people who are not a part of this stupid movement brings unnecessary suffering. People who support these fools are only endangering their own lives. I tell you this: they will certainly be arrested, punished, and deported!"

Bogdan Stashynsky suspected that the Russian was referring to his own family, and Captain Sitnikovski soon left him in no doubt. It was known, he said, that the Stashynsky family was on the side of the OUN, that one of the young man's sisters was directly connected with the partisans. However, there was one way in which he might protect his family and, at the same time, do important political work for the state. "Think it over," said Sitnikovski, with meaningful emphasis.

There was no need to think it over; Stashynsky saw that he had no choice. By cooperating, he could prevent the deportation of his family, and when the assignment was completed, he could go back to his studies. Or so he thought. He signed a special pledge of agreement and was given the cover name of Oleg.

As Oleg, he spied on his family and other residents of the village, reporting on their political feelings. In January, 1951, as a supposed fugitive from the Security Police, he asked for refuge in an OUN underground group. With the help of his sister, this was arranged. His assignment was to learn the name of the assassin of the pro-Soviet Ukrainian writer, Jaroslaw Galan. In a short time, he was successful, and Galan's murderer was liquidated. This act uncovered Stashynsky's role as a Soviet spy among his own people. Captain Sitnikovski pointed out that since Stashynsky could no longer return home, his best option was to join the MGB on a full-time basis. Again feeling that he had no choice, Stashynsky agreed.

His third mission was to carry out espionage activities against OUN resistance groups near Lemberg. Afterward, he was sent to an intelligence school in Kiev, which he attended for two years. Among other things, he learned German and took on the alias of Moros.

In 1954, Moros was instructed by his superiors to try and gain the forgiveness of his parents, which he genuinely wished to do. The past had been so filled with pain, troubled by mixed loyalties, and embittered by the forced deportation of several hundred thousand Ukrainians, that the Stashynsky family considered itself blessed to remain intact. All—or almost all—was forgiven. The prodigal son told his parents that he had a job in Kiev, but he failed to inform them that his employer was the KGB.[2]

During that year Stashynsky assumed a new identity. After careful and thorough instruction, he became Josef Lehmann, a German national, born one year earlier than Stashynsky in Lukowek, Poland. The real Lehmann was dead, and in acquiring his identity (or legend, as it is called in intelligence terminology) Stashynsky visited Lukowek and other places where Lehmann had lived. To complete the legend, he was dispatched to Dresden, in the Soviet Zone of Germany. There, as Josef Lehmann, he was issued identity papers of a stateless person as well as a driver's license from the People's Police. Later, he met his KGB control, Sergei Alexandrovitch Demon at Karlshorst. The Russian made it clear to his new charge that he would be spending a lot of time in West Germany, and that his assignment would center on the activities of Ukrainian émigré groups such as OUN and on their leaders: Stetzko, Bandera, and Rebet.

Stashynsky spent the year of 1955 in further training and firmly establishing his cover. In April, he was given a job as a metal puncher in a Soviet-administered plant in Zwichau. This was to establish a genuine certificate of employment in the name of Lehmann. At the end of the year, he moved to East Berlin and, under Sergei Demon's instructions, passed himself off as an interpreter for the Trade Bureau. By 1956 he had made his first trip to Munich, and by the autumn of 1957 he had visited the city many times, engaged in a wide range of espionage activities. He had met an unidentified Ukrainian who had agreed to work for the KGB under the condition that recent photographs of his family be produced. From this person Stashynsky attempted to learn a number of things: Were demonstrations being planned against Khrushchev and Bulganin during their forthcoming visit to London? Was there conflict among the émigré groups? How much use were U.S. and German Intelligence agencies making of these groups? What were the travel plans of Vitali Bender, editor of *Ukrainski Visti?*

Stashynsky met with this mysterious contact three times, supplying him with chemicals and special paper for sending messages in invisible ink and an ample supply of money. He informed the man that the KGB would bring his wife to a meeting in West Berlin as proof of its good faith. At their meeting in August, 1956, the contact was unaware that Stashynsky was using a concealed camera to photograph him; but when they met for the last time in February, 1957, they were both unaware that an Allied Intelligence agent was photographing them. On two trips Stashynsky left parcels of money for the contact at dead drops (prearranged hidden locations, selected for depositing and picking up messages and money). At a location near Frankfurt am Main, he also left money and coded information for another agent. On a later mission, he was sent to a town in southern Germany to observe American troops. This was a job of reconnaissance: ascertaining numbers, units, types of equipment, etc. However, most of Stashynsky's spying was targeted against the Ukrainians in Munich.

Bogdan enjoyed the highly paid espionage game. He liked to visit West Berlin's well-stocked shops and cafés. The girls were friendly, and he had money in his pockets. Then he fell in love with Inge Pohl, a young woman who worked in West Berlin and lived with her family in Dallgow, a suburb west of Berlin in the Soviet Zone. She believed that he was Josef Lehmann and that his frequent business trips were in connection with the Bureau of Trade.

Although Inge occupied much of his time, Bogdan worked hard at his job. When Stashynsky reported to his KGB control, Sergei, at Karlshorst in September, 1957, he had developed into a professional. Always quick-witted, perceptive, and observant, through his training and assignments he had become adept at the art of surveillance. He knew how to be unobtrusive, to guard against being followed, to operate as an undercover agent, and to play a role. On that September day, appearing before Sergei, he had learned the tricks of his trade well.

"The time has come," Sergei announced, rising from behind his desk. "A man from Moscow is here to see you."

The man from Moscow was a KGB technical expert. He brought forth a weapon which Stashynsky had never seen before. Essentially, it consisted of a seven-inch metal tube that could be broken down into three sections. The first section held a firing pin, powered by a 1.5 volt battery which made its action noiseless. Instead of bullets, it fired the contents of a pellet containing deadly prussic acid. The poison was colorless and odorless. Anyone who breathed the gas at close range would be dead in seconds, the Moscow expert explained, and long before an autopsy could be performed all traces of the killing agent would disappear.

"It has been used with 100 percent success," Sergei said.

"For your safety and protection," the technician explained,

"you swallow one of these sodium thiosulphate tablets before shooting the gun. And then, immediately after firing, you crush this amyl nitrate ampoule and inhale."

While the man from Moscow assembled the weapon and matter-of-factly demonstrated its operation, it swiftly dawned on Stashynsky that he was to be the user. He was so shocked by the realization that he could not bring himself to touch the gun. His one wish was to leave the room, to get away from Sergei and from this man who acted as if he were describing the workings of a new toy and not a deadly murder weapon.

The next day, when Stashynsky reported to Sergei, the man from Moscow was in the office again. He was fondling a small dog. They all got into Sergei's car and drove to a forest. Making certain no one was about, Sergei tied the dog to a tree.

"Take one of these," the man from Moscow said, offering Stashynsky a pill.

He obeyed numbly and then was handed the tube gun. "It's ready to fire," the man from Moscow told him.

The dog wagged his stubby tail and licked Stashynsky's ankles.

"Shoot him," Sergei ordered, pointing at the dog.

When they left the woods, Sergei carried the dog's collar and leash. The weapon had made no sound; neither had the dog. The prussic acid looked like water. Sick and dazed, Stashynsky knew full well what was to come next.

That day Sergei ordered him to kill Lev Rebet.

"It was like a nightmare to me, that I was now to kill an unsuspecting human being," Stashynsky was to reflect. "I felt as if I were caged in. I knew that one must not kill, but on the other hand I could not refuse to carry out the orders of my superiors, considering the organization to which I belonged. Every time I saw a married couple in the street I would imagine how dreadful it must be for a woman to suddenly lose her husband. At such moments I was convinced that I would never be able to carry out such an order. But then I tried to justify such a murder. And I recalled the acts of violence of the OUN in my native village. I told myself that after all Rebet was an enemy of the Soviet Union since he was preventing immigrants from returning there and was also responsible for their becoming agents of a foreign power. I did not know what to do. After a while I no longer used the word 'kill' to myself but only 'fire the weapon.' I tried to persuade myself that the situation was the same as in a war when the aim justifies the means and orders have to be carried out come what may."

He wanted to tell Inge, but he dared not. There was no one

he could tell unless he defected and that, too, was out of the question. The West was a frightening place, hostile to all he had been taught and believed.

On October 8, Sergei gave him his final instructions. The gas pistol was concealed in a special tin made to look as if it contained sausages. The weapon was loaded, the safety catch set. He had ten days in which to accomplish his mission. He was given one pill for each day and a single piece of gauze with antidote on it.

"You will depart on schedule," Sergei said, "You will return no later than the eighteenth. Here are your travel documents. You will go in and return as Siegfried Dräger. At all other times you are Lehmann. Before you return, burn your Lehmann identification. You will carry out your instructions at No. 8 Karlsplatz. After it is done, dispose of the weapon. Do you have any questions? Good. I'm sure you'll succeed."

In his room at the Stachus Hotel the next evening, Stashynsky spent a sleepless night. In the morning he rose and breakfasted on an antipoison pill. After dressing, he took the spray gun from its container, wrapped it in a piece of newspaper, put it in his inside coat pocket, and went to Karlsplatz. There he took up an unobtrusive position near a trolley stop and awaited Rebet's arrival.

He watched and waited, praying that his victim would not appear. If he did not arrive, there would be no need to act, for his orders had been explicit. Nothing had been said about hunting or tracking the man; the killing must be carried out at the prescribed spot, or not at all.

For two days he waited. At the end of each day he told himself, "If he comes, then I shall have to do it; if he doesn't come, then my orders for the day are finished."

On the third morning, he was beginning to relax a little in the belief that he would get through this day as he had the previous two, when he saw Lev Rebet get off the trolley and start walking toward No. 8. The actual sight of his victim hit him like an electric shock. His heart began to pound. Mechanically, he moved.

Stashynsky reached the building before Rebet. He entered and went up the rickety stairs to the first floor. In the silent, dimly lit corridor, he stood, waiting, breathing hard. The sound of the front door opening below came up to him as a thunderous echo. He took the gun out of his pocket, unscrewed the safety catch, and started down the stairs. The older man climbed up the staircase towards him.

Assassin and victim met. Rebet's luminous eyes shone, their expression faintly quizzical. Stashynsky's right hand moved. He pointed, fired, and heard the deadly hiss. Rebet gasped and fell forward; his murderer raced down the remaining steps past him. In the entryway Stashynsky paused to crush the amyl nitrate pellet and inhale the contents. Then he was out in the street, walking as rapidly as he could, trying not to run. He crossed the streets in a daze, traveling by rote until he came to the Kögelmühlbach, a stream behind the Hofgarten. Flinging the weapon into the water, he slowly began to regain control of himself. As he walked, more normally now, he suddenly noticed that the sun was shining, that people looked happy. He felt as if he were waking up from a nightmare.

But later, when he crossed the Lenbachplatz, he knew it had not been a dream. From a distance, he could see No. 8 Karlsplatz where he had carried out his orders. A crowd was gathered in front of the building, and a police car was stationed near the entrance.

After his return to Karlshorst, Stashynsky completed a report for Sergei. He wrote: "In a town that I know I met the object that I know and greeted it. I am sure the greeting was a success."

It was. About 10:40 A.M., on October 12, 1957, Lev Rebet was found dead on the stairs of No. 8 Karlsplatz. After an autopsy, the cause of death was given as heart failure.

Sergei and his KGB superiors were elated over Stashynsky's success, but he continued to feel tormented by guilt. However, he had been in the game long enough to know he must keep his true feelings from his masters. His relationship with Inge only added to his misery as she began to question him about his sudden depression.

A year passed in which Stashynsky, among other assignments, carried out a reconnaissance mission in Rotterdam. He reported the identities of the mourners at a memorial service for Colonel Konovaletz, the founder of OUN, who had been murdered by the Soviets in 1938. Then, in the autumn of 1958, the same deadly routine began again. He took on a new identity for travel purposes, becoming Hans Joachim Budeit of Dortmund. In January, 1959, as Budeit, he began to make "business" trips to Munich. This time, the target of his spying was a Ukrainian writer called Stefan Popel.

Popel was, in fact, Stefan Bandera, who had given the eulogy at Konovaletz's memorial service. Long recognized as the principal political leader of OUN, Bandera's efforts toward the establishment of an independent Ukraine dated back to the days of the Russian Revolution when he had fought as a partisan against the Red Army. During World War II, he had served in both French and British Intelligence and, following the war, in the Gehlen organization and U.S. Intelligence. Throughout his career, Bandera had remained a hero for two million anti-Soviet Ukrainians. He was a relentless and implacable foe of the Kremlin; his agents worked not only in the Ukraine, but in East Germany and Hungary as well. Bandera's name was high on the list the *Mokryye Dela* had marked for death and, once again, Stashynsky was told that he had been chosen as the assassin.

Stashynsky found out where Bandera lived by looking up the name Stefan Popel in the telephone directory. He began to follow him, as he had Rebet, learning his movements and habits. In the midst of his tracking, he was unexpectedly summoned to Moscow. In the case of Rebet, Stashynsky's instructions had come from Sergei Demon. Now he received his orders from a much higher KGB official, Georgi Aksentevitch. "A decision has been reached by the highest authority," Aksentevitch said, "Bandera must be liquidated in the same manner as Rebet."

He had been prepared to learn that he must kill again, but even so, it was difficult to hide his feeling of revulsion. "It will be much more difficult than Rebet," he argued. "Bandera is armed and travels with a bodyguard."

His arguments were useless. Stashynsky returned to Berlin carrying a double-barreled spray pistol, false documents, and orders to assassinate Bandera. On May 10, as Hans Budeit, he arrived in Munich. Along with the weapon and antidote pills, he brought a key with five interchangeable bits so that he could open the front door of No. 7 Kreittmayerstrasse, the building where Bandera lived.

Two days later, while watching the house, he saw Bandera drive his Opel into the secluded garage area. No one else was around. "In a few more minutes he'll no longer be alive," Stashynsky thought, moving toward the enclosure. "But he hasn't harmed me in any way. He's a human being like me . . . I can't do it!"

He turned and ran again to the bridge over the Kögelmühlbach. Holding the pistol over the railing, he fired it and then threw it in the water. At first, he felt relieved. Then, terror overwhelmed him. He had disobeyed orders! There was no doubt in his mind of the consequences if he were found out. But Stashynsky had not been trained in the arts of subterfuge and deceit for nothing; he calmed down and began to invent an explanation for his failure.

The next day he went back to No. 7 Kreittmayerstrasse. Inserting the key in the lock of the front door, he worked it back and forth until it snapped off. Next, he bought a set of files and filed his aluminum apartment house key to approximate the original. This, too, he managed to snap off in the lock. Reporting to Sergei, Stashynsky showed him the broken keys, indicating how much effort he had expended in trying to enter Bandera's house. Because he knew that the KGB very often spied on its own spies, he explained that he had seen

Bandera in the courtyard the day before but had not been able to kill him because of the presence of some passers-by.

Sergei accepted his report and asked him to make a sketch of the original key. A few days later, he sent Stashynsky back to Munich to try out four more keys on the lock at No. 7. One of them worked. Stashynsky did not receive new orders to kill Bandera, but he was instructed to find out where a Ukrainian exile calling himself Dankiw lived. Dankiw was the alias for the former Ukrainian Prime Minister Jaroslaw Stetzko, and Stashynsky realized that Stetzko was scheduled to be next on the list after Bandera.

As the months went by and no more mention was made of Bandera, Bogdan began to relax. He and Inge were now engaged. In August, he made his annual visit to see his parents. Then, in October, Sergei presented him with a new double-barreled gas pistol and issued the order: "Kill Bandera."

Stashynsky moved automatically. He remembered the steps and executed them in well-rehearsed succession: swallowing the anti-poison pill for breakfast, leaving the hotel, watching Bandera's office at 67 Zepplinstrasse, taking the tram to Kreittmayerstrasse, watching No. 7 and its garage area until exactly 1:00 P.M., praying that Bandera would not arrive, and then leaving quickly, relieved that another day was over.

On October 15, he saw Bandera's Opel parked in front of the office building. Stashynsky watched the car all morning. At high noon, Bandera emerged from the building in the company of a woman. They drove off together.

"Good!" Stashynsky sighed. The chances were that Bandera would not arrive home before one o'clock, and if he did, the woman would be with him.

Just before the hour, he saw Bandera drive into the garage area. He was alone. The climax was at hand. As if watching someone else, Stashynsky saw himself run across the street, fit the key in the lock, and enter the foyer of the house. In the dim light, he saw the elevator and a flight of stairs next to it. He started toward the stairs. On the landing above, a door opened, and a woman's voice called out, "Auf wiedersehn!"

He turned away, moving toward the elevator, not wanting the woman to see his face. Later, he was never sure whether he went up to the first floor by the elevator or by the stairs. He only knew he got there. He heard Bandera open the door below, and just as he had with Rebet, Stashynsky began to walk down the stairs. This time the meeting was at the door. Bandera was carrying a basket of tomatoes on his right arm. His key had stuck in the lock and he was struggling to get it out with his left hand. Seeking delay, Stashynsky bent down, pretending to tie his laceless shoes. Then straightening up, he moved to the door where Bandera still stood, holding the key. Grabbing the door with one hand, Stashynsky turned to Bandera and asked "Won't it work?" And suddenly, before the victim could reply, he raised the murder weapon concealed in a newspaper and fired both barrels pointblank into his face.

In November, Bogdan Stashynsky was presented to the Soviet KGB chief for East Berlin. The general was effusive. Cognac in hand, he toasted the young man and told him: "Comrade, you have executed an important government commission. For this you have been awarded the Order of the Red Banner. It will be presented to you in Moscow by Comrade Shelepin himself."

The recipient was not moved by the signal honor. He knew that no amount of self-rationalization could erase the reality of his guilt. Stashynsky had been obsessed with the memory of the killing since shortly after his return from Munich, when he had seen a newsreel of Bandera's funeral showing his body in the coffin, surrounded by his grieving family. Later, when he learned the results of the autopsy, Stashynsky's anxiety increased. The autopsy attributed Bandera's death to potassium cyanide poisoning, and the verdict was that the victim had been murdered.

"Until the excitement dies down," the Soviet general continued, "you will remain in Moscow where you will undergo further training for new missions in the West." He raised his glass in salute.

Stashynsky said little in reply. His reticence was judged a quality of his character; his superiors did not read into it withdrawal. An agent who has successfully carried out two cold-blooded executions is not expected to show emotion. Not even with Inge could he be outgoing, since he could neither confess his crimes nor tell her the nature of his work. Again, she was aware of a change in him; he was unusually silent and subdued. However, she believed his explanation that he was sad because he had to go on a long business trip to Poland. At the end of November, he left for Moscow.

Upon his arrival, the department head to whom he reported briefed him on his new training. He would perfect his German, he would learn English, and he would drop Inge Pohl. Marriage with a foreigner was not permissible for a KGB agent. Stashynsky argued that by marrying Inge he would be giving himself additional cover wherever he was sent.

"I can only advise you to think over the matter very carefully," the KGB official answered.

Stashynsky had been pushed too far. He was not prepared to

give up the woman he loved. A few days later, at a meeting with his department chief and with Aksentevitch, who had given him the original order to kill Bandera, he was presented to Alexander Shelepin, director of the KGB. He was the highest-ranking official Stashynsky had ever met. Prior to taking over as director in late 1958, Shelepin had been a member of the Central Committee of the Communist party of the Soviet Union.

In presenting him with the Order of the Red Banner, Shelepin pointed out that the document of award had been signed by none other than Voroshilov, then chairman of the Presidium. When the conversation touched on Stashynsky's bright future in the KGB, Bogdan seized the opportunity to press his desire to marry Inge. It was a bold move, over the heads of the others present. He told Shelepin that before asking Inge to marry him, he had assured himself of her sincere admiration for the Soviet Union. He promised that she would be an important adjunct to future missions. Ignoring the scowls and interjections of his immediate superiors, Stashynsky pressed his case. Finally, Shelepin good-humoredly agreed, but stipulated that certain conditions must be met. Inge must come to Moscow to prove that she was politically trustworthy and would support her husband in his work. Having been awarded the Order of the Red Banner, Stashynsky left the meeting feeling that he had won something far more important.

Before his return to Berlin, he was given the ground rules he was to follow in his relationship with Inge. He was to tell her that he was employed by MFS, not the Trade Bureau, and that his work was politically important to the East German state. If she agreed to help him in his work, he was to bring her to Moscow in January, 1960; if she refused, he was to come alone.

On Christmas Eve, 1959, in defiance of orders from Sergei to stay out of West Berlin, he met Inge at her office. Together, they left for Dallgow to spend Christmas with her parents. On Christmas Day, Stashynsky revealed to her that he worked for the KGB, but he could not bring himself to disclose that this work was to assassinate anti-Communist leaders.

After the first shock had worn off, she took his hand and said, "I love you, Bogdan, and I'll stick by you, but we must go over to the West at once."

He shook his head. "No, I don't trust them there any more than I trust them here. They might send me back, and if they didn't we'd be hunted."

"What then? What can we do?"

"You can come to Moscow with me. I'm to have more training

Alexander N. Shelepin, former head of KGB, who decorated Bogdan Stashynsky for his successful assassinations of anti-Communist leaders.

in German so that I become perfect in it. After I complete my studies, they'll send us to the West, and we can decide what to do then."

Inge told her parents that she was accompanying Stashynsky to Poland on a business trip. The KGB supported the story by forwarding all Inge's letters, postcards, and presents via Warsaw. But if the KGB's subterfuge was convincing to Inge's parents, her own attempt to convince Bogdan's superiors in Moscow that she was a loyal Soviet supporter was even more successful. Permission to marry was granted.

They returned to East Berlin. On April 23, 1960, a double ceremony took place, first at the registry office in Berlin-Mitte and then at the war-ruined Golgatha Kirche. The KGB did not approve of the church ceremony, which was performed in deference to the wishes of Inge's family, but again Stashynsky argued that it would add to his cover of respectability. After the wedding, there was a celebration at the home of the bride's parents. The newlyweds' gaiety was considerably restrained, however. Their happiness was overshadowed by the knowledge that they would be beginning their married life in Russia.

In May, under the name of Krylov, they left for Moscow, again telling Inge's parents that they were off for a long business sojourn in Warsaw. The Stashynskys' life in Russia fulfilled their worst expectations. Their new home was a single bug-infested room. While a KGB tutor worked on perfecting Bogdan's German, Inge was given a grand tour of Soviet museums and factories so that she could be duly impressed. Instead, she became more discontented daily.

"How can you be so blind?" she asked her husband, "when you are not stupid in other respects?"

He was not blind; he wanted to get out. The problem was twofold: how to escape, and what would happen to him once they were in the West. Each day his antagonism burned brighter, fueled by another action of his superiors. His mail was opened and censored. He was followed. Inge was followed. Finally, Inge's resentment flared up over the bugs.

Inge had had enough! Either the bugs would leave their bed or she would leave. Stashynsky attacked the job, pulling the mattress away, going after the iron framework with matches. And then he found another kind of bug—an electronic one. Wide-eyed, they stared at each other.

From then on, whenever they had anything of importance to say to each other, they wrote it down, or waited until they were walking alone. Longingly, they looked forward to the end of the year and the day of their promised visit to East Berlin. Once there, they would escape to the West.

In September, Inge informed him that he was going to be a father. When he announced the good news to his control, the answer was, "Either she can have an abortion or we'll place the child in a home. A child is undesirable for you at this time."

"You go to hell!" Bogdan rasped and stalked out of the room.

At one time such an outburst to a superior would have earned him a tour in a labor camp, but now he was permitted a certain leeway. After all, he was a two-time assassin, an award winner, and he was being specially prepared for new assignments. His masters had no wish to jeopardize the considerable investment in time and effort they had made in him. The KGB backed off.

As the year ground on, the Stashynskys drew solace from their dreams of escape. Shortly before the anticipated day of departure, however, they learned that their request to travel to East Berlin had been refused. Now irrevocably determined to make a break, Bogdan took Inge for a long walk. For the first time, he told her the true story of his past.

Stashynsky devised an alternate plan for escape. If they were not going to be allowed to travel together, at least he would see that Inge returned home to Dallgow. Once there, she must pretend illness to delay her return to Moscow. After the baby was born, she was to write to Shelepin and beg for a visit from her husband. If that did not work, he would have to figure out some other way to outwit his captors. In the meantime, they must devise a simple code for use in their letters.

Again taking advantage of his privileged position, Stashynsky pressured his superiors into allowing Inge to visit her parents. She was not well, he said, and her parents were becoming suspicious, wondering why their daughter, supposedly in Poland, could not come and see them. In January, 1961, Inge left for Dallgow for what was to be a short stay. There she managed to convince the KGB agents assigned to watch over her that she was too ill to make the return trip to Moscow before her baby was born. On March 31, Inge gave birth to a son, Peter. She sent her husband a telegram, informing him of the new arrival. Overjoyed by the news, Stashynsky realized that the time had come to attempt his escape.

The next day, when he was introduced to Yuri, his new control, Stashynsky reported the birth of his son and requested permission to visit his wife and child. The request was promptly rejected. Yuri countered with an order for Inge and the baby to come back to Moscow. Again, Inge managed to delay her departure. However, from the tone of her husband's letters, she soon saw that his chances of coming West were nonexistent. Resignedly, at the beginning of August, she went about getting the necessary travel documents to return to Russia. And then tragedy struck.

On August 9, Stashynsky received a heartbroken call from his wife. Peter had suddenly fallen ill and died. "You've got to come!" she cried, "You've got to come!"

When he approached Yuri, Bogdan was calm enough to offer a practical argument. He could not vouch for his wife's reaction if he were not permitted to be with her now. She was distraught, unwell, frantic. There was no telling what she might say or do. She could disregard her training and ruin everything! He must go to her immediately.

The next day he was permitted to leave by military aircraft, escorted by Yuri. When they landed, they were met by local KGB agents who informed Stashynsky that he must remain at Karlshorst until it was determined whether the Americans, discovering that he was a Soviet agent, had poisoned his son to lure him back to Berlin. Stashynsky was sure the KBG story was false, contrived so that he could be kept under surveillance.

Inge was brought to Karlshorst, and he tried to comfort her. As she clung to him, he realized the irony of their situation; Peter's death had brought them together when all else had failed. The funeral of their son was to provide their sole opportunity to escape.

On August 11, they were told that the baby had died a natural death, and they could go to Dallgow to make preparations for the funeral which would take place on the following day. Yuri told them that he would be the only agent accompanying them to the funeral, but Stashynsky knew they were under constant KGB surveillance. Inge's apartment house, her parents' home, both were being closely watched.

When they were finaly alone, walking to the quarters assigned him, Stashynsky said, "Inge, we're going to be watched tomorrow just as we have been today. After the funeral, it will be too late. There'll be no chance."

"Oh God, what can we do!" she whispered.

"There is only one possibility, we must try to escape *before* the funeral. They will not expect it."

"Oh, no."

"It's the only way! We'll go to your place first. There'll be a back entrance. There's some woodland there. We might make it."

She began to cry, but nodded her head in agreement.

When they departed for Dallgow in the morning, Yuri was in the car with them. As they pulled up in front of the house where Inge had her room, her husband saw that he had been correct. There were men watching them from cars parked at both ends of the street. They left Yuri and went into the building. There they found Inge's sixteen-year-old brother, Fritz.

"Fritz, you can show us the way through the woods," Inge told the surprised boy.

While the occupants of the KGB cars kept watch at the front of the house, the trio slipped out through the back door. Using trees and shrubs as cover, they walked through the forest into the center of Dallgow. Then they walked three miles to the town of Falkensee, where they left Fritz. Stashynsky knew that once they were missed, the word would go out to look for them at all zone checkpoints. He hailed a cab, flashed his credentials, and told the driver to "go like hell!" His one ace was that even though he was traveling under the name of Krylov, he still carried the official identification of Josef Lehmann.

"Try to act natural," was the only advice he could offer his wife as the taxi pulled up at the zone barrier. The cab approached the gate house, drawing near to the lowered peppermint-striped crossing bars. Flashing a friendly smile, Stashynsky presented his credentials to the guard. The wait was brief, but agonizing. He didn't dare to look at Inge. Then his documents were handed back with a salute and a return smile.

Upon reaching the Spandau district, they changed cabs. They saw no sign of pursuit and did not stop again until they reached the Schönhauser Allee S-bahn station in East Berlin. There, on August 12, 1961, Bogdan Stashynsky—KGB man, assassin, defector—boarded the elevated train with his wife, Inge, and rode the short distance to Gesundbrunnen in the Western Zone. Luck rode with them. The next day, the Soviet Union closed down the border between East and West Berlin, cutting off all traffic, and began the building of the wall. If the Stashynskys had delayed twenty-four hours, they would have been trapped in the Soviet Zone.

When Stashynsky first told his story to Western Intelligence officers, they were highly skeptical. But after exhaustive investigation, they realized that the defector was not lying. All the details checked out: the airline passenger lists, the bits of broken keys in the lockbox at No. 7 Kreittmayerstrasse, his descriptions of the weather on the two days of the assassinations, the names he had used on the hotel registers in Munich and Frankfurt. Furthermore, he brought identity papers and a testimonial signed by the Director of the Scientific Research Institute (a cover name for a KGB department). This document not only attested to his successful work from March, 1951, to December 28, 1960, the date of the testimonial, but also stated that "for successful activity in working out an important problem he was decorated with the Order of the Red Banner, in accordance with a decree of the Presidium of the Supreme Soviet of the USSR of November 6, 1959."

A month after Stashynsky's defection, before it had been announced publicly in the West, the KGB and the East German Security forces launched a propaganda campaign, claiming that Bandera had been assassinated by a Ukrainian emigrant named Myskiv, who was an agent of the BND, the West German Intelligence service. Myskiv himself, the Soviets asserted, had then been killed by the BND. Western Intelligence refuted the Soviet statement, presenting evidence that Myskiv was in Italy on the day of Bandera's murder and had died of natural causes on March 27, 1960.

The case, reported widely throughout the non-Communist world, became a *cause célèbre,* and although the Soviets and the East Germans did their best to discredit Stashynsky's confession, they failed. The thirty-one-year-old ex-spy could have received the death penalty, but because of his confession and the impression he made upon the court, the sentence was eight years.

Bogdan Stashynsky was released from prison in 1966. As was done for the Gouzenkos, a new identity was prepared for him and his wife. But no one could say they would live happily ever after, for the spy who crosses a border to rid himself of old fears necessarily takes on new ones. And in Stashynsky's case, he would always know that whereas once he was the hunter, now he was the hunted.

CHAPTER FIVE

The Illegal
Rudolf Ivanovich Abel –The Spy with Six Faces

After World War II, the techniques of Soviet espionage changed. The KGB and the GRU in the United States and the NATO countries began to rely on Soviet legal and illegal agents, rather than on members of an *apparat* who were native to the country in question.

In the United States, the legal Soviet spy entered the country either as an official member of the staff of the Soviet Embassy, or as a UN representative. Usually, when the legal agent was found guilty of espionage, he was declared *persona non grata* and sent home. In the period between 1960 and 1964, forty-six Soviet and Soviet bloc diplomatic officials—twenty-eight attached to the UN—were caught spying in the United States and expelled from the country.

Soviet illegal agents in America are spies who come into the country bearing false identity papers, posing as U.S. citizens or legitimate refugees. Such an agent goes through a long period of preparation and training to build up his legend, and once on the scene, he may wait years before he is signaled to carry out a specific act of espionage. Illegals are also called "deep cover" agents, or "sleepers."

As a result of World War II, the agent's technological equipment was greatly improved. With a shortwave radio he could listen to Radio Moscow to receive instructions, which might be included in a news broadcast, a music program, or a talk on art. He could also listen in on an assigned frequency and pick up coded information. With a transceiver and an assist from a small generator, he could use his shortwave radio to transmit information. Through the use of an automatic sending key, his messages could be compacted and sent out in short bursts, at the rate of 240 words a minute. He had an assigned code for receiving, as well as a different code for every day of sending.

A new soft-film process had been developed to strip away the hard outside covers of the film so that the message could be folded up and placed in a small container, such as a hollow pencil, without cracking the film. Often, the spy would put his message into a magnetic container. Then, he would stick the container onto the metal portion of a preselected dead drop. His contact, whom he might never see, would make the pickup and leave funds or further information.

Agents also began to use a new method of sending information: the microdot. Developed by the Germans during World War II, microdotting is the photographic technique of reducing an entire page of material to the size of a normal period. When the message is received, it is blown up back to its original size. The microdot can be placed under the stamp of a letter, in the context of a letter, or tucked in the spine of a magazine.

In the post-World War II period, Soviet agents entering the United States had three outside sources from whom they obtained their information: pro-Communist collaborators; contacts who could be bought; and contacts who could be recruited through blackmail. Often the legal agent would spot a potential contact at an embassy function, or at some other social affair. After a long period of careful cultivation, he would make a cautious approach. Sometimes the individual would report the attempt to the FBI. The FBI would then coach him on how to respond, and the game would be played out until the FBI decided to send the Russian diplomat home.

Much of what U.S. Counterintelligence knows about the operations of the KGB and the GRU has been supplied by defectors from both Soviet services. During the fifties more than a dozen important Soviet and Soviet bloc espionage officers crossed over to the West. It was through one such defection that the most celebrated espionage case of the decade came to public light.

* * * * *

On a gray day in November, 1948, the S.S. *Scythia* docked in Quebec after an uneventful voyage from Cuxhaven, Germany. Among her 1,587 passengers were many of foreign origin, either coming to seek a new beginning or returning from a visit to the "old country." One of them was a lanky, bald man with a large nose and a weak, tucked-in chin and mouth. His thin face looked birdlike, with bright, perceptive eyes peering out from under tufted eyebrows. His clothes were nondescript. According to his U.S. passport, his name was Andrew Kayotis, and he was an American citizen, fifty-three years old. His arrival in Canada was routine: immigration officials promptly processed his papers, customs officers checked his baggage, and he left.

In fact, Andrew Kayotis had never sailed on the *S. S. Scythia*. The real Andrew Kayotis had been a naturalized U.S. citizen who in July, 1947, had returned to his birthplace in Lithuania, where he died. The man who walked down the *Scythia*'s gangplank, bearing Kayotis's identification, was a Soviet spy. Once across the U.S. border, he shed the Kayotis identity and, chameleon-like, assumed a different outer skin. For the next sixteen months he spent considerable time traveling around the country, leaving no trace. But in April, 1950, he emerged out of the shadows with a new identity; he had become Emil Robert Goldfus, a semiretired photoengraver, forty-eight, born in New York City on August 2, 1902, of German parents.

The newly risen Emil Goldfus rented a furnished apartment on the West Side of upper Manhattan. Unobtrusive, scholarly, and charming, he merged into the community around him. Living quietly, he went his careful way, playing the role of a well-educated, displaced European intellectual. To see him on the street—walking with a slight stoop, wearing his unvarying costume of slacks, tweed jacket, and, in summer, a straw hat—no one would surmise that he was fluent in five languages, expert in the technology of radio mechanics, photography, microfilming, and microdotting, and skilled in fashioning hidden recesses in articles such as pencils, screws, bolts, cuff links, tiepins and coins. Even among those who became friendly with him, none guessed that he held the rank of colonel in the KGB, having served Soviet Intelligence since 1927.

One acquaintance of Emil Goldfus's who certainly suspected nothing was Alan Winston, a Columbia University student. Winston wanted to become an artist. Goldfus sympathized; that was his desire too. He became the young man's father confessor and mentor, a man interested in art and music. In the course of their friendship, Winston allowed his older friend to put his life's savings of $15,000 in his safe-deposit box at the Manufacturer's Trust Company.

Emil Goldfus also took on another identity, that of "Milton," a retired English businessman. Playing the role of Milton, he went to dine one evening in June, 1950, at the home of Morris and Lona Cohen. Morris Cohen had fought in Spain in the American Lincoln Brigade and served in the U.S. Army during World War II. For years Cohen had been an active Communist, and Lona strongly subscribed to her husband's political views. Two months after inviting Milton to dine, the Cohens disappeared from the country. (A decade later, the Cohens would become better known to the public as Peter John Kroger and Helen Joyce Kroger, London book antiquarians. Along with a Soviet national calling himself Gordon Lonsdale and two others, they were convicted of stealing British naval secrets for Russia.)

Only Soviet Intelligence knows the exact nature of the clandestine espionage carried on by Emil Goldfus in the years between 1949 and 1952. What information he microfilmed, microdotted, concealed in his tiepin, left in one of his containers at dead drops, or sent on his Hallicrafters shortwave radio is not known. However, it is known that the volume of his work was so great that he signaled headquarters that he could use an assistant. As a result, on a day in August, 1952, a meeting was held at a private home in Moscow. Four men were present: Vitali G. Pavlov, of Canadian network fame, now the assistant director of the American Section of State Security; Mikhail N. Svirin, on vacation from his diplomatic position as first secretary of the Soviet Mission at the United Nations; an agent named Stoyanov; and the subject of the conference, Reino Hayhanen.

Hayhanen, a short, chunky, fair-haired young man, had been building a legend since 1948, in the name of Eugene Nicolai Maki. The real Eugene Maki was born in Idaho. In the late 1920s, the Maki family went to Finland on a visit and disappeared. The new Eugene Maki's story was that when he was eight years old he traveled to Estonia with his mother and lived there with her until her death in 1941. His father had died in 1933. Since 1943, Maki's story continued, he had lived in Finland.

To help build this legend as Maki, Hayhanen had a photostat of Eugene Maki's birth certificate. In addition, on July 3, 1951, when he paid a call at the U.S. Legation in Helsinki, seeking a passport as a native born citizen, he had established a bona fide work record as a blacksmith's helper, a repairer of safes, and an auto mechanic. He also carried affidavits, which he had bought, attesting to his residence in Finland since 1943. His legend was well-established and costly, purchased with considerable expenditures of time and money.

After a year's wait, Hayhanen received a passport as Eugene

Maki. At this time, Emil Goldfus asked for an assistant, and Hayhanen was assigned the job. He crossed the border in a trunk of a car and reported to Soviet Security headquarters at 2 Dzerzhinski Street. There, he took a three-week cram course in espionage techniques, including soft-film processing, cipher methods, and English. Previously, while serving in Estonia for background purposes, English had been one of the subjects he studied during his training. His progress had been poor. It was equally poor in Moscow, but his superiors felt that the calibre of his intelligence was such that once in the United States his English would improve rapidly. After all, he had received praise for his work as a counterintelligence officer in the Finnish-Russian War. He had worked his way up the NKVD ladder by first translating documents, then interrogating prisoners, and later selecting and recruiting agents to send into Finland.

When Hayhanen arrived in Moscow in August, 1952, his superiors were sure that they had made a sound choice. As an agent in Estonia and Finland, he had carried out his instructions perfectly, even to the extent of marrying a Finnish girl, Hannah Kurikka. Hannah was a simple, good-looking young woman who became a dutiful, unquestioning wife. She remained completely unaware that her husband already had a wife and son in Moscow.

Hayhanen was given the code name of Vic and told that his superior in the United States was called Mark. His American contact was to be Svirin, a thin-lipped man with sad eyes and a prominent nose, whom Vic knew only as Mikhail. Mikhail's assignment was to assist Mark in his work.

What kind of work?

In his imperfect English, Hayhanen later described his mission as obtaining "all information what you can look for from newspapers or official way by asking for, I suppose, legally from some office, and espionage information, the kind of information what you get in illegal way. That is secret information, military information or atomic secrets."

To assist him in establishing his cover in the United States, Hayhanen was given $5,000 and a salary of $400 a month, plus $100 for his travel expenses. An additional wage was to be paid to his Russian wife. Svirin briefed him on the location of three dead drops for hiding messages: a bridge over a footpath in Central Park, a lamppost in Fort Tryon Park, and a hole in the wall on Jerome Avenue in the Bronx. Signal areas for indicating that a message had been left in a drop were to be set up using selected subway and train stations and a certain street light in Brooklyn. The system was simple: a horizontal chalk mark meant there was a message waiting.

After the message was picked up, he was to leave a vertical mark.

Pavlov had a farewell warning: "In espionage, we are always at war. If real war comes, there won't be time for you to move, and even if you no longer have communication with us, you will continue your work."

After receiving word of his promotion to the rank of major, Hayhanen went back to Helsinki, once more crossing the border in a car trunk. In October, he left Hannah and traveled to England where he booked passage on the *Queen Mary*. His arrival date in the United States was October 20, 1952. Mikhail Svirin had preceded him by a month and was working as a UN diplomat and living with his wife, Raissa Vassilievna, in an upper West Side apartment.

Hayhanen took a furnished room in a transient hotel on East Fiftieth Street. Hampered by his faulty English, he moved with extreme caution. A week after his arrival, he furtively placed a red thumbtack on a white sign which said "Be Careful of Riders" next to a bridle path in Central Park. In Moscow, Svirin had instructed him to use this signal to indicate his safe arrival.

A month later he deposited his first message at the Jerome Avenue dead drop in the Bronx. In the message, Hayhanen confirmed his arrival signal, said he was ready to start operating, and asked for more money. The response which he collected from the same drop told him it was too soon to talk about such matters.

On the twenty-first of each month, he boarded the BMT subway and rode to the stop at the Prospect Park station. There, sporting a blue tie with red stripes and smoking a pipe, he strolled to the Lincoln Road exit and waited for a contact. Six months after his first trip, someone approached him. Hayhanen recognized the man immediately; it was Svirin.

They retired to the men's room, where the diplomat handed Hayhanen a package containing letters from home and a May Day greeting from his superiors in Moscow. Then they left together on the same train. Hayhanen got off first.

At their next meeting, Svirin told him there would be no more personal contacts between them.

In the spring of 1953, Hayhanen made contact with a Finnish sailor whose code name was Asko. They arranged dead drops and a thumbtack signal. Asko served as a courier, bringing letters from Hayhanen's relatives and messages from Moscow.

As the weeks and months slipped by and he continued to make his rounds, Hayhanen began to feel more and more isolated. He had always liked to drink, and now he began to drink heavily. Hannah had arrived in February, 1953. They quarreled. She did not drink.

She did not like the city, the run-down place they had moved to in Brooklyn, nor the strange way in which her husband behaved. Once she had been impressed with his self-assurance; now she saw him becoming sloppy and careless. Soon this carelessness was to result in evidence of espionage reaching the FBI.

On a summer day in 1953, James Bozart, a bright thirteen-year-old newsboy, was making his weekly collection at an apartment building on Foster Avenue in Brooklyn. A customer had given him a quarter and five nickels in change, and as the newsboy was walking down the stairs, he dropped the coins. When he picked them up, he saw that one of the nickels had split in half and one of the halves had a microfilm in it.

"It was a picture of a file card or an index card," he said later. "There seemed to be a row of numbers on it."

The boy turned his find over to the police who, in turn, passed it on to the FBI. The bureau put its cipher experts to work, but they were not expert enough to crack Hayhanen's personal code, which was designed to be used only by himself and his Moscow control. At the time, if the decoders in Washington had been able to translate the microfilmed numbers, they would have read the following:

> We congratulate you on a safe arrival. We confirm our receipt of your letter to the address 'V' repeat 'V' and the reading of letter Number 1.
>
> For organization of cover, we gave instructions to transmit to you three thousand in local (currency). Consult with us prior to investing it in any kind of business, advising the character of this business.
>
> According to your request, we will transmit the formula for the preparation of soft film and news separately, together with mother's letters. It is too early to send you the Gammas. Encipher short letters, but the longer ones make with insertions. All the data about yourself, place of work, address, etc., must not be transmitted in one cipher message. Transmit insertions separately. The packages were delivered to your wife personally. Everything is all right with the family. We wish you success. Greetings from the comrades. Number 1, 3rd of December.

The microfilm message lay undeciphered for four years, until Hayhanen supplied the FBI with his code. That it reached the FBI in 1953 was a measure of the extent of Hayhanen's ineptness.

In the spring of 1954, Hayhanen and Hannah moved out of the city to a sparsely populated spot near Peekskill, New York. The move may have been made under orders or because they both longed to live in the country. But the country air failed to rehabilitate Hayhanen. He drank more than anyone around, was unfriendly to his few neighbors, and made himself conspicuous by treating Hannah badly. He continued his work routine, driving to the city to check the drops, but for weeks no message came. It was not until August, almost two years after his arrival in the United States, that Hayhanen had his first meeting with Mark, his Russian superior—the lean, quiet man who publicly called himself Emil Goldfus.

As to what Emil Goldfus had been doing in the long interim between his request for an assistant and the eventual meeting, the overt record is tenuous and obscure; the covert record, nonexistent. Until December, 1953, he continued to live on Riverside Drive at Seventy-fourth Street. Alan Winston was his only known friend. Winston had no suspicion that his fatherly companion was a Soviet agent. They dined together frequently, visited art exhibits, and discussed all kinds of subjects. Then in December, not long before Winston was due to enter the army, Emil Goldfus moved to Brooklyn Heights, renting a one-room studio in the Ovington Building at 252 Fulton Street.

The Ovington was a seven-story, red-brick building, full of aspiring artists and writers. Emil Goldfus, playing the role of the retired photofinisher who had saved his money so that he could devote his time to painting, took over room 505 and set up shop as an artist.

Most of his fellow tenants were young men who had not yet been successful in their careers. Two of them, Burt Silverman and David Levine, became his close friends. They introduced Goldfus to other writers and artists. Although at first his new acquaintances were curious about something mysterious, something enigmatic, that they sensed in the Goldfus personality, soon they accepted him at face value. As individualists, they valued their own privacy and granted Goldfus his. His old-world manner, his affability attracted them; his adaptability, his range of knowledge and interests impressed them. After hearing Segovia play Bach on the radio one night, Goldfus went out and bought a guitar, and six months later he was playing Segovia, Bach, and de Falla on the instrument. He applied his technical craftsmanship to many fields. He fixed things; he built things. On one occasion, when the building elevator refused to work, he brought out his own tools and repaired it. In addition to his paints and paintings, his studio became cluttered with all kinds of objects and artifacts: photographic equipment, books, mechanical parts, a Hallicrafters shortwave radio, and a clothesline. The clothesline was generally festooned with dripping white handkerchiefs, since

Rudolph Ivanovich Abel, Russia's "master spy," caught and convicted in the United States.

The Illegal 117

Goldfus suffered from sinus trouble and used many handkerchiefs in the course of a day.

Goldfus did more than play the role of the artist; he worked hard at his painting and offered opinions about art. His own canvases, largely still lifes and portraits of people living in poverty, reflected a bleak realism. Ostensibly, he kept regular hours, arriving at the studio about 10:00 A.M., and usually leaving around 7:00 P.M. Secretly, however, he would return to his studio at night, when everyone else had departed, to receive shortwave radio messages from Moscow. Almost always, he seemed uninvolved in politics, unconcerned over what was going on in the nation and the world. Only once did the secret face of the man reveal itself.

Late one night, Burt Silverman came to the building with his fiancée, Helen Worthman. Seeing a light under the door of 505, the couple knocked and were welcomed in by Goldfus. He brewed some coffee. Helen, noticing the Hallicrafters radio, asked if he could get European stations on it. He could, Emil told her, and fiddled with the dial until they heard some music. They sat quietly, listening to the music from overseas. When it ended, the announcer spoke in a language the couple did not recognize. While the announcer was talking, the telephone rang in Silverman's studio down the hall. He went to answer it. The call was from a friend. Helen and Goldfus strolled into the studio, and the friend asked who was there.

"Oh, that's Helen and Emil," Silverman said and joked, "We were just listening in on Moscow."

The friend laughed. After the conversation ended, Silverman turned to find Goldfus staring at him angrily. "Don't ever say such a thing on the phone again," Emil snapped. "Even in jest."

Burt realized that Goldfus was angry. After reflection, Silverman felt ashamed. Goldfus was right—at this time you should not joke about Communist conspiracies! Chastened, he accepted the older man's rebuke.

So Emil Goldfus continued to play his role and receive the applause of his unsuspecting audience. Reino Hayhanen, however, was, as always, encountering problems.

In August, at the RKO Theater in Flushing, Queens, Hayhanen met Goldfus, the man he was to know as Mark. The meeting had been arranged by dead drop. Hayhanen wore his colorful tie, puffed his pipe in the men's room, and kept his password ready. The man who finally entered did not stand on intelligence ceremony.

"Hello," he said brusquely. "I am Mark. Never mind about passwords. I know you are the right man." Then, striding from the room, "Come outside."

The opening at the base of this lamppost, in Fort Tryon Park, New York City, was used as an espionage "dead drop" by Abel and his fellow spy, Reino Hayhanen.

The Illegal   119

Hayhanen was shaken. The older man was cold, official, authoritative. Thrown offstride by the openness of the approach, Hayhanen followed him dutifully.

But if Hayhanen was upset, so was Mark. He soon discovered that in nearly two years on the scene, Vic, as Mark called Hayhanen, had set up no business cover, although he had been given $3,000 to do so. He was amazed at the poor quality of Vic's English, annoyed at the ineptness of his technique in microdotting and making soft film, and dumbfounded that the man had not been taught Morse code. Mark looked his assistant over and disapproved strongly of what he saw. Pasty-faced, sloppy, obviously nervous and in need of a drink—what kind of incompetent clod had Moscow sent him?

Mark determined to set up an efficient operation; they would have weekly, even biweekly meetings, and three new drop locations were to be added to the list. He would handle Vic's money. Vic must find a suitable cover job. Mark ordered Vic to learn his trade; he must practice photography and practice Morse code. At subsequent meetings, he gave his assistant frequent tests, checking him to see if he had perfected his skills.

Vic's resentment grew. He detested Mark, detested his arrogance, his self-discipline, his superior knowledge, and his manner of treating his assistant, not as a major in the KGB, but as a chauffeur. And often, following Mark's instructions, that is what Vic became. On one occasion, he drove Mark up into Westchester County to the Croton Reservoir, where they tested a shortwave radio that Mark was going to give him. On another trip, they drove to Hopewell Junction near the Taconic Parkway, looking for a house to buy to convert into a secret radio station, but found prices too high. Similar field trips were taken to Pennsylvania and New Jersey. One day, Mark had Vic drive him to Red Bank, New Jersey, to search for a contact, Sergeant Roy A. Rhodes of the U.S. Army, whose code name was Quebec. They discovered that Quebec did not live in Red Bank. On two separate journeys, Mark sent Vic alone to locate potential spies, one in Arleigh, New Jersey, and the other in Quincy, Massachusetts. Both missions were unsuccessful.

In the case of Sergeant Rhodes, who had previously worked for the Soviets while attached to the U.S. Embassy in Moscow, Mark felt he would make a good agent if he could be located. Contacting Moscow for more information, Mark was told that the sergeant's sister lived in Salida, Colorado. Hayhanen telephoned her and learned that Rhodes's address was Fort Huachuca, Tuscon, Arizona. Mark told his assistant that he would look up the sergeant at a later date.

Time and time again, Mark emphasized that Vic must find cover

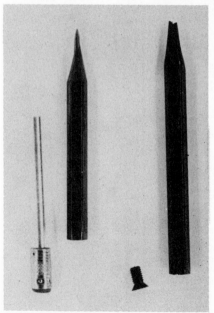

Shaving brush, flashlight battery, cufflinks, pencil and other articles converted into containers and used by Abel for smuggling microfilmed messages to Moscow.

work. He decided that Vic was to open a photographer's shop. And so, on March 29, 1955, Vic, as Eugene Maki, signed a three-year lease for an empty store and a four-room apartment at 806 Bergen Street in Newark, New Jersey. The location was in a dismal neighborhood of small shops, far from the center of the city. The store was to be converted into a photoequipment outlet. However, Vic did not have enough money to buy the necessary supplies, so late one night Mark took him to the Ovington Building and gave him equipment from his own storage room, including a shortwave radio.

Permitting his assistant to visit his place of operations was a surprising lapse in good judgment for an espionage agent of Mark's calibre. Perhaps Mark was influenced by the knowledge that he would soon be leaving the area; during this period he informed his subordinate that he would be returning to Russia for his first vacation in almost seven years. Vic would be in charge in his absence.

Shortly before Mark's departure in July of that year, the two spies drove to Bear Mountain Park and buried $5,000 in two packages. The money, Mark informed Vic, had been sent from Moscow to be given as a gift to Helen Sobell, the wife of Morton Sobell. Sobell, whose code name was Stone, had been convicted of espionage in the Rosenberg case, and was, at the time, serving a thirty-year sentence in the penitentiary at Atlanta. Mark said that on several occasions he had attempted to deliver the money to Stone's wife, but that her apartment was being watched by the police. Now, Vic was assigned the task of handing the money over to Mrs. Sobell. He was to make contact by letter, mentioning the name of the man who had recruited Sobell.

Vic wondered: was Agent Stone's wife a spy, too?

Mark was not sure, but he explained that the usual procedure was for a husband and wife to work together as agents.

Later, Vic would inform Mark that he had turned the money over to Helen Sobell as instructed, telling her to spend it carefully. Actually, during Mark's absence, he dug the money up and kept it for himself.

Before leaving, Mark once again assumed the role of Emil Goldfus. Goldfus told his friends at the Ovington that he was going to California to try and sell some photocopying equipment he had developed. He said good-by to Burt Silverman, paid the superintendent, Harry MacMullen, several months rent in advance, and, on the third of July, he left. He was to be gone nearly a year.

In that year, Eugene Maki did not open a photoequipment shop. He did drink heavily and Hannah joined him. Neighbors on Bergen Street heard their quarrels. Nightly, the street resounded with the raucous clamor of Maki shouting, Hannah screaming. In one drunken brawl, Hannah stabbed her husband in the leg, and a neighbor called the police. On another occasion, Maki had an automobile accident and was almost arrested for drunken driving. In the summer of 1956, he moved back to Peekskill. As a discreet spy, his performance in New Jersey had been unique. Everyone on Bergen Street noticed him; no one forgot him.

By the spring of 1956, Burt Silverman had become concerned about the long absence of Emil Goldfus. Harry MacMullen also was worried about the missing tenant. He told Silverman that the rent was due; unless Goldfus showed up by the end of the month, he would be evicted. And then, the day after Silverman's conversation with MacMullen, Goldfus reappeared. He had suffered a heart attack while in Texas, he told Silverman, and was hospitalized for four months. Silverman was upset. Why hadn't Goldfus let his friends know about it? Goldfus sighed. He hadn't wanted to bother anyone with his troubles. He was all right now. His business trip had been a failure, but that was life. No need to weep. What was new?

What was new was Mark's realization that he was forced to take action on the problem of Vic. For a considerable period of time, Mark could not make contact with Vic because he did not show up

Birth certificate used by Rudolph Abel to assume the identity of Martin Collins, an American citizen.

for appointments. After they finally met, Mark notified Moscow that his assistant needed a vacation. The message came through by dead drop; Moscow thought a vacation for Vic was an excellent idea, too. He was to obtain a new passport as soon as possible and travel as a tourist. To reassure him, he was also informed that he had been promoted to the rank of lieutenant colonel.

Vic was not reassured; he was terrified. Reino Hayhanen was a drunk and a bumbler, but he had a strong instinct for survival. He knew that he had done nothing to earn the promotion, and that his vacation trip was probably destined to end in Siberia.

Mark spent many weeks making arrangements for the trip. Vic was to travel by ship to Le Havre, train to Paris and West Germany, and plane from Germany to Moscow. If, for any reason, this route had to be abandoned, he was to go to Mexico City, where a Russian official would meet him in a specified bar with further instructions. In case he could not use his United States passport, Mark gave him a birth certificate in the name of Lauri Arnold Ermas. Maki buried this certificate in the basement of his Peekskill house; one false identity was enough for him. He was ordered to inform his friends of his impending departure. He had no friends, only neighbors, and he told them over and over again that he was "gonna shoot pictures in Paris."

At the beginning of the new year, Mark instructed him to buy his ticket and depart. He told Vic to leave the notification of his sailing date in a special drop set up for that purpose in a staircase in Prospect Park, Brooklyn. Vic left this message:

"I bought a ticket to next ship—Queen Elisab. for next Thursday—1.31. Today I could not come because 3 men are tailing me."

By the middle of February, Vic still had not sailed. He remained in Peekskill, drinking and growing increasingly terrified. Mark ordered his assistant to meet him at the Prospect Park drop. They met, although Vic had some trouble finding Mark, who had hidden behind some bushes until he was certain they were alone. Mark demanded an explanation. Vic said that he had been unable to sail because the FBI had taken him off the ship and questioned him. Mark repeated the instructions: Vic must sail immediately. Once more, he detailed the route Vic was to follow. Patiently, he told Vic that he appreciated the strain under which he had been living, but once he returned home, everything would be better. He instructed him on what to do in Paris. He was to call KLEber 3341 to contact the Soviet Embassy. He was to identify himself by saying, "Can I send through your office two parcels to the USSR without Mori Company?" As a last lesson, Mark issued exact instructions on how to operate Parisian telephones.

Finally, on April 24, the reluctant spy departed. He arrived in

Paris after six days of alcoholic deliberations about his future. First, he made the required telephone call. Then, sporting his blue tie with red stripes and smoking his pipe, he met his Russian contact, who gave him $200 for the rest of his trip. The next night the two agents met again. They did not speak, but Vic was hatless and carried a magazine in his hand to signal that he would be leaving for West Germany the next day.

That night, after the meeting with the Russian, Vic went to a movie and returned to his hotel. But agent Vic did not leave Paris the next day. In the morning, Reino Hayhanen walked down the busy

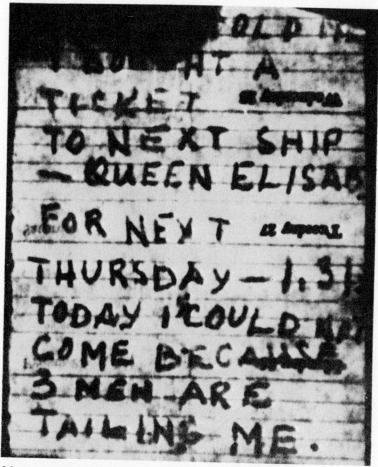

Message written by Hayhanen and left at "dead drop," informing master spy Abel that he planned to leave the United States on the Queen Elizabeth.

Rue de Rivoli, passed the Place de la Concorde, and entered the American Embassy. There, he announced himself as a lieutenant colonel in the KGB with information to offer.

While Reino Hayhanen was submitting to the long, agonizing ordeal of interrogations, investigations, and self-recriminations which defectors undergo, Emil Goldfus seemingly remained unaware of the fatal blow his assistant had dealt him. For some time, Goldfus had been moving in and out of a series of hotels, registering under different names. For most of 1956, he lived in the Embassy Hotel at Seventieth Street and Broadway. In September, he checked in at the Ben Franklin on West Seventy-second Street. At each hotel, he registered as "E.R. Goldfus" and listed Burt Silverman as the person to be notified in case of emergency. He stayed at the Ben Franklin until April 17, 1957. Then, on April 19, five days before Hayhanen sailed on the *Liberté,* he went to the Broadway Central Hotel, where he signed his name as Martin Collins. Collins gave Chicago as his address but left blank the place marked "In Emergency Notify."

He stayed at the Broadway Central for a week. During that time, Collins spent one night in the role of Emil Goldfus, dining with the newly married Burt Silverman and his bride. Goldfus told the Silvermans, who were planning to leave shortly on a European honeymoon, that he, too, was going away. His doctor had ordered him to a warm climate for a rest cure for his sinus trouble.

On April 28, Goldfus, as Martin Collins, checked into the Plaza Hotel in Daytona Beach, Florida, giving his home address as the Beekman Hotel, New York City.

He remained in Florida until May 7, painting a seascape. On May 7, three days after Reino Hayhanen defected to the Americans, Martin Collins returned to New York, checking into the Latham Hotel on Twenty-eighth Street, just east of Fifth Avenue. At first, he stayed away from the Ovington. On May 21, he went to the hotel doctor for a smallpox vaccination, telling him he was planning to travel. Two nights later, he took the subway to Emil Goldfus's studio and walked into a trap.

Hayhanen had remembered his visit to Mark's studio and led the FBI to the address. Agents were posted all over the area: around the Ovington Building, in the park across the street, two blocks away in the Hotel Touraine, and in the nearby Brooklyn Federal Post Office. More agents were walking around the neighborhood, looking inconspicuous.

FBI Special Agent Neil D. Heiner, watching studio 505 through powerful binoculars from the twelfth floor of the Hotel Touraine, described what he saw from his vantage point: "I could see a male figure moving around in the room. From time to time, he would pass in front of the light. . . . I could see this man was middle-aged and was bald-headed. He had a fringe of gray hair around the edges. He was wearing glasses . . . and he showed himself only momentarily. My view of the entire room was obstructed, except when he stood in front of the window. The light remained on, and at about one minute before midnight, I saw this man in back of the light put on a dark brown or dark gray summer straw hat, and it had a very bright white band. The band stood out. About a minute later the light went out."

The distinctive white-banded hat continued to stand out. Just after midnight, Special Agent Joseph C. McDonald saw leaving the building a man wearing a hat that matched Agent Heiner's description. Carrying his coat over his arm, walking at a leisurely pace, the man strolled down Fulton Street to Clinton, up Clinton to Montague, and then around the corner to the BMT Borough Hall subway station. McDonald followed him. In the station, the two men entered the elevator together, and went down to the subway platform. The older man walked to the end of the platform. McDonald, mixing with the crowd, watched his man turn and walk right past him as a train came clattering in. He saw him board the next-to-last car. Just before the doors closed, McDonald stepped into the last car. From his seat, he could not see the straw hat and the white band. When the train pulled into the next station, McDonald looked through the windows to see if his man was getting off. Convinced that he was still on the train, McDonald moved to the car ahead where he could watch the straw hat. He rode with his man to the City Hall stop, where they both got off.

They came up out of the subway into the warm spring night. The sidewalks were sparsely populated. Agent McDonald moved cautiously now, following the white hatband and trying not to signal its owner that he was being stalked. They moved north on Broadway to Chambers Street, where the quarry stopped on the corner. McDonald ducked into a doorway and waited. After a few minutes, a New York City bus appeared. The man on the corner stepped aboard, but there was no time for McDonald to do so. McDonald quickly hailed a cab. The pursuit continued to Twenty-seventh Street and Broadway. There, McDonald saw his man get off the bus and start walking towards the east. He followed. At Fifth Avenue, the chase turned north for a block, then east again on Twenty-eighth Street.

But when McDonald reached the corner of Twenty-eighth Street and Fifth Avenue, his man had vanished. He made his report, and the FBI resumed surveillance of the Ovington Building.

Three weeks later, on the night of June 13, the same scenario was enacted again, with a different ending. The cast was the same: the man with the straw hat and the FBI agents following him. The scene was the same: the Ovington Building, the subway, and the streets of Brooklyn and Manhattan. This time, however, the chase concluded with the agent following the straw-hatted man to the Latham Hotel. Now, the FBI knew where he was living.

This was not all the FBI knew about Mark–Goldfus. In the nearly six weeks since the defection of Reino Hayhanen, the FBI had learned all the assistant could tell them about the lieutenant colonel and his associations. Through photographs of Soviet UN diplomats, the FBI had identified "Mikhail" as Mikhail N. Svirin. They knew about Hayhanen's bosses—Alexander M. Korotkov, who was the assistant director of PGU, the KGB's department of external espionage, and Vitali G. Pavlov. With Hayhanen's aid, the FBI had finally translated the microfilmed message found in the nickel turned in four years before by newsboy James Bozart. After Hayhanen drew a floor plan of his house and showed the agents where to dig, they unearthed a cache of espionage evidence including a microfilm written in English, giving information on the activities of U.S. Army Sergeant Roy A. Rhodes. Inserted inside a hollowed-out bolt which was placed in a Dugan bread wrapper, the microfilm read as follows:

> Quebec. Roy A. Rhodes. Born 1917 in Oilton, Oklahoma, U.S. Senior Sergeant of the War Ministry, former employee of the U.S. Military Attaché Staff in our country. He was Chief of the garage of the embassy.
>
> He was recruited to our service in January, 1952, in our country which he left in June, 1953. Recruited on the basis of compromising materials but he is tied up to us with his receipts and information he had given in his own handwriting.
>
> He had been trained in code work at the Ministry before he went to work at the embassy but as a code worker he was not used by the embassy.
>
> After he left our country, he was to be sent to the School of Communications of the Army C.I. Service which is at the city of San Luis, California. He was to be trained there as a mechanic of the coding machines.
>
> He fully agreed to continue to cooperate with us in the states or any other country. It was agreed that he was to have written to our embassy here special letters but we have received none during the last years.
>
> It has been recently learned that Quebec is living in Red

Bank, N.J., where he owns three garages. The garage job is being done by his wife. His own occupation at present is not known.

His father, Mr. W.A. Rhodes, resides in the U.S. His brother is also in the states where he works as an engineer at an atomic plant in Georgia together with his brother-in-law and his father.[1]

What the FBI did not know was the answer to one question: why was Emil Goldfus–Mark–Milton–Martin Collins, a colonel in the KGB, who had been operating in the United States for eight and one-half years, acting in this puzzling manner? Two weeks after Hayhanen's defection, Goldfus came back to New York from Florida when he could easily have returned to Russia via Mexico. Was he unaware that his assistant had not reached Moscow and had gone over to the Americans? It certainly seemed so. Goldfus wore a hat that was a beacon. He followed a routine at a time when routine should have been avoided at all costs. He appeared not to realize that he was being watched.

The FBI made the necessary legal preparations in order to act. One week after the second chase, they were ready. At 7:00 A.M., on June 21, 1957, FBI Special Agent Gamber knocked on the door of room 839 of the Hotel Latham. The sound awoke the naked man sleeping inside the hot, cluttered room.

"Just a minute," he muttered groggily. Beside him on the night table was a Hallicrafters shortwave radio, the aerial running up the wall, across the ceiling, into the bathroom, and out the window.

The colonel's own words describe what happened next:

Without putting on my clothes, I opened the door a few inches to see who was there. Three men pushed their way in. They said they were agents of the FBI and showed me identification cards in their wallets. They told me to sit down on the bed. Still naked, I did so.

For the next five minutes the three men, who said their names were Phelan, Gamber and Blasco, talked to me. They said, we know all about you; that they had been following me and knew all my agents. They urged me to cooperate. I told them I didn't know what they were talking about; I had a right not to talk and I did not wish to do so. After a while, I received permission to, and did, put on my underwear shorts.

(He also was given permission to fetch his false teeth from the bathroom.)

Throughout the questioning they addressed me as "colonel" although I had never used the title or any similar title in the United States.

The agents informed the colonel that they had information concerning his involvement in espionage. If he cooperated, one of the agents would "call his immediate superior at the New York FBI office and report the degree of cooperation." If he did not cooperate, he would be arrested immediately. The colonel refused the offer. Two agents of the Immigration and Naturalization Service (INS) moved into the room.

"What is your name?" one of them asked.

"Martin Collins," came the reply.

"We are placing you under arrest." Taking the warrant from his pocket, the agent read: "Whereas from evidence submitted to me, it appears that the alien Martin Collins, alias Emil R. Goldfus, who entered this country from an unknown point in Canada. . . ." When he had finished citing all the whereases in the lengthy official document, he said to the accused, "You are entitled to consult a lawyer. It is also your constitutional right to remain silent."

The colonel chose to remain silent. The INS agent then informed him that he would be taken to Immigration headquarters. He could bring his possessions with him. The room was now crowded with both FBI and Immigration officers, and the latter group began to rummage through everything within the room and the bathroom. Each item the occupant owned was searched and investigated. Clothes, books, cameras, medications, toilet articles, and paints were scattered around the room. The miscellany was an ordinary assortment of everyday belongings except for a few odd items: birth certificates in the names of Emil R. Goldfus and Martin Collins, a certificate of vaccination recently issued to Martin Collins, photographs of Morris and Lona Cohen, $6,500 in cash, and a bankbook in the name of Emil Goldfus.

The agents took his clothing from the closet and dresser and piled it on the bed. They permitted him to dress, carefully inspecting each item before he donned it. When they began stuffing his clothing into his suitcases, he asked to do the job himself. He packed with care, folding each piece of clothing neatly. Some objects he discarded, tossing them into the wastebasket. These included painting supplies, pencils, an ebony-finished block of wood, kleenex packages, papers, and half a dozen books. While the colonel was repacking, he was watched closely by Robert E. Schoenenberger, supervisory investigator for INS. Later, Schoenenberger described how he caught the colonel "in the act of removing some papers from his bag and attempting to slip them inside the right sleeve of the jacket he was wearing. I reached down and pulled his hand up and took the three pieces of paper.

"Two of them were strips with but a few lines on them. They had Spanish words on them. One started out with the word 'Balmora.' The other started out with 'In.' It looked like 'In Mex.' I noticed the word 'Chihuahua' in the body of it. The other was a piece of paper like graph paper with number groups on it, five numbers in a group. I suppose there were eight lines, eight or ten lines."

The arrest took an hour and fifteen minutes to complete—from the apprehension through the search, the packing, and the payment of the hotel bill. At 8:15 A.M., the handcuffs came out. The Immigration agents left, hustling their manacled prisoner into a waiting car.

The FBI men stayed in the hotel. Obtaining signed permission from the hotel manager, they returned to room 839 and began their own search. They spent three hours going through everything in the room, but the search divulged evidence that more than justified the expenditure of time. Digging into the filled-up wastebasket, they unearthed what they were looking for—physical proof of espionage operations. One of the pencils the colonel had discarded was hollow and contained microfilm. The block with the ebony finish held a small pad with 250 wafer-thin pages of numbers. They also found a paper with a partly encoded message on it. All these objects were dispatched to the FBI laboratory in Washington.

In the meantime, the colonel was taken to Immigration headquarters at 70 Columbus Avenue where he was photographed, fingerprinted, questioned, and searched again. Once more he was asked to cooperate; once more he refused. He doodled on a pad while he was questioned. One of the agents asked him what the doodles were.

"Logarithm tables," the prisoner answered.

Late in the afternoon, he was driven to Newark Airport in the company of two INS agents. There, he was escorted on to a DC-3 aircraft which took off, heading south. Some hours later, when the plane began its landing approach to Mobile, the colonel showed how well he knew the land below by asking, "What are we doing in Alabama?" He said he had calculated the plane's course by watching the sun, noting the direction they were heading, and estimating the speed of the aircraft. After refueling in Mobile, they took off again. At half-past four in the morning, they landed in Brownsville, Texas. A car was waiting to take the prisoner to the Federal Detention Camp for Aliens at McAllen, Texas.

He slept for a few hours. Beginning at nine o'clock in the morning, he was interrogated over and over by FBI and Immigration agents. He refused to answer most of the questions. But three days after his arrival, he made a confession. He said that his real name was Rudolf Ivanovich Abel and that he was a Russian citizen. He also admitted he had entered the United States illegally. He had, he said, found a large sum of American money in a ruined blockhouse in Russia and taken the money to Denmark, where he bought a forged U.S. passport. Using this passport, he had gone to Canada in 1948 and then to the United States.[2]

This was his story, and he stuck with it through the next three weeks of solitary confinement and questioning. To choose his attorney, he went through a classified directory and selected a local firm, Stofford, Atlas, and Spilman. On June 27, at a formal hearing, accompanied by his lawyer, Morris Atlas, he admitted to being an illegal alien. Asked by the special inquiry officer, "Do you admit your deportability in this charge?" Abel answered, "I accept deportation."

Accept deportation? He hoped for it, longed for it.

He did not know how much the FBI had found out about him. As an illegal alien, the penalty under law was deportation, the only escape route open to him.

After the hearing, there followed a long period of interrogation. "I was questioned daily by various FBI agents," Abel later reported. "They stated over and over again that if I would cooperate, they would get me good food, liquor, an air-conditioned room in a Texas hotel and they could assure me of a $10,000 a year job with another United States government agency." But Colonel Rudolf Ivanovich Abel was not Lieutenant Colonel Reino Hayhanen. He had spent years disciplining himself to accept the knowledge that some day he might be apprehended. He was a true professional. He refused to cooperate, and the agents questioning him began to realize that he never would.

The Department of Justice continued to prepare the case. A Brooklyn Grand Jury heard testimony and on August 7, Abel was indicted. The indictment charged him with three crimes: conspiracy to transmit atomic and military information to Soviet Russia (maximum penalty—death); conspiracy to gather such information (maximum penalty—ten years in prison); conspiracy to remain in the United States without registering with the State Department as a foreign agent (maximum penalty—five years in prison).

The press had a field day. Abel's rank of colonel was featured. He was called "the highest ranking espionage agent ever caught in this country" and the *resident,* or head, of the Soviet espionage network for the United States. In later newspaper accounts, the area of operations he commanded grew to encompass all of North America and Mexico. He became "the Master Spy."

Extradited from Texas, arraigned on the charges, and held in Manhattan's West Street Jail, the accused waited to be tried. Still, no defense lawyer had been chosen. Abel had requested that John Abt, an attorney who had defended many alleged Communists, be assigned to defend him. Abt refused to take the case. After some delay, the Brooklyn Bar Association found the perfect man for the job, James B. Donovan. Donovan had graduated from Harvard Law School. During World War II, he had been a Naval Intelligence and OSS officer, and later he had served as associate prosecutor at the principal Nuremberg trial. After the war, he went into private practice. A Catholic, forty-one years old, and prematurely silver-haired, Donovan was respected by his colleagues not only as an astute and gifted attorney, but also as a man who could not possibly be accused of sympathy for communism.

Excited about what he viewed as a "fascinating legal assignment, however unpopular or hopeless," as he described it later, and aware that the American system of justice was on trial along with his client, Donovan took on the case.

When the trial opened on Monday, October 14, 1957, the Cold War had become frigid. On October 5, the Russians had astounded the world with the launching of Sputnik. In its lead editorial of October 13, the *New York Times* strongly criticized "bellicose, Soviet moves" since the launching. Andrei Gromyko had told the UN that the United States and West Germany were out to block all disarmament plans. Simultaneously, Krushchev had charged, in an interview with columnist James Reston, that Secretary of State John Foster Dulles had sent State Department official Loy Henderson to the Middle East to help Turkey organize an Arab attack on Syria. Turkey was warned by the Soviet premier and the Soviet press. On October 16, Dulles counterwarned that a Soviet attack on Turkey would bring prompt U.S. retaliation. The Hungarian uprising of the previous October was still fresh in the public mind. It was no time for a Soviet "Master Spy" to expect public opinion to be objective. Rudolph Abel was lucky to have James Donovan to represent him.

Between the accused and his defender, there swiftly developed a firm bond of respect and sympathy. They had much in common. Both men had worked in the intelligence field, which led them to accept the need for espionage by both sides. In addition, both shared an interest in art and had quick minds, stubborn and determined. Later, Donovan was to describe Abel as "an intellectual and a gentleman, with a fine sense of humor. . . . I found him intriguing. As a man, you could not help but like him." The trial lasted eleven days, but the relationship between Donovan and Abel was to last much longer.

James Donovan soon realized that he had the task of defending a client who was obviously guilty of espionage, since, if nothing else, the physical evidence seemed irrefutable. When Donovan saw how much evidence there was of spying, he said to his client, "It's incredible. You violated most of the basic rules of espionage with all that paraphernalia lying about."

Abel answered, "I tried to get rid of everything."

And when Donovan questioned him on his major error—taking Hayhanen to his studio—his response was equally weak. "I couldn't believe he was so stupid, such an incompetent," Abel said. "I keep thinking he couldn't be this bad, they never would have sent him. I was sure it was part of his legend that he was preparing to become a double agent and go to work for the FBI as a defector."

Donovan was troubled. He knew that it would be a difficult, grueling trial. He needed time, and he needed a plan of action. Before the trial began, he launched his counterattack, a one-two legal punch. Because Abel had been arrested and held in Manhattan on a civil charge, even though he was to be tried in Federal Court in Brooklyn on a criminal charge, Donovan instituted a civil action in the form of an affidavit in Manhattan Federal Court in Foley Square. The affidavit moved to have all physical evidence removed from the case on the grounds that it had been illegally obtained. The basis of his argument was the Fourth Amendment of the Constitution, "that government agents had seized in his home a person and all his property, without a criminal warrant for his arrest or a public search warrant; secretly transported him to an alien detention camp in Texas and held him forty-seven days, the first five incommunicado."

In his motion, he also said, "Because the methods used by the government trapped a suspected enemy agent, the average citizen would not become alarmed, nor be shocked. In such a case, he would feel the end justifies the means. But under our law the constitutional guarantees apply to everyone of us as well as to a suspect like Abel."

On October 2, Judge Sylvester J. Ryan dismissed Donovan's illegal search and seizure motion, but granted permission for him to bring a similar petition in Brooklyn where the criminal trial was to take place. But with the selection of the jury to begin the next day, Donovan had no time to try again. Further, he realized that there was little chance of an appellate court in another district reversing Judge Ryan's ruling.

Rudolf Abel's trial took place in the Brooklyn Federal Courthouse within sight of the Ovington studios, and the crusty, eighty-year-old presiding judge, Mortimer W. Byers, pointed out the building to the jury. Donovan, with the help of two young and able assistants, Tom Debevoise and Arnold Fraiman, tried to show that

Colonel Abel had been illegally detained, that the FBI had used the Immigration Service to make a civil arrest when a criminal action was involved in the hope of turning the colonel into a double agent. But this second legal punch also failed to connect. Judge Byers's response was negative: "I should be very reluctant to have any court assume the function to tell the FBI how to perform their functions."

The government case ground on, built largely on the testimony of Reino Hayhanen. In his three days on the witness stand, he provided a detailed account of what the newspapers called "the life and times of a Russian spy in the United States": the assignments from Moscow, the drops and signal areas, the hollowed-out coins, the microdots, the coded transmissions. Donovan tried to discredit Hayhanen, but although he was able to expose him as an alcoholic and a liar, he failed to cast doubt on the defector's testimony on the espionage activities in which he and Abel had engaged.

The prosecution's second major witness was Sergeant Roy A. Rhodes. Rhodes took the stand and admitted that he had been a Soviet agent. He also stated that he had never met or talked to either the defendant or Hayhanen, and that he had stopped spying in 1952. Donovan tried to have the soldier's testimony stricken from the record, since Rhodes's case was not directly connected to Abel's. Again, the defense lawyer was unsuccessful.[3]

The government called twenty-seven witnesses. Day by day, they produced the evidence, consisting of the vast array of espionage equipment found in the defendant's hotel room, studio, and storage room. One of the microfilms in the hollow pencil was a broadcast schedule, giving dates, times, and radio call-letters for shortwave broadcasts. Six others were letters from Abel's wife, Hellen, and his daughter, Evelyn. Read into the record, they presented a picture of two lonely women, fiercely devoted to husband and father. One reporter covering the trial wrote, "As the attorney droned through the letters, Abel's steel cage of self-discipline almost cracked. His face grew red and his deep-set eyes filled with tears."

However, during most of the trial, Abel's control was perfect. Even when listening to the testimony of the man who had betrayed him, he showed no indication of the resentment, the hatred, he must have felt. He sat quietly, taking notes, keenly interested in the proceedings. At no time did he take the witness stand.

In his summation before the jury, Donovan began by stressing that the first count against his client, which carried the death penalty, was the charge that he had conspired to transmit national defense and atomic energy information to the Soviet Union. "What evidence of national defense information or atomic information has been put before you in this case?" Donovan asked the jury. "When you and I commenced this case, certainly we expected evidence that this man is shown to have stolen great military secrets, secrets of atomic energy and so on."

Donovan went on to describe Abel as "a devoted husband, loving father . . . a very brave patriotic man serving his country on an extraordinarily hazardous military mission and who lived among us in peace during the years."

In concluding his summation, Donovan told the jury: "Abel is an alien charged with the capital offense of Soviet espionage. It may seem anomalous that our Constitution guarantees protection to such a man. The unthinking may view America's conscientious adherence to the principles of a free society as altruism so scrupulous that self-destruction must result. Yet our principles are engraved in the history and the law of this land. If the free world is not faithful to its own moral code, there remains no society for which others may hunger."

The prosecution answered each one of Donovan's arguments, stressing the physical evidence of espionage which corroborated Hayhanen's testimony, insisting that Abel was "a master spy, a real pro," and concluding by emphatically reminding the jury: "This is a serious offense. This is an offense directed at our very existence and through us at the free world and civilization itself, particularly in light of the times."

There was no real disagreement among the jury members as to Abel's guilt. At 12:15 A.M. on October 25, the jury filed out to deliberate, and at 4:50 P.M. a verdict was reached. Rudolf Abel was found guilty on all three counts.

Judge Byers set November 15 as the date for sentencing. In the interim, Donovan submitted arguments against imposition of the death penalty: the possibility that "in the foreseeable future an American of equivalent rank will be captured by Soviet Russia or an ally—at such time an exchange of prisoners through diplomatic channels could be considered to be in the best interests of the United States"; that it was still possible that Abel would cooperate; that "it is absurd to believe that the execution of this man would deter the Russian military"; that the prosecution had failed to submit evidence to prove that Abel actually "gathered or transmitted any information pertaining to the national defense."

On November 14, the Soviets broke their silence on the case. A story in the *Literaturnaya Gazeta* described the affair as "a hoax, a low-brow crime-fiction," concocted by the FBI.

On November 15, Judge Byers sentenced the defendant to thirty years in prison on count one, ten years in prison and a fine of

$2,000 on count two, and five years in prison and a fine of $1,000 on count three.

The colonel accepted the verdict calmly. As a military man, as a skilled agent, he could not do less. He had been trained to maintain stoicism, to wear a mask at all times, to endure.

"That wasn't bad," Abel commented to Donovan after the verdict. "What you said up there was quite well done." Now he wanted to discuss the appeal. It was an appeal James Donovan would carry all the way to the highest court. On March 29, 1960, the Supreme Court ruled to sustain the findings of the lower courts.

In the long interval, the convicted spy served his sentence in the Atlanta Federal Penitentiary. His mind remained lively, and he kept busy. In charge of making Christmas cards, he was accepted and respected by his fellow prisoners.

At the beginning of 1959, permission was granted for Abel to receive mail from his wife and daughter. But permission for him to answer was revoked by the Justice Department on the grounds that in his letters he was sending coded information to the KGB. Abel protested bitterly. In February, Donovan also received a letter signed Hellen Abel. Bearing an East German return address, the letter began, "I am taking the liberty to write you after having learned from the newspapers about your most humane attitude towards my husband, Rudolf Abel."

Donovan saw the message as the first link in a chain of communication between the U.S. government and someone behind the Iron Curtain. He replied, keeping the Justice Department informed, and a correspondence was begun. Donovan later wrote: "I regarded the letters as the amateur and transparent work of a Soviet Intelligence unit. To me, the letters meant only one thing: someone over there was very much interested in the future of my client."

In the spring of 1960, an event occurred that radically changed the life of Colonel Rudolf Abel. On May 1, Francis Gary Powers, an American CIA pilot flying a U-2 spy plane on a mission to get photographs of missile sites, was shot down over the Soviet industrial center of Sverdlosk, more than 1,200 miles inside the Soviet border. His plane, equipped with cameras, tape recorders, radios, and radars, survived in surprisingly good condition. So did Powers.

The pilot and the wreckage of his plane were put on public display in Moscow. The U-2 incident became the Soviets' greatest propaganda triumph of the Cold War. President Eisenhower took full responsibility for the flights. At a press conference, the president reviewed the Abel case as an example of Soviet espionage in this country. In an editorial, the *New York Daily News* suggested that

The Glienicker Bridge between East and West Berlin, where Abel was exchanged for U-2 spy Francis Gary Powers.

Abel and Powers be swapped, stating: "Abel is of no further value."

It would take nearly two years of intricate maneuvering and secret negotiations to bring about the swap. On one side, representing the United States, was James Donovan; on the other was the supposed Hellen Abel, an East German lawyer named Vogel, and a ranking KGB official, Ivan Schischkin. Abel and Powers's father played subsidiary roles, but Donovan carried the ball, finally going into East Berlin to hammer out an acceptable agreement.[4]

Thus, on a cold, clear morning in early February, 1962, two small groups of men gathered at either end of the Glienicker Bridge, which spans a lake between East and West Berlin. At a signal, four men from each group moved forward to the center of the bridge. This was the way Donovan remembered the meeting:

> Powers and Abel moved forward with their bags and crossed the center line. Neither looked at the other. . . . They walked to our end of the bridge. Abel paused. He asked Wilkinson for the official pardon, saying, "I'll keep this as sort of a diploma." Then he put down the bag, extended his hand to me and said, "Good-by, Jim." I replied, "Good luck, Rudolf."[5]

When they parted, Francis Gary Powers returned to the Western side, having served eighteen months of an eighteen-year sentence, and the spy, Colonel Rudolf Ivanovich Abel, after nearly five years in prison, went in from the cold.

His accuser, Reino Hayhanen, had not been so lucky. Some time between July, 1961, when he participated in a taped interview with David Brinkley of NBC, and November of that same year, when the interview was seen on TV, he died. Reportedly, he was killed in an automobile accident on the Pennsylvania Turnpike, but private investigations revealed no official record of such an accident. Some assume he died of a result of alcoholism; some are certain that he was killed by the KGB. There are no facts to substantiate any story. His death remains a mystery.

Mystery also obscures the last years of Abel's life. In 1965, the year after the Kremlin saw fit to pay homage to Richard Sorge and his *apparat*, Rudolf Abel was awarded the Order of Lenin in recognition of his long and distinguished career in Soviet Intelligence. That much is known. As for what he was doing during the period following his exchange, Soviet reports placed him all over the world. It was reported that he was teaching younger men the fine art of the intelligence trade; that he was in Saigon; that he was in Leipzig; that he was retired and living in the Soviet Union.

On November 15, 1971, Moscow announced the death of sixty-eight-year-old Colonel Rudolf Ivanovich Abel. His obituary commanded headlines around the world. The press lauded his achievements: he had hidden his identity for nine years; he had played various roles with great skill; he had been a master craftsman in the techniques of obtaining and transmitting secrets. But today, as then, the story of the "Master Spy" must end with questions. What secrets? What information did he steal during those nine years? Who stole it for him? Who *was* Rudolf Abel?

Only Moscow can supply the answers.

CHAPTER SIX

The Diplomat
George Blake – The Triple Agent Who Was Double-Crossed

Soviet agents have always followed an elaborate system of rules. Russian espionage has even developed its own vocabulary: *treff*—the secret meeting; *parol*—the password; *dubok*—the dead drop; *yavka*—the safe house; *chuzhoi*—an agent who spies for money; *suyaznyie*—the courier. The language of Soviet espionage has its own slang, too: a shoe is a passport; a passport forger is a cobbler; a roof is a cover for illegal activities; a music box is a radio transmitter. Whether the spy is a legal or an illegal, he follows the rules and uses the language because this is the safest method of operation.

In his training, which may take place at the KGB Institute or at another one of the more than fifty KGB or GRU schools, the would-be agent learns the rules. If he is judged to have special talents, he is taught on an individual basis.

He also studies all the skills essential for success in his trade. Proficiency in a foreign language is extremely important, and with the language must go a knowledge of the society into which the agent is to be injected. At various times, there have been news reports of a replica of an American town, set up as a training school by the KGB, where agents live with townspeople who resemble, in every way, the residents of an American small town. It has also been reported that Rudolf Abel, after his return to Russia, was a teacher in such a training school.

Often, after graduation, an agent is sent to a foreign country simply to observe the people and customs and to make reports on his observations. He, in turn, is observed, and when he returns to Moscow, he sits down with his superiors and goes over the evaluations of his behavior.

The agent wends his careful way in the shadow world of intrigue, following the established rules. As already illustrated, the success or failure of his mission may depend on many factors. Certainly, his actions must always be plotted with great care. In plotting, Soviet Intelligence has achieved some of its most notable successes through the use of a spy who is neither a legal nor an illegal, but a man apart —the double agent.

Former CIA Director Allen Dulles called the double agent "one of the most intriguing figures in the annals of espionage. He is in touch with two, usually opposing, intelligence services, and is spying for each against the other or against the other's territory." [1]

The double agent may assume different guises: he may be a spy who, while serving as an agent for his own country, is secretly working for the enemy; he may be a spy for his own country who pretends, under orders, to be working for the enemy; he may be a spy for his own country who pretends, under orders, to be working for the enemy, and actually is.

The best known Soviet double agents in the first category were Donald MacLean, Guy Burgess, and Harold Kim Philby. All were British agents who were actually Soviet spies.

In the third category—the man who is, in fact, a triple agent—there is no spy who compares with George Blake, whose astonishing feats of treachery placed him in the annals of espionage as the prototype of the secret agent, the master of duplicity.

* * * * *

W hen George Blake was charged with offenses under the Official Secrets Act in London's Old Bailey on May 3, 1961, he was thirty-eight years old, a happily married man, and the father of two small boys. Until a month before his trial he had served as a ranking British Intelligence officer.

As one lawyer in the court expressed it, "George Blake was

the kind of man I would have been glad to have in my home."

However, the British government had good reason not to admire Blake's character, and in passing sentence the lord chief justice, Lord Parker, told the defendant and the world why:

> Your full written confession reveals that for some years you have been working continuously as an agent and spy for a foreign power. Moreover, the information communicated, though not of a scientific nature, was clearly of the utmost importance to that power and has rendered much of this country's efforts completely useless. Indeed, you yourself have said in your confession that there was not an official document of any importance to which you had access which was not passed to your Soviet contact.
>
> When one realizes that you are a British subject, albeit not by birth, and that throughout this period you were employed by this country—your country—in responsible positions of trust, it is clear that your case is akin to treason. Indeed, it is one of the worst that can be envisaged other than in time of war.

The case had been shrouded in mystery. The hour-long trial proceedings were open to the public and press for only eight minutes. For the remaining fifty-two minutes, the trial was held *in camera,* behind locked doors and shuttered windows, with only the principals present. Blake was charged with five offenses under the British Official Secrets Act, and after his own confession, he was quickly found guilty on all five counts. His acts had badly compromised British Secret Service operations in Europe, as well as the confidential internal decisions on which British foreign policy was based. After the verdict, Lord Parker sentenced the defendant to forty-two years in prison. It was the longest sentence in modern British history for *any* offense. Blake was so shocked by the severity of the sentence that he collapsed and was hospitalized.

After Blake recovered, he appeared to adjust to prison life. One of 317 prisoners in cell-block D of the grim Victorian keep known as Wormwood Scrubs Prison in the Kensington section of London, he was liked and respected by prisoners and guards alike. The length of his sentence impressed his fellow inmates, who appreciated his ability to offer words of encouragement to others when his own lot was so much worse. For five years, he followed prison routine, giving no trouble. But in the stone silence of his cell, George Blake was patiently planning his escape.

There had been many escapes; escape had been a way of life to him. The first escape was in Holland. He was seventeen, then, and his name was George Behar.

In the spring of 1940, after the Wehrmacht's blitzkrieg invasion

George Blake, British foreign service officer and trusted British double agent who became a Soviet spy.

of the Low Countries, the German internment camp near Amsterdam was filled with a mixed bag of "aliens and suspects" of different nationalities rounded up by the Gestapo and SS troops. One of these prisoners was George Behar, a former student at Rotterdam High School. Before the Nazi attack, George had been uninterested in politics. Quiet, introspective, the brightest student in his class, he was considering the priesthood of the Lutheran church as his future vocation. The bombing of Rotterdam irrevocably changed his life.

His father, Albert Behar, who had died in 1936, came from an aristocratic family of Sephardic Jews. Albert Behar had been born and raised in Cairo, Egypt, but he and his family were classified as "British protected persons." During World War I, Behar served with distinction in the British army and received a number of awards for gallantry. He carried a British passport. Although George's mother was Dutch and he had grown up in Holland, he considered himself British. After the German invasion of Holland, George's mother and two sisters escaped to England through the help of a friendly British Intelligence officer, Commander Child. Before George could join his family, a member of the Dutch Nazi party turned him in to the Germans, denouncing him as a British subject.

In the internment camp, a number of languages were spoken, and because he was fluent in English, German, and French, George was able to communicate with his fellow prisoners and learn his way around the camp. He was mature and poised for his age, and he possessed the ability to adapt quickly. He had survived the bombing of Rotterdam which had destroyed the city and killed thirty thousand of its inhabitants. He would never forget it, and he would never forgive it. He had seen the conquerors come goose-stepping, and he dreamed of defeating them. He was determined to escape.

He did it alone, making his own plans, choosing his own time. The camp was under heavy SS guard. It was his first escape, and there is no record of how he accomplished it.

Once free, he began making his way eastward toward the home of his uncle, Anthony Beijderwellen, who lived in Warnveld. To get there, he had to travel across most of Holland, ducking field patrols, moving by night, hiding in the day. He arrived safely in mid-October, but his uncle knew that his nephew's safety was only temporary, and he arranged to have George taken on as a farmhand in a nearby village. By November, George was looking around for other young men to join him in resisting the invaders. He became an *onderduiker*, a fighter in the Dutch underground. At first, it meant little more than cutting telephone wires and slashing tires. Nevertheless, if caught, the penalty could be death. He took the name Max van Vries. When a country-wide resistance movement, the *Orde Dienst,* was formed, Max van Vries became a trusted member.

Soon the Gestapo had a price on his head. At age eighteen, life had become a series of escapes.

One of his fellow underground fighters said of him: "He never seemed to be tired. He was a youngster, but men twice his age accepted his authority without a murmur. He seemed to be shy but he had a strong personality and could make quick decisions which were right when older fellows would bite their nails and scratch their heads." [2]

The life of a Dutch resistance fighter was further imperiled by the success of German Intelligence in penetrating the *Orde Dienst.* In the period of a year and a half, fifty out of fifty-four agents dispatched to Holland by the British Secret Service Special Operations Executive (SOE) were dropped into the hands of waiting Germans.

Churchill had given SOE the order to "set Europe ablaze." In attempting to do so through subversion and sabotage, preparing for the day of invasion, SOE worked together with all the resistance movements in occupied Europe. In the case of the Dutch, agent after agent was captured by the Gestapo. But George Behar–Max van Vries remained free. During the summer of 1942, he had been given the assignment of trying to find Professor Jambroes, the most important Dutch resistance leader to have been parachuted into Holland. Unknown to George, Jambroes had been betrayed and captured, and the Gestapo was hunting his contacts. Fortunately, while searching for Jambroes, George again met Commander Child. Child warned George that the Gestapo was on his trail. Why not get out? He could follow the SOE escape route across Europe to Spain and Gibraltar. Once in England, his experience would be of great value to the Dutch headquarters of SOE. The Commander's advice made good sense, George thought.

In July, 1942, a youthful Trappist monk with a "shining morning face" crossed the Dutch frontier into Belgium on a bicycle. The border guards paid little attention to him. His papers identified him as Brother Peter. Brother Peter pedaled on to Brussels and a safe house, a relay point on the escape route which Child had outlined for him. From there he made his way to France. The trip was uneventful until he reached the flat farm country near Lille where he was stopped by a German police patrol. *A Trappist monk, hey? Brother Peter, hey?* They'd check his identity soon enough in Lille. He could get off his bicycle and come with them in the car. Exposure was very near when suddenly bombers appeared overhead and bombs began falling. The young monk took to his heels, while his captors took to the nearest shelter. Once again, George's luck held; the door on which he happened to knock was that of a local resistance leader. Through this man's help, George reached Paris, hiding for a time in a monastery near Sacré Coeur. From Paris, he went on to Lyon and finally into Spain. But once across the rugged frontier, Spanish border guards arrested him, and he ended up in an internment camp near Barcelona. The British Embassy in Madrid was informed, and eventually George was released. He reached England in the beginning of 1943.

He arrived with high hopes and great expectations. He thought he would be greeted with open arms. Instead, he was looked upon first with suspicion and then with disinterest. He was detained and interrogated at a center called the Royal Victoria Patriotic School. This was a routine procedure all escapees had to undergo to make sure they were not spies. Previously, George's background had been checked by intelligence authorities in Gibraltar, and he strongly resented this further investigation of his record. When he was released, he immediately applied to the War Office for an intelligence assignment, only to be turned down. The one bright spot was that he had found his mother and sisters again. But the days of hit-and-run, the exciting and dangerous days of escape, seemed over.

Finally, Commander Child came to his aid again. The commander had made his way back to England soon after George. Through the British officer's recommendation, George entered the Royal Navy and in May, 1944, he received a commission as a sublieutenant in the Volunteer Reserves. His espionage skills were finally recognized, and he was posted to the Dutch section of SOE. He was given a desk job, but he soon moved into the field. The end of the war found him assigned as an interpreter on the staff of Field Marshal Bernard Montgomery. He was present at the unconditional German surrender at Limburg Heath in Holland—a moment to savor after the horror of Rotterdam.

By the end of World War II, George was twenty-two years old. He had changed his name to Blake, as had his mother and sisters, perhaps because they felt it sounded more British than Behar. The war was over for George Behar. But for George Blake another secret war was about to begin.

Six years lay between the end of World War II and his next escape. In that period, he served British Naval Intelligence in Hamburg, first interrogating former U-boat captains and then reporting on Soviet Intelligence activities. It was his first encounter with the Russians, and he went overboard, overdoing security, overdoing his reports, flouncing around in his cloak and dagger, and generally making his superiors tired of his antics. Spying on the Russians afforded George the opportunity to do what he most enjoyed, to match wits with an enemy who was worthy of his steel. To be better prepared for the battle, he saw that a knowledge of Russian was essential, and he asked his superiors if he could be sent home for such training. They readily agreed. Anything to get the "mad Dutchman" out of their hair!

By the spring of 1948, Blake had completed his studies at Cambridge. He was assigned to the Far Eastern Department of the Foreign Office. Two important rules were waived to permit Blake to enter the Foreign Service. The first rule was that only candidates born in the United Kingdom could be admitted; the second was that the candidate must have a university degree. George was born in Rotterdam, and he had never obtained a degree. But because of his intelligence background and his fluency in five languages, the Secret Intelligence Service (SIS) put aside the rules, and he joined the Foreign Service as a vice consul.

In the fall of that year, Vice Consul George Blake became assistant to Captain Vyvyan Holt, *chargé d'affaires* of the British Legation in Seoul, South Korea. The Communist takeover of China had made Seoul an important British post for gathering information. Furthermore, as Blake soon realized, Seoul was a tinderbox. Each day, the threat of an attack from North Korea became more apparent. Through Blake's ability to make friends with the Koreans, he was able to contribute valuable data to Captain Holt's dispatches. When the attack came, on June 25, 1950, it was no surprise to the British Foreign Office.

The invaders occupied Seoul quickly. Once again George Blake heard the staccato clatter of machine guns, the snap of small arms, the wild shouts of rampaging mobs. And once again he was captured. In the presence of his captors, he handled himself with coolness and courage; he was the perfect picture of the British official taking adversity with a stiff upper lip.

There was much to take. With Captain Holt, Consul Norman Owen, and a small group of foreign civilian and church officials, he was questioned for days. First he was interrogated in Seoul, while the legation was being looted, and then in Pyongyang, the North Korean capital, where he was interned with other important foreign civilians, elderly churchmen, and nuns.

An incident occurred which shows the fortitude which Blake displayed before his captors. When he was being questioned in Seoul, sporadic shooting was still going on in the city. A bullet came in the window and thudded into the table next to his chair. The North Korean interrogating officer shrugged and said, "the boys are having fun."

Blake slammed his fist down on the table, splattering ink from a bottle on the officer's face and uniform. "I want to have some fun, too!" he shouted.

The officer apologized.

In early September, Blake and his fellow prisoners were packed in a train, ten to each compartment, and shipped north. Their destination was Man-po, a village on the Yalu River. The journey lasted one week. In the train, U.S. POWs were crammed into open coal cars; many of them died of their wounds en route.

Throughout the journey and the wretched months at the Man-po camp, George Blake helped his fellow prisoners. Commenting on his behavior, Commissioner Herbert Lord, who had been head of the Salvation Army in South Korea before his capture, said: "He (Blake) turned his hand willingly to any kind of job, cooking, cleaning, and all the other chores we had to do. . . . He did it all with good humor, always ready to help others." [3]

Life at Man-po became an increasingly bitter ordeal as the Communists began to sustain reverses at the front. After General Douglas MacArthur's counterattack at Inchon in September, the North Koreans were cut off and faced a major military defeat. The farther north the advancing U.S. column rolled, the harsher grew the treatment of the internees.

On October 9, with the weather growing very cold, the prisoners were herded out onto the road and marched fifteen miles to Ko-Sang Djin, another village on the Yalu River. Their ranks were swollen by a host of other captives: exhausted South Koreans, wounded and starving GIs, and nuns from various religious orders. As they stumbled along, shivering in their threadbare clothes, they could hear the heavy thump of approaching artillery and the roar of American bombers overhead. The desperate condition of many in the line of march made a quick rescue imperative if they were to survive. The excited and confused actions of their captors gave the prisoners hope that their release was near. Blake decided to be the instrument of that hope.

It was not until they were turned around again some days later and marched back to Man-po that he saw his chance. In their absence, Man-po had been bombed, and the ruins were still burning as the weak internees painfully straggled in. The cold was intense. There was little food, and the guards regularly shot groups of South Korean prisoners to reduce the mouths to feed. In the night, when the fires were doused as a protection against air raids, Blake decided to make his move.

Down flat, on his stomach, he snaked past the sentries and crawled out of the camp. His pulse quickened; it was the old game again. He headed south, moving cautiously through enemy territory, stumbling up steep hills in the frigid darkness. Dawn found him in a valley, on the lookout for an advance American patrol. While he was searching for a U.S. unit, he ran straight into a North Korean patrol.

Taken to the officer in charge, Blake was pronounced a spy and sentenced to be shot immediately. His hands were tied behind his back, and he was pushed in front of a wall. The soldiers' rifle bolts snapped, ready for the execution. In a last-minute effort to save his life, he shouted at the officer in Russian: "I'm not a spy! I am a civilian internee, a British diplomat. I went out of the camp at Man-po and I lost my way!" [4]

The North Korean knew Russian and was impressed by his captive's command of the language. Instead of killing Blake, the officer treated him to a meal and a pack of cigarettes and had him escorted back to Man-po. It was Blake's first failure to escape.

Blake was returned just in time to join another long march. Of the several hundred prisoners who began the march, more than one hundred perished. They died at the hands of their guards, shot when they dropped out of the column. They died of exposure to the cold. They died of exhaustion. The dying were pushed into ditches, buried in unmarked graves.

On November 8, the march ended at a new prison camp, but the ordeal continued. Throughout the winter, with the temperature often falling to thirty below zero, the internees suffered from the cold, from illness, and from malnutrition. Many died. Of the nearly 800 U.S. POWs in the camp, 460 did not live to see the spring of 1951.

George Blake withstood the inhuman treatment with great courage. On one occasion, feverish and weak, he refused to obey a guard's order to carry 100 gallons of water from the river. As a punishment, the guard forced Blake to kneel in the snow until he had nearly frozen to death. When a fellow prisoner, British journalist Philip Deane, tried to reason with the guard, he was told he, too, would be punished. Deane later described the scene:

> The guard accused us of insulting the Koreans, and of not carrying the amount of water laid down by the regulations. We replied that this was not so. The guard said he would teach us not to lie, and he beat us with the butt of his rifle, kicked us and slapped us.
>
> George Blake, who got the worst of it, smiled through the ordeal, his left eyebrow cocked ironically at the guard, his Elizabethan beard aggressively thrust forward.[5]

In the fall of 1951, Russian and Chinese specialists arrived to begin serious attempts to brainwash the British "reactionary" prisoners. The key figure in the brainwashing of George Blake was the Soviet agent, Gregory Kuzmitch, nicknamed "Blondie." Kuzmitch, highly trained and sophisticated, had an excellent command of the English language and considerable firsthand knowledge of the West. His assignment in Korea was to win, by mental persuasion, converts to the Communist cause. Ironically, after the end of the Korean War, Kuzmitch defected to the Americans and went to work for the CIA.

In his confession, after his arrest in 1961, George Blake maintained that he became a Communist during his captivity in Korea. However, everyone who suffered through that period with him found it difficult to believe that he was brainwashed at this time. Later, Gregory Kuzmitch said that aside from expressing sympathy for the downtrodden and a feeling of disillusionment over Western policies in Korea, Blake made no move to become a Soviet agent.

Fellow prisoner Jean Meadmore, a French diplomat, was even more emphatic in his disbelief. "I cannot believe that George Blake was such a good actor," he said, "and we such poor psychologists that we could not have realized he was a Communist, was becoming a Communist, or even that he was a potential convert to communism. . . ." [6]

Still, George Blake said that he was indoctrinated in Korea. He defected on three conditions, Blake asserted: that he would not inform on his fellow prisoners, that he would receive no preferential treatment, and that he would receive no payment for his work.

On April 23, 1953, almost three years after his capture in Seoul, Blake returned to Great Britain. He came back in the company of six fellow prisoners. Mysteriously, they had been freed three months before the final armistice was signed and before any of the other United Nations prisoners were released. The party of seven received a royal welcome home. All were suffering from an assortment of serious ailments. George Blake was given a long leave in which to recuperate.

When he started work again, it was as an official of the Secret Service (MI6), controlled by the Foreign Office. At his office he met a beautiful young girl, Gillian Allan, who had been assigned to him as a secretary. They fell in love, but Gillian had to convince George to accept the idea of marriage. Yes, he loved her, but there were problems, he said. He was reluctant to burden her because of his work; he was being trained for a difficult intelligence job overseas. He had peculiar habits, and he did not want to settle down. Besides, he was a foreigner, half-Jewish, and he was not sure her parents and family would accept him. Then, too, his salary was low.

Gillian dismissed his doubts, and the marriage took place on September 23, 1954. In March, 1955, Blake was informed that in one month he would be sent to Berlin.

According to the evidence disclosed in the indictment at his trial, the Soviet Union was using Blake as a double agent throughout this period. From the time he reported for duty after his recuperation leave until his departure for Berlin, George was meeting with his Soviet contact in London and passing on to him every intelligence document of value which he could procure or photograph.

Ironically, in the six months before the newlyweds departed for Germany, British Intelligence was training Blake so that he could work as a double agent for Britain in Berlin. Thus, while he was actively engaged in betraying his country, he was being trained to pretend to become a traitor. The situation must have provoked some chuckles in Moscow.

At this time, Berlin was the world's focal point of the conflict between East and West. Thousands of agents from both sides swarmed about in a *danse macabre* of violence, intrigue, and espionage, each side seeking to discover the secret strategy of the other. Into this seething cauldron stepped George Blake.

Again, according to the indictment against him, Blake began communicating information to the enemy on the very day he and Gillian arrived in Berlin on April 14, 1955, and he continued to do so until their return to England four years later in April, 1959.

His office was in the Olympic Stadium Buildings, headquarters for British Intelligence in Berlin; his apartment was located in the select residential section of Charlottenburg. He and Gillian lived a quiet existence. Few of their neighbors got to know them, and they seldom participated in the social life of the British colony. Theater and concerts were their main diversions. Their first child, Anthony, was born in 1956.

British Intelligence was highly satisfied with George Blake's performance as an agent during his tour of duty in Berlin. To the Olympic Stadium Buildings he brought back what appeared to be valuable Soviet secrets, and he was responsible for catching several Communist spies. Actually, his success was engineered by the KGB. In order to enhance Blake's status with British Intelligence, the KGB was willing to sacrifice some minor agents, usually Germans, and to leak a certain amount of secret information. At the same time, following the instructions of the British Secret Service, Blake was turning over to the Russians information selected by British Intelligence. Of course, what the British did not know was that Blake was supplying the Russians with much more valuable secrets than those contained in the documents chosen for him at the Olympic Stadium Buildings.

In this period, Blake handed over to the KGB two categories of secret documentation. On the level of espionage, he passed on the names of agents working for British, U.S., and German Intelligence, as well as the locations and tasks of their networks. On the level of political strategy, he turned over all the plans and reports formulated in Berlin for the British government in its negotiations with the Soviets. Often, after everyone in the office had gone for the day, Blake would stay late, locked in by guards, supposedly working, but instead photographing documents with his Soviet-issued Exakta camera.

Some of the episodes in which Blake was involved during the years he worked at British Secret Service headquarters in Berlin illustrate sharply the dangers of the game he was playing.

At this time, one of the great coups of Allied Intelligence was the construction of an 1800-foot tunnel from the U.S. Zone at Radow into the East German Zone at Alt Glienicke. The tunnel was designed to monitor and tape-record all telephone calls between the Soviet and German ministries throughout East Germany, and all calls between Karlshorst, Warsaw, and Moscow. The major telephone lines had been expertly tapped and were monitored by a staff of U.S. army technicians. The listening post operated for over nine months before it was discovered by the Russians in April, 1956. Although none of the operating technicians were caught in the act, the tunnel was found crammed full of electronic bugging equipment. Its function was unmistakable, and the East Germans and Soviets had a propaganda field day. Some 90,000 East Berliners were given a conducted tour of the tunnel.

A limited number of senior intelligence officials knew of the existence of the tunnel. George Blake was one, and he promptly revealed the secret to the Russians. However, an intensive investigation at the Olympic Stadium Buildings failed to expose him. Nor was he suspected after another episode of betrayal, which also took place in 1956.

Two floors below the Blakes' apartment lived Lt. Gen. Robert Bialek, former inspector-general of the East German People's Police. At the time of his defection to the West in 1953, the general had been in charge of the East Berlin Section of the State Security service of the East German Communist party. Now he worked for British Intelligence. The general was in constant fear for his life, and special precautions were taken to protect him. He lived under an assumed name; no one in the building knew his real identity, except George Blake.

Ordinarily, the general never traveled anywhere without a body-guard, but one night he went for a walk with his dog. Two burly kid-napers flung themselves on Bialek and dragged him into a waiting car which sped away to the Eastern Zone. British Intelligence soon learned that the general had been put to death in East Berlin. An investigation failed to reveal the name of his betrayer.

In all, it was estimated that George Blake, during his tour of duty in Berlin, betrayed more than fifty agents working for British, U.S., and German Intelligence. Four of these were members of NTS, the anti-Communist organization formed by *emigré* Russians in Ber-lin. For some time NTS members had been operating with success behind the Iron Curtain and in Russia. Then Blake came to know about their daring work. The KGB grabbed them. Several months after they disappeared, they were produced at a show trial in Mos-cow, where their "confessions" were made public. Even though only a few British and American officials knew the identity of the NTS members, Blake escaped once more. He was not suspected.

He was not even suspected after the affair of RAF Group Cap-tain Cedric Masterman, who was arrested in Czechoslovakia on charges of photographing airfields. After a strong protest from the British Foreign Office, Masterman was released, but the disturbing fact to British Intelligence was that only four officers at the Olympic Stadium Buildings knew of Masterman's mission. Blake was one of them.

The strangest episode in George Blake's career as a triple agent occurred when the British Secret Service instructed him to make contact with Horst Eitner. Eitner, a German agent working for the British, was handling a network of a dozen agents in the Eastern Zone, and Blake was ordered to improve the operation. He was not to let Eitner know his real identity, so he reverted to the past and once again became Max van Vries, a Dutchman working for the British. As van Vries, Blake rented a furnished room near the Eit-ners' apartment.

In personality and character, Horst Eitner was the exact oppo-site of George Blake. Loud, brash, Eitner's political loyalty was to the highest bidder. Yet, the two men became friends. Their associa-tion lasted several years. Blake was a frequent visitor to the Eitners' apartment, often bringing gifts to Eitner's crippled child. They worked closely together, but each kept one fact secret from the other. Unknown to each other, unknown to the British, *both* were working for the Russians.

After four years of triple-dealing, George Blake was ordered by the KGB to ask for his recall to London. His Soviet superiors felt that Blake would now be more useful to them at a desk in the Foreign Office. The British Secret Service agreed to Blake's transfer because George said that the KGB was growing suspicious of him.

The Blakes came home in April, 1959. In that same month, Gillian gave birth to their second son, James. A few weeks after George's return, he was busily photographing secret documents of state and passing them on to his Soviet contact.

After September 17, 1959, Blake enjoyed a vacation from his espionage work. He had been transferred to the Middle East division of the Foreign Office and was taking preliminary training prior to being sent to the Middle Eastern College for Arabic Studies (MECAS) in Lebanon. During his training he was no longer able to put his hands on secret papers. Perhaps, too, he wanted a respite from his labors of betrayal.

In September, 1960, the Blakes arrived in the charming Lebanese village of Shemlan where MECAS was located. Blake was one of fifty students drawn from the Foreign Office and from business firms, banks, and oil companies. The Blakes settled into an easy and relaxed way of living.

His stay at Shemlan was the most tranquil period of George Blake's adult life. There were no escapes and no need for any. The air was spiced; the breeze was mild. Bright flowers grew profusely under palm, pine, and cypress, and the land rolled gently down to the sea. The bombs of Rotterdam, the death march of Korea, the intrigues of Berlin—all were forgotten.

But, unknown to Blake, forces from the past were at work. In the same month the Blakes arrived in Lebanon, Horst Eitner was arrested by West German Intelligence (BND) as a double agent. He claimed to have been forced to work for the Soviets. Thrown into prison, Eitner faced the possibility of life imprisonment. At some point before his arrest, he had learned that his old friend, Max van Vries–George Blake, was also a Soviet agent. Eitner wrote Blake and asked him for help.

Blake did not answer. By March, 1961, Eitner was tired of staring at stone walls and angry at Blake's lack of response. He asked to talk to the judge who was preparing his case. To the German official, Eitner confessed: he had become a Soviet agent through a British agent who was also working for the Soviets. His detailed accusation was passed on to British Counterintelligence. At first, the officials working on the investigation considered Eitner totally unreliable, a liar who would concoct any story to save his own neck. Nevertheless, security officers began to do some checking. The men who had directed Blake's operation in Berlin were questioned. The investigation was more a matter of routine than urgency, however, until Colonel Anthony Alster defected to the West.

Alster had been chief of the Polish Secret Police before his defection. In questioning him, British Intelligence began to amass a frightening file of evidence against George Blake. Alster supplied detailed reports on some of George Blake's activities.

The days of tranquillity at Shemlan ended with a telegram from the Foreign Office. It was phrased in careful terms since SIS did not want to alert Blake. Would he come to London for important consultations? There was no hurry; he could delay until after Easter. Blake said good-by cheerfully to Gillian, who was expecting their third child, and promised to return shortly.

He arrived in London on Monday, April 3. On Tuesday morning, he reported to the Foreign Office. He was taken to the office of the head of the Secret Service, where he was introduced to two detectives who took him to the police station. At police headquarters, he was charged with offenses under Section 1(c) of the Official Secrets Act.

On May 3, his brief trial took place. British newspapers were not permitted to write in detail about the case, because the government had sent out D-notices, a special method of press censorship used in matters of national security.

However, even with the limited newspaper coverage of the trial, the outcry in the House of Commons against the Macmillan government was fierce, the questions scathing. Nineteen sixty-one was a very bad year for British Intelligence and the Conservative party. A month before Blake's arrest, the Portland naval spy case had filled the headlines. Colonel Molody, a Soviet illegal, had been operating in England for six years as a Canadian businessman under the name of Gordon Lonsdale. With the assistance of Lona and Morris Cohen, known as the Krogers, and two English accomplices, Henry Houghton and Ethel Gee, both employed at the Portland Naval Base near Southampton, Molody had been forwarding British and NATO naval secrets to Moscow. When arrested on January 7, 1961, Molody carried a shopping bag full of top-secret naval plans, including detailed information concerning Britain's first atomic submarine.

It was on the heels of this dramatic saga of Soviet espionage that George Blake was brought to trial. Before his trial, Blake had made a full confession; at the trial, he had nothing to say in his defense. His life was ruined, his marriage wrecked. There was no escape route open to him now, only forty-two years of stone walls and barred windows.

By the fall of 1965, Blake seemed to have become a model prisoner. Although considered the most important prisoner at Wormwood Scrubs, he was no longer made to wear bright patches on his prison garb to signal him out to the guards. His cell had a Bokhara rug on the floor and prints on the wall. There were flowered curtains on the window, which looked out on the bowling field and aviary. He had books and a radio and was taking a correspondence course in Arabic through London University. Every Sunday, when the prisoners were allowed to visit each other, Blake held open house for a select group of fellow convicts. Blake and his visitors often listened to BBC critics discussing the arts.

Blake's only regular visitor from the outside was his mother. Gillian had come to see him in the beginning of his term, but they both realized there was only pain and no future in their relationship. She had known nothing of his duplicity. He told her she must make a new life for herself and the children. Reluctantly, she agreed, for even with time off for good behavior he would be sixty-six years old before he was eligible for release.

Throughout this period, the Special Branch of Scotland Yard and the Security Service (MI₅) were kept busy with tips and rumors of plots to get George Blake out of prison. A helicopter was going to rescue him; a man disguised as a guard was going to climb over the wall and take him away; the Russians had a plan to enable him to escape to East Germany and then to the Soviet Union. In each case, security officials conducted a thorough investigation, but could find no basis in fact to any of the rumors. Nevertheless, with so many stories of plans to rescue Blake, special precautions were taken to watch him carefully. Questioned about the escape rumors, Blake laughed them off, saying that he was resigned to prison life.

Despite his public assurances that he had accepted his fate, privately, George Blake had resolved to turn rumors of escape into reality. He knew that he would not be able to get out without assistance. The Soviets could not help him, which meant that his only chance was to find someone in prison who could. By September, 1965, he believed that he had found the person he was looking for. His name was Sean Bourke, a fellow prisoner.

Bourke was an Irishman from Limerick who had been an active member of the Irish Republican Army. Blake had met him at a prison English literature course soon after Bourke had arrived at Wormwood Scrubs in the fall of 1961.

The Irishman was serving a seven-year sentence for having sent a bomb through the mails to a police constable. Having spent four years obeying prison rules, Bourke was looking forward to parole.

During the four years, he and Blake had become close friends. Bourke admired Blake's quiet courage. He said of him, "though he was serving the longest prison sentence ever passed in a British court of law, Blake did *his bird* (his sentence) better than any prisoner I had ever met."

Blake respected Bourke's abilities, too. The Irishman had become editor of the prison magazine *New Horizons*. In this position, he was granted more privileges than any other convict in Wormwood Scrubs. Blake realized that Bourke was motivated by a profound dislike of British authority. He would do anything to get revenge for his own misfortune. In addition, he was clever and daring.

Having decided that Bourke was the man he needed, Blake asked for his help one day as they took their daily before-meal stroll on the ground floor of the cell-block. He suggested that Bourke think it over for a few days before giving his decision. Bourke did not have to think it over. After the first shock wore off, the idea of springing the most notorious spy in the Western world appealed to him enormously.

"I'm your man!" he said. And George Blake could have chosen no better.

Thirteen months were to pass between Blake's first planning session with Sean Bourke and the actual escape attempt. They were months filled with frustration and tension.

Bourke was finally released from prison on July 4, 1966. For seven months before his release, he lived in a building within the prison walls called the hostel. During this period, he participated in the prison rehabilitation program. In the morning, he left the prison for work in a factory, returning by ten forty-five in the evening. Except for his employer, no one at his place of employment was aware that he was a prisoner.

The relative freedom of action enjoyed by Bourke gave him an opportunity to work on the escape plan. A prison trusty, named Peter, was brought into the plot to act as courier, and Bourke communicated through him to Blake, using a simple code. Both realized that once Bourke was released from prison, this method of contact would be difficult. Then, Bourke came up with a flash of inspiration. He informed his hostel chief that he needed money for a new suit, and with the cash he bought a compact pair of two-way radios. They were small enough to fit in a pocket and had a range of five miles.

At a performance of the prison drama group, Peter received Blake's radio from Bourke and smuggled it to Blake as they sat watching the play. From then on, the prisoner in his cell and his accomplice in the hostel were able to converse with each other.

Bourke's code name was Fox Michael, and Blake's was Baker Charlie. For protection, they used an exchange of passwords which Bourke selected. The Irishman would begin by reciting the first line of a poem by Richard Lovelace, "Stone walls do not a prison make, nor iron bars a cage."

Blake would respond, "Minds innocent and quiet take that for a hermitage."

Then Bourke would add, "Richard Lovelace must have been a fool," and Blake would conclude, "or just a dreamer." [7]

The two-way communications system proved remarkably efficient. While Bourke remained in the hostel, the reception was excellent; both men were able to whisper and hear each other clearly. But having overcome one difficulty, they were faced with two other major problems. How was Blake going to get out of Wormwood Scrubs, and once out, where was he going to go?

With his genius for devising escape stratagems, Blake finally developed a plan. At each end of the cell-block was a narrow window that began at the second level and extended to the building roof. The window was eighteen inches wide, divided into six sections. Each section was framed by cast-iron bars. If the bottom bar and the window it framed could be neatly broken, an opening of twelve-by-eighteen inches would be formed, through which Blake could crawl.

Outside, at the base of the window, was the apex of a slanted shed roof which formed part of a porch entrance to the cell-block. The porch roof sloped down into a covered way which joined D and C cell-blocks. Blake's plan was to climb out the window, down the roof, onto the covered way, and drop to the ground. He would then be about sixty feet from the eighteen-foot-high wall at the south end of the building.

Blake had carefully ascertained that during his exit and descent, he would be out of the sight of any of the guards. Only when he broke for the wall could he be observed. But he felt that by then it would be too late for anyone to stop him. Since he and Bourke would be in constant radio contact, on receiving his signal, Bourke would throw a rope ladder over the wall, and he would be up and over within a few seconds. Bourke would have a car waiting.

It was a bold scheme, requiring courage, patience, and nerve. Its audacity reflected its originator. The plan called for accurate, split-second timing. Its ultimate success would depend on Blake getting out of the window unseen, and on Bourke arranging a getaway to a safe place.

From the outset, Blake and Bourke were aware that there were major obstacles to overcome. Money was the first. Neither man had any. Bourke estimated that the cost of a car, a hideaway, and a fake passport, together with the expense of getting Blake out of the country, would come to a minimum of £700 (about $1,600). At Blake's suggestion, Bourke approached the prisoner's mother and sister, but the Irishman soon came to the conclusion that involving Blake's family might compromise the effort. Bourke began seeking financial aid elsewhere.

This was a slow and time-consuming process. The months ground on. On July 4, 1966, Bourke was given his final parole and set free. Although now he had more time to devote to planning the escape, he also was faced with the problem of maintaining communication with Blake. Bourke found a place to live near the prison, but the prison wall and other obstructions prevented radio contact. In order to reach Blake, he had to get very close to the wall, and he was afraid of being spotted.

Bourke worked out a solution. Nightly, he scaled a spiked fence enclosing a park adjacent to the prison. Lying flat on the grass, Bourke whispered the opening words, "This is Fox Michael, calling Baker Charlie. . . ." He was in a dangerous position, for the roads around the park were patrolled, and, as he learned from another newly released prisoner, the authorities had grown suspicious of radio communication going on inside the prison and were monitoring likely frequencies.

Somehow, Bourke escaped detection. From a friend, he borrowed enough money to buy a car, but making contact from a car was still a risky business. Bourke would park on Artillery Road, close to the prison wall, across the street from Hammersmith Hospital. At six o'clock on Saturday evening, around the time that visitors to the hospital were beginning to arrive, Bourke would sit inside the car, sniffing a bunch of chrysanthemums which concealed his radio. As he sniffed, he would talk to Blake.

During the months of preparation, Bourke's reconnaissance of the neighborhood was so thorough that he had explored every street and alley in the area. He knew how long it took to drive from point to point, at various times, and under different conditions of traffic and weather. He left nothing to chance. He made a rope ladder, using steel knitting needles to reinforce each of the rungs and insure quick passage. In his room, he practiced how to hold and throw the ladder accurately.

In this period, two events occurred that almost ended the entire escape venture. In June, 1966, four prisoners escaped from cellblock D. After this, Bourke and Blake were afraid that Blake would be sent to a prison where security was tighter. Then, two months later, four British police constables were shot down in cold blood on a street close to the prison. Security throughout the Kensington area was intensified; policemen were stationed on every street. Bourke had to be more careful than ever.

All this time, Blake continued to play the role of the model prisoner. However, secretly, he was diligently studying all the details of the planned escape route. He memorized the movements, the routine, and the location of every guard within the cell-block and on the wall. To the second, he knew how long it would take him to move from the ground floor to the window on the second-floor landing. In his cell, he made a rough dummy the size of the space to be opened and practiced wriggling through it.

Bourke and Blake chose Saturday as the day on which the escape would take place, since fewer guards were on duty during the weekend. Six o'clock in the evening was selected as the time to begin, because between five and seven o'clock prisoners were allowed to leave their cells to see a movie, watch television, or to fraternize. To force the cast-iron bar and to break the window, Blake was to have the assistance of Peter, the trusty. First, Peter would cover the window with paper, using chewing gum as glue. Then the glass would be broken, but no sound would be made, because the glass would stick to the paper. The pieces would be carefully removed. To snap the bar, Peter had a small automobile jack, which had been smuggled into the prison by Bourke.

On October 15, 1966, Bourke began making final preparations. The escape was to take place on October 22. He rented a two-room ground-floor flat at 22 Highlever Road, a short walk from the prison. This apartment was to serve as Blake's hideout after the getaway. Bourke paid four weeks' rent in advance and told the landlady that he was a journalist who traveled a great deal.

At noon on October 22, Bourke parked near the prison wall in a spot exactly opposite cell-block D, sniffed his chrysanthemums, and went over last-minute instructions with Blake. Blake reported that most of the prisoners would be attending a movie in the cell-block recreation hall.

At 5:30 P.M. the moment of action came. Blake had joined a large group of prisoners watching a wrestling match on television. Men were milling around, and the room was noisy with shouts, hoots, and wisecracks. In the gray light, he casually walked away from the gathering, strolled around, and went up to the second-floor landing, joining Peter at the window. Now it was 6:00, the time set for Bourke to signal. Anxiously, Blake waited, but there was no word. Five minutes passed, eight minutes—what had happened to Bourke?

What had happened was that, after all Bourke's careful planning and reconnaissance, he had been trapped in an unexpected traffic jam. Everything was ready for the escape. On the back seat of the car, he had neatly spread out his coat and hat for Blake to put on. In his lap was a pot of flowers with the radio; in the trunk was the rope ladder. But he was unable to move. The rain pounded down, and the cars fanned out in all directions. Waiting for the traffic to unsnarl, Bourke had to fight to remain calm.

It was 6:10 before Blake heard the familiar call on his radio. Unlike Bourke, he had his nerves under tight control. He knew this was just the beginning. Bourke gave the signal for Peter to break the window and the bar. Blake stood on the landing to make sure that no one approached. The job took three minutes, but at the moment Blake was ready to go through the window, Bourke whispered that he was being watched and switched off.

A van had driven past, then returned and parked, shining its headlights on Bourke. The driver stepped out of the truck, holding a dog on a leash, and began to approach Bourke. Bourke realized that he must be a park patrolman. There was only one thing Bourke could do and that was to leave. He drove around the long block.

By the time he had returned, it was 6:30. The van was gone, but a car was parked where the van had stopped. Was it another police car? Bourke drove around again and glanced in the car. A young man and woman were embracing in the front seat. He had to get them to move. Climbing out of his car, he stood in the rain staring at them until they drove away.

It was 6:40 before he could resume radio contact with Blake.

Blake's voice came back over the radio, speaking quickly, "I can't delay any longer. They're on their way back from the cinema. I must come out now. No time for explanation. Over!"

"Okay, go ahead!" Bourke hissed.

"Right. I'm coming out now."

Through the small opening, Blake wriggled out into the rain and dark. It took no more than a moment for him to slide down the roof, onto the covered way, and down to the ground. He called Bourke, "I'm out! Throw the ladder!"

But again, the unexpected had occurred. Visitors to the hospital were arriving, parking on both sides of the street. With headlights shining on him, Bourke was unable to throw the ladder to Blake without being observed.

Blake crouched by the covered way, fifteen yards away from freedom, knowing a police patrol would be passing soon. His calls became urgent.

"Fox Michael, come in, please! I cannot wait much longer. . . . You must hurry! There's no more time! I expect to be taken at any moment! . . . Come in! You must throw the ladder now, you simply must!" [8]

It was now 7:00. Both men knew that this was the time a check was made on all prisoners. Blake was at the point of no return; he could not go back into the cell-block.

Bourke climbed up on the roof of his car and threw the ladder, knowing that any passing car would catch him in the act. Jumping off the car, he held on to the rope, pressing his head against the stone wall, waiting for Blake to make the climb, waiting for the alarm to be sounded, ready for a fight.

Now, Bourke was at *his* point of no return. He waited in agony, unable to hear Blake making the ascent. He could not feel any strain on the rope. If someone was climbing the ladder, who was it? Was he helping Blake, or a guard?

"For God's sake, man, hurry up!" [9] he muttered. Then, looking up at the wall, the rain pouring down on him, he saw two hands appear, clutching the stone coping, and finally the white blur of a face emerged.

It was Blake.

Blake stared down at him, not moving. Bourke's control broke, and he shouted, "Come on, man! Come on! . . . Jump! Jump!"

Blake swung over the wall, teetered on the edge, and dropped. Bourke tried to break his fall but failed. Blake's body thudded onto the road. His head hit the ground.

At that moment, a car swung into the road and came slowly towards them, its headlights illuminating the scene. Bourke's car concealed Blake, who continued to lie still. Frantically, Bourke, using the car door as a shield, managed to drag the half-conscious man into the back seat. Blake was groaning. Bourke drove quickly off.

By now, Blake had regained consciousness. His face bleeding, his wrist broken, he cautioned Bourke to calm down. By the time they reached the flat on Highlever Road, Blake had put on the coat and hat Bourke had supplied.

After their safe arrival, Bourke left to get rid of the car. He parked it in a section of London far from Wormwood Scrubs Prison. At 9:00 P.M., the two men listened to the details of the escape on television. They toasted each other, Bourke raising his glass and quoting with a wry grin, "Mischief, thou art afoot; take thou what course thou wilt."

The hue and cry was immediate and sustained. A huge manhunt was underway, directed by Scotland Yard's Special Branch. A

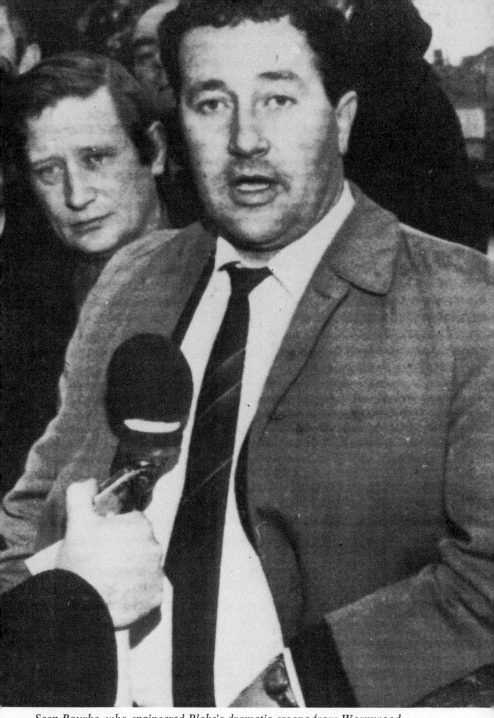

Sean Bourke, who engineered Blake's dramatic escape from Wormwood Scrubs prison in London.

The eighteen-foot wall of Wormwood Scrubs prison over which George Blake climbed to make his escape.

close watch was placed on all airports and ports, and the Soviet and East European embassies were also put under careful surveillance. But the object of the hunt lay low, hidden almost in the shadow of Wormwood Scrubs.

Later, Sean Bourke wrote an exciting account of how the escape was engineered, from which details have been drawn here. In it, he told how he and three friends helped to get George Blake out of England and behind the Iron Curtain.

Bourke claimed that Blake did not leave England until December of that year, and that he followed immediately afterward, knowing that Scotland Yard was hard on his trail. Bourke reached Moscow and remained there for two years, returning to Ireland on October 22, 1968, the second anniversary of Blake's escape. Since then, British authorities have been trying to bring about Bourke's extradition, without success.

Bourke went to Moscow as Blake's firm friend, but returned as his enemy. He declared that once Blake was in the Soviet Union, he became cruel and ruthless, and that he actually tried to convince the KGB that his rescuer be liquidated.

In 1970, George Blake was hailed for his services by the Soviets and awarded the Order of Lenin, Russia's second highest honor. Interviewed by *Izvestia,* he told with pride how he had outwitted and betrayed those with whom he had worked.

George Blake has been called a hero, a traitor, a double agent, and a triple agent. Though we now know much about his extraordinary career, one major question remains unanswered: *Why?* The words of those who knew him well throw light on many different George Blakes. Sean Bourke said of him: "He's a born traitor. Blake does not betray for ideals; he betrays because he *needs* to betray. If Blake had been born a Russian, he would have betrayed the KGB to the British. That's how he's made." [10]

After his arrest, his wife, Gillian, said: "George liked to be a power behind the scenes, but not to be obviously powerful. He wanted to know all sorts of things that were going on. And he liked to have a hand in them, though nobody need know it."

Perhaps a great French writer who never knew Blake best explained his motivation. Honoré de Balzac described a spy as someone who craves the excitement of being a criminal while keeping the character of an honest man.

No other spy in the annals of espionage courted excitement more ardently than George Blake. He sought danger as the moth seeks the light, mesmerized by the flame that would destroy him.

CHAPTER SEVEN

The Networks
Better Relations – Better Espionage

The continuing thrust of Soviet espionage was visible throughout the decade of the sixties, as in each year major spy cases were brought to public light in the West. The effect of these revelations was particularly damaging in Great Britain, where the Portland naval spy case and the Blake case shook the foundations of British security. But the end was not in sight for the British. In 1962, John Vassal, a thirty-eight-year-old Admiralty clerk, confessed that for seven years, under threat of blackmail as a homosexual, he had been turning over to the Soviets top-secret information. The following year brought the Profumo scandal in which it was revealed that John Profumo, British minister of war, was sharing the favors of callgirl Christine Keeler with a GRU agent, Captain Yevgeny Ivanov. Adding to the embarrassment of the Macmillan government was the defection of Kim Philby to Moscow in 1963. Philby had held a position of trust in the foreign service; his defection revealed that he had been working for Soviet Intelligence for years.

In 1963, attention was finally drawn away from England's security problems by those of other nations. In June of that year, Colonel Stig Wennerstrom, a Swedish Air Force officer, was charged with stealing U.S. and NATO military secrets for the Soviets. In October, the FBI broke up a Soviet *apparat* engaged in trying to obtain the plans of the Strategic Air Command's electronic communications system. Four Soviet agents and an American engineer, John

A happy Soviet spy. Igor A. Ivanov, after being sentenced to 30 years in prison for espionage in the United States, is allowed to leave for a visit to Russia, subject to return when his appeal was to be heard. He never returned.

Butenko, were caught in the act. Three of the Soviets, who were attached to the UN, were declared *persona non grata* and were sent home. The fourth, thirty-three-year-old Igor Ivanov, a chauffeur for Amtorg, did not have diplomatic immunity and was held for trial with Butenko.

In December, 1964, both men were given thirty-year sentences, but Ivanov never went to jail. He remained free on $100,000 bond posted by the Soviet Embassy, while his case was appealed all the way to the Supreme Court. His movements were restricted, but he enjoyed the distinction of being the first spy ever arrested in any country who remained out of jail after conviction.

In 1965, the Soviets attempted to exchange Ivanov for Newcomb Mott, an American textbook salesman, but the U.S. government refused the offer. While visiting Kirkenes, Norway, as a tourist, Mott had accidentally crossed the almost totally unmarked Russian border at Boris Gleb. He had then turned himself in to border guards and spent the next three months in solitary confinement in Murmansk. Brought to trial, he was found guilty of illegal trespass and sentenced to eighteen months in a labor camp. In January of 1966, he died under unexplained circumstances.[1]

In 1971, Ivanov was permitted to go home to Russia to visit family and friends, on the condition that when his trial came up again, he would come back to the United States. One observer of the case commented, "It is not a return anyone would want to bet on."

Aside from these two cases, in 1963 eleven other cases of Soviet espionage were brought to light. Four of these involved spies operating in the United States. The others occurred in Australia, Iceland, Turkey, and France. Of the four in the United States, two involved American military service personnel. These were the first cases in which men in uniform were apprehended as Soviet spies since the conviction of Sergeant Roy A. Rhodes, after the trial of Rudolph Abel in 1957. More were soon to follow.

On January 7, 1965, Boris V. Karpovich, information counselor at the Soviet Embassy in Washington, was expelled from the country on the grounds of having been "implicated in an indictment for espionage." A former Air Force airman second-class, Robert Glenn Thompson, was arrested at the same time and arraigned on a three-count charge that he had conspired over a period of years to pass military secrets to the Soviet Union. The FBI had evidence that Thompson had been a paid Soviet agent in Berlin from 1957 to 1963. Karpovich had worked with Thompson and with another Soviet spy, Fedor D. Kudashkin, who was, at the time, second secretary of the Soviet UN delegation. Thompson was found guilty of the charges and on May 13, 1965, he was sentenced to thirty years in prison.

One month before Thompson was sentenced, Army Sergeant Robert Lee Johnson and former Army Sergeant James Allen Mintkenbaugh were also arrested by the FBI and charged with having sold military secrets to the Soviets over a twelve-year period. According to the charges, Johnson, assigned to Army Intelligence, had sought out the Soviets while stationed in Berlin in 1953. He offered to sell them information, and the offer was readily accepted. Several months later, Johnson recruited Mintkenbaugh to help photograph the steady stream of documents flowing in to his desk. In 1956, both men were honorably discharged from the army, but Johnson, under Moscow's orders, reenlisted. Mintkenbaugh continued to act as Johnson's contact until 1959. After 1959, both men continued to serve the Soviets in different capacities. As a U.S. intelligence courier stationed in Europe and later, at the Pentagon, Johnson was able to pass on secrets ranging from details of the Nike-Ajax antiaircraft missile to plans in case of war.

Johnson and Mintkenbaugh were sentenced to twenty-five years in prison on July 30, 1965. On May 19, 1972, Johnson's son, Robert Lee Johnson, Jr., a twenty-two-year-old Vietnam veteran, visited his father at the federal penitentiary at Lewisburg, Pennsylvania. The two had not seen each other in many years, and when they met, the son produced a knife and killed his father.

In June, 1969, a number of publications in West Germany, Italy, France, and England received copies of a "top-secret" Pentagon document. The plan, called "Plan Number 10–1," detailed operational Defense Department strategy in case of nuclear war with the Soviet Union. According to this document, the United States planned to drop atom bombs on German cities and to use bacteriological and nerve gas weapons in the anticipated guerrilla conflict that would follow. Publication of the plan created a great deal of anti-American feeling throughout Western Europe. According to the unsigned letter accompanying the report, Major General Horst Wendland, a key official in the West German Intelligence service (BND) who had committed suicide some months before, had turned the plan over to the anonymous writer of the letter with instructions to release the document in case of his death.

According to Western Intelligence, "Plan Number 10–1" was actually conceived, written, and disseminated by the KGB Disinformation Department.

The Disinformation Department, or Department D, was created in 1959 by Soviet Intelligence and became an integral part of Soviet espionage activities. The purpose of Department D, as described by the CIA, is to "defame and discredit" the United States and its policies through the use of "false, incomplete, or misleading information that is passed, fed, or confirmed to a targeted individual, group, or country."

The CIA estimates that Department D turns out between three hundred and fifty and four hundred derogatory items annually. "Plan 10–1" was such an item. A UPI report, datelined September 8, 1969, summed up the story:

> The magazine *Stern* today published details of what it called a top-secret U.S. military plan that outlines atomic, chemical and biological warfare plans from the Atlantic to the Caucasus Mountains in the event of a Soviet take-over of Western Europe.
> The magazine *Der Spiegel* said the plan was sent to *Stern* and the American magazine *Ramparts* by the Soviet KGB disinformation section. *Der Spiegel* said the KGB was attempting to sow confusion among the people of Europe and the Western allies. The Soviets got Plan 10–1 along with many other secret U.S. documents from Sergeant Robert Lee Johnson, 46, a former U.S. courier. According to *Der Spiegel* . . . these activities already known about, indicate an offensive in military and political thinking unknown since the days of Hitler.

In May, 1971, a Czech Intelligence officer who had served two years as deputy chief of the Czech Disinformation Section, defected to the West. His testimony included descriptions of types of disinformation and the techniques employed to utilize them.

The major explained:

> There are basically three types of operations: disinformation, which means to feed an enemy . . . with false information so that the counterpart, the enemy, makes wrong decisions.
> Second type are propaganda operations. It may seem strange that Soviet-bloc Intelligence spends so much time on propaganda when every Communist-bloc country has a large official apparatus for the same purpose. It is true that Soviet-bloc Intelligence takes over the role of propagandist abroad whenever for ideological, moral, or tactical reasons, the official propaganda institution can't do that. So, for example, Eastern European Intelligence services do not hesitate to do propaganda of Fascist character in the name of some nonexistent Fascist organization if it serves the purpose. It is actually black propaganda as the real source is covered and the world public opinion doesn't know that it was initiated in Eastern Europe.
> Then there is the third type called influence operations which are the most demanding and very rare. These operations are based on the activities of so-called influence agents, Communist agents working in non-Communist countries, who have

Growing Numbers of Soviet-Bloc Officials in the United States

How Many There Are

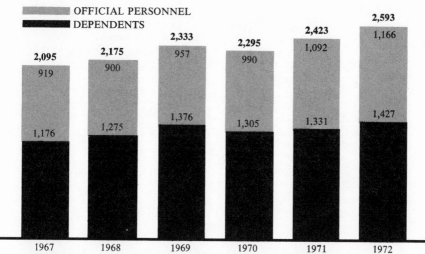

OFFICIAL PERSONNEL
DEPENDENTS

	2,095	2,175	2,333	2,295	2,423	2,593
	919	900	957	990	1,092	1,166
	1,176	1,275	1,376	1,305	1,331	1,427
	1967	1968	1969	1970	1971	1972

Excludes couriers, members of special delegations, and other officials temporarily in the United States.

Where They Come From

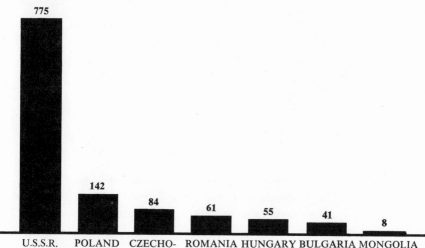

U.S.S.R.	POLAND	CZECHO-SLOVAKIA	ROMANIA	HUNGARY	BULGARIA	MONGOLIA
775	142	84	61	55	41	8

As of 1972

Source: Federal Bureau of Investigation, United States Department of Justice, 1972.

important positions in the government political parties or in Parliament. They can get instructions from East European Communist Intelligence services, for instance, how they should react in Parliament, in a parliamentarian discussion or if they occupy an important position in an enemy's intelligence service, what to do in order to make it less efficient. . . .

. . . It is very easy for the Communist Intelligence service to start an anti-American operation in Africa, Asia, or Latin America because of anti-American movements and opinions which objectively exist there. Disinformation operations of the Communist Intelligence services parasitize on these existing American streams.

I can give you an example of an operation which was carried out in 1964 and 1965, aiming at undermining the American position in Africa. Three forgeries of American documents were produced in Prague. The purpose was to reveal the United States as the major conspirator and enemy of the left-oriented African regimes. The first one was a forgery of a letter by the American Ambassador in Leopoldville to the Congolese Ministry of Foreign Affairs. . . . Together with the other two written in similar spirit, these forgeries were to prove American conspiracy against the leftist Tanzanian government. They were leaked to Tanzanian government officials. . . . In this operation, Oscar Kambona, the Minister of Foreign Affairs of Tanzania, presented the forgeries to the public as proof of the American conspiracy. And that was the start of a big anti-American campaign, not only in Tanzania but, I would say, all over the African continent. Tanzanian President Nyerere hesitated to believe in these forgeries; he asked the American authorities for proof and shortly after that the American authorities presented the facts proving that all these documents were forgeries. President Nyerere accepted that, but the campaign continued, because actually the press did not want to believe that they were forgeries.[2]

The testimony of the Czech major was revealing in still another area, the relationship between Soviet Intelligence and the intelligence services of their satellites. The major listed fifty countries around the world in which the Czech Intelligence service was active in one form or another. With this figure can be placed estimates by *U.S.News & World Report* that in 1963 there were more than two hundred and fifty thousand Soviet-directed spies working against the West.

Among the estimated two hundred and fifty thousand agents enlisted by Moscow was a United States officer, Lt. Colonel William H. Whalen. When he was arrested by the FBI on July 12, 1966, he bore the grim distinction of being the only U.S. officer ever charged with spying for the Soviet Union. Because of a heart condition, Whalen had retired from the army in 1961, at the age of forty-six, after twenty-one years of "distinguished service." At the time of

Sergei Edemski, (left) Soviet military attaché in London, taking in the information volunteered by a British soldier during a military exercise in England. Previously, when he was military attaché in Washington, Edemski secured military secrets from Lt. Col. William Whalen, U.S.A., who was later convicted as a Soviet spy.

his retirement, he had been an intelligence aide to the Joint Chiefs of Staff. He had served in U.S. Intelligence since 1947. He had first come under FBI surveillance in 1959 when he was observed meeting with two Soviet Embassy officials, First Secretary Mikhail M. Shumaev and Colonel Sergei A. Edemski. The meetings continued intermittently, taking place in shopping centers in Alexandria and Arlington, Virginia, not far from the Pentagon.

The indictment against Whalen charged him with revealing: "information pertaining to atomic weaponry, missiles, military plans for the defense of Europe, information concerning the retaliation plans of the United States Strategic Air Command, and information pertaining to troop movements, documents and writings relating to the national defense of the United States."

On March 2, 1967, Whalen was sentenced to fifteen years in a federal penitentiary. By then, the two Soviet officials had left the country, Edemski going to the Soviet Embassy in London and Shumaev returning to Russia.

Still another American serviceman was arrested for espionage in 1966. He was Air Force Sergeant Herbert Boeckenhaupt. Born in Mannheim, Germany, he had come to the United States with his parents at the age of five. When stationed at the Pentagon as a radio operator in the Air Force Headquarters Command, he contacted the Soviet Embassy, and in June, 1965, he began to meet on a regular basis with an employee on the staff of the embassy's commercial counselor. On May 27, 1967, Boeckenhaupt was convicted of conspiring to transmit defense secrets and sentenced to thirty years in prison.

Since 1967, only one American, military or civilian, has been indicted on charges of spying for the Soviet Union. He was Walter Perkins, a thirty-seven-year-old Air Force master sergeant and the top intelligence noncommissioned officer at the Air Defense Weapons Center, Tyndall Air Force Base, Florida. When Perkins was arrested in Panama City, Florida, he was charged with having in his possession five secret documents which, if passed on to the KGB, would have seriously jeopardized the United States defense system. When arrested, he also carried an airplane ticket to Mexico City and a map of the city, as well as instructions for getting in touch with the Soviets. Perkins pleaded guilty, maintaining that while in an alcoholic stupor, he believed that he could swap secret documents in return for the release of three American POWs in North Vietnam. Perkins was sentenced to three years in prison on August 11, 1972.

Nineteen sixty-seven was a bad year for Soviet Intelligence. In March, Western Counterintelligence uncovered a vast GRU spy

Soviet Network Disrupted by Western Counterintelligence

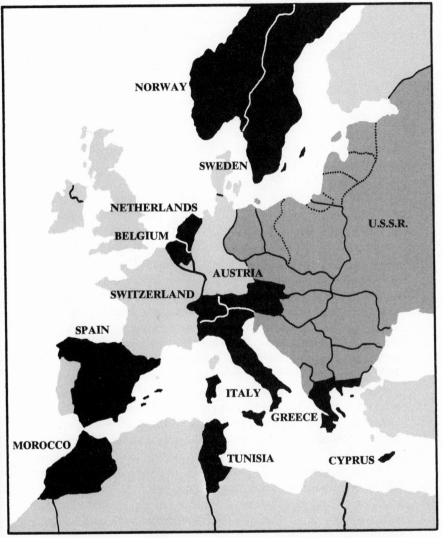

Map shows twelve countries where a massive network of Soviet spies was discovered in April, 1967, by Western Intelligence agents. Some were arrested, some expelled, and others fled before they could be caught.

Source: *U.S.News & World Report.*

network, with cells operating across the face of Europe and into Africa, "from Scandinavia to Somalia." Headquarters for this huge *apparat* was an antique shop in Turin, Italy, run by a skydiver, Giorgio Rinaldi, and his wife, Angela. Rinaldi had used his skydiving as a method to travel around Europe, with the purpose of enlisting recruits. He had been extremely successful.

The network's aim was to penetrate NATO and obtain details on military bases and operations, troop and ship movements, weapons, and new equipment. NATO communications were a prime target for agents in ten European countries and four in the Mediterranean area. Moscow wanted various categories of information: locations of radio transmitters, frequencies, and power facilities; accurate counts on air traffic at all NATO bases; and detailed reports on the attitude of the governments and the peoples of the host countries toward NATO and the U.S. troops on their soil.

When the network was broken, it was estimated that over two hundred agents were serving it. This puzzled Western Intelligence because, previously, standard Soviet operating procedure had been to keep *apparati* small and to have a series of rings independent of each other. Subsequent developments were to indicate this change marked a shift in Soviet Intelligence policy.

While Rinaldi might have excelled as a skydiver, as a spymaster he committed a serious fault—he kept detailed records. The result was that a long list of Soviet officials were expelled from the countries in which they were posted. Those sent home included Russians representing such agencies as: Aeroflot in Holland and Cyprus, Tass in Belgium, and the International Telecommunications Union in Switzerland. Diplomats and members of the staffs of Soviet embassies in Rome, Athens, and Nicosia were also ordered to leave. At the same time, non-Russian agents of the Soviet Union were arrested in Norway, Sweden, Belgium, Austria, Spain, Greece, and Cyprus.

The breaking of this network had taken years of painstaking counterintelligence work. The investigation had begun when Western Intelligence agents observed Rinaldi meeting with a known Russian spy. From then on, Rinaldi was watched. A longtime Marxist, he suddenly began moving in right-wing circles. In 1959 he married a former Fascist, Angela Maria Antoniola. Shortly afterward, they opened an antique shop in Turin and began to spend a great deal of money. Rinaldi acquired a chauffeur, Armando Girard. Both men traveled frequently, making separate trips, Rinaldi visiting Montreux, Switzerland, and Girard driving to France and Spain.

Italian monitoring stations began to pick up coded radio messages, emanating from a station in the vicinity of Moscow. The

Giorgio Rinaldi, Italian skydiver, who directed a Soviet spy network extending from Scandinavia to Somalia.

transmissions were sent out at the same hour every night. Although cryptologists could not break the code, a definite link was detected between the radio messages and the two suspects. Whenever a short message was transmitted, Rinaldi departed the next day for Switzerland; when a long one was received, Girard would head for France or Spain. During this period, Rinaldi and his wife traveled secretly to Moscow, via Paris, using false identity papers.

By March, 1967, Italian Counterintelligence was ready to move. After a long radio transmission was picked up on March 9, agents attempted to trail Girard as he drove his Volkswagen toward the French border. Customs checkpoints were set up on a twenty-four-hour basis at spots along all the routes that would bring him back to northern Italy. On March 15, Girard returned and drove into the trap. His car proved to be a treasure trove of microfilmed intelligence reports. Agents in Turin were alerted and the Rinaldis were quickly picked up. Under questioning, the skydiver confessed. Among other details, he gave the cipher key to decode the Russian broadcasts. As a result, on the night of March 20, Soviet diplomat Yuri Pavlenko was caught in the act of picking up intelligence material at a dead drop near Rome. Announcement of Pavlenko's expulsion set off shock waves in some faraway places. Soviet officials assigned to missions in Casablanca, Tunis, and Tokyo headed home without being asked to leave.

In November, 1967, Soviet Intelligence suffered still another blow when Lieutenant Colonel Yevgeny Y. Runge, a thirty-nine-year-old KGB officer, defected with his wife, Valentina, and their seven-year-old son, Andrei. In his confession, Runge described the increasing use by Soviet Intelligence of illegal agents in the United States, the British Commonwealth, Western Europe, and Japan.

In September, 1971, the British government announced that it was expelling one hundred and five Soviet diplomats and representatives as spies. One week later, the Belgian government announced that it was sending home thirty-two. A *New York Times* correspondent wrote, "Soviet espionage appears to be growing around the world —particularly in the West—while Western and Soviet officials negotiate about reducing tensions. . . ." Once again, Soviet Intelligence found itself where it most disliked to be: on the front pages of the world's newspapers.

* * * * *

itain expels 10
ssian diploma
SPY
PURGE

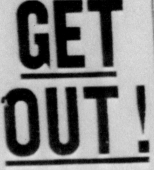

GET
OUT !

Britain expels 90
Soviet agents after
tell-tale spy drama

Defector puts finger on
Russia's secret army

Daily

Why Britain is expel
105 Russian diplom

CONC
SABO

BRITAIN
KICKS OUT
105 SPIES

HEATH BEATS 'SABOTAGE

*Sensation caused in Britain by exposure and expulsion of 105 Soviet
spies, as shown in these London newspaper headlines.*

In 1970, eighty-three Soviet diplomats were attached to the Soviet Embassy in London. The number had been frozen in 1968, as a result of a spy case, one of twenty-seven such cases exposed by the British over a ten-year period. However, in addition to the eighty-three diplomats, there were more than four hundred and fifty Russians attached to other agencies: the Soviet trade delegation, Intourist, Aeroflot, Tass, the Russian Wood Agency, the Moscow Narodny Bank, Ranzo, and a civil-engineering and road-building equipment firm called UMO. How many of the total number of Russians posted in England were legal agents was known only to the KGB and the GRU, but, as indicated elsewhere, 50 percent would be a conservative estimate.

From examination of the location and activities of one Soviet agency in England, a pattern of clandestine operations emerges. In 1967, the Soviets set up the UMO firm in England. UMO established its main base at Letchworth, with depots in Herts, Doncaster, and York. Twenty Russians ran UMO, with the help of a staff of seventy Englishmen. UMO's headquarters in Letchworth was next to Great Britain's largest computer factory. Some of UMO's Soviet personnel lived in an apartment building in the market town of Baldock, Hertfordshire. Fronting the building was a poorly lit, bush-lined path; at the end of the path stretched the flood-lit, barbed-wire perimeter of one of the most secret research laboratories in the country.

The function of the laboratory was to supply the British armed services with a wide range of secret equipment such as gas lasers, semi-conductor lasers, and lasers for aerial photography, as well as navigational aids for atomic submarines. Of the fifteen flats in the Hillcrest apartments, which faced the laboratory, nine were occupied by Russian "mechanics and engineers." The only restriction British authorities placed on the Russians' activities was the requirement that they notify local police before traveling to their outlying depots.

The UMO branch in Doncaster, set up in 1970, was under the direction of Vyatcheslov Patushkov. He and his four Soviet assistants, described as "technicians," lived in a house in Kirk Sandall, which was located a short distance from the RAF headquarters of No. 1 Group Strike Command. UMO's road-building equipment, supervised by Soviet personnel, was used on Highway M-5 in Somerset, close to the British Aircraft Corporation's Concorde aircraft works.

Thus, a small Soviet commercial operation managed to domicile some of its people a stone's throw from a top-secret electronics laboratory, place others not far from a vital RAF installation, set up headquarters next to an important computer factory, and employ its technicians in the vicinity of the corporation involved in the development of the supersonic Concorde aircraft.

British Intelligence was not blind to what the Russians in UMO and other agencies were doing. In October, 1970, when Soviet Foreign Minister Andrei Gromyko came to London to discuss means to improve Anglo-Soviet relations, Sir Alec Douglas-Home, the British foreign secretary, raised the matter with him. In the course of their talks, the name of Fedor D. Kudashkin was brought up. Kudashkin had been exposed by the FBI as a KGB agent in the Robert Glenn Thompson case in 1965. Gromyko was anxious to have Kudashkin's visa application accepted by the British so that the agent could be assigned to the Soviet Embassy in London. Stressing the need to improve relations between the two countries, Gromyko suggested that Sir Alec write to him on the extracurricular activities of Soviet officials in England.

On December 3, 1970, the British foreign secretary did so:

You will remember that on October 28 at the Soviet Embassy in London, I mentioned to you the case of F. D. Kudashkin. As you requested, I have gone carefully into this case. F. D. Kudashkin's activities in the United States were referred to in court proceedings which were reported at length in the *New York Times* of March 9, 1965. I enclose a copy of that report.

If you read it you will certainly understand why my colleagues and I regard F. D. Kudashkin as unacceptable for any appointment in this country. I hope you will agree that in the interests of our relations, it would be better that we should both regard the visa application made on his behalf as having lapsed.

The case of F. D. Kudashkin is by no means isolated, and it is with regret that, after the enjoyable and constructive discussions I have had with you in London, I find myself constrained to write to you about the scale and nature of the intelligence activities conducted by Soviet officials in this country and about the frequency of the attempts which have been made in recent months to introduce into this country officials who, in the past, have been engaged in such activities.

In 1970, alone, we have refused visas to more than a half a dozen Soviet officials assigned to this country because we had every reason to suspect, on the basis of what we know about their previous activities, that if they were admitted to this country, they would not restrict themselves to work which we regard as legitimate and conducive to the maintenance and development of good relations.

Most of the men to whom we have refused visas have been appointed to the Soviet trade delegation. I know that the Soviet trade delegation is not directly subordinated to your ministry, but since you, as minister of foreign affairs of the USSR, are concerned with all matters which affect the foreign relations of your country, I wish to invite your attention to the number of cases which have come to light of late in which members of the Soviet trade delegation have been found to have engaged in totally inadmissible activities.

This year alone, permission to stay in this country has been withdrawn from four members of the Soviet trade delegation. Since I had occasion to speak to you about F. D. Kudashkin, two new cases, one of them particularly serious, involving members of the Soviet trade delegation, have been brought to my attention. And I am told that a visa application had recently been submitted for A. P. Safronov whom we know to have engaged in inadmissible activities when he worked at the Soviet trade delegation between 1962 and 1966.

The competent Soviet authorities will be able to give you full information about the various kinds of inadmissible activities which have been conducted from the Soviet trade delegation. They have included the running of agents, instruction in the use of clandestine techniques, the offer and payment of considerable sums of money to persons resident in this country either to suborn them or to secure their help in obtaining classified information (both official or commercial) or commodities subject to embargo on other restrictions.

You will be aware that Her Majesty's previous Government felt compelled to place a limit on the growth of the staff of the Soviet Embassy in 1968. Even so, since last August, we have had to request the withdrawal of L. Y. Yeshukin, and the attempt to support F. D. Kudashkin to the embassy has awakened old suspicions. When you were in London, you said that Anglo-Soviet relations could not be described as bad, but that more could be done for their development and improvement. In this letter I have indicated a field which is becoming an increasing obstacle to the development of our relations, and with regard to which the kind of improvement of which you spoke would be most welcome.

The representations which Sir Denis Greenhill made on the subject to Vice Minister Kozierev earlier this year appear, from subsequent development, to have been ignored. I hope that this personal letter to you will be handled in the spirit of your opening remarks to the Prime Minister and myself during your visit to London.

Nine months later, on August 4, 1971, Sir Alec wrote another letter to Gromyko, saying:

I have received with interest Sir Denis Greenhill's reports of his conversation with Mr. Kozierev and yourself, in which you both referred to the allegedly hostile and provocative activities of the "British special services" against the Soviet Union and its citizens and against Soviet agencies in the United Kingdom, and in which you argued that these alleged activities did not contribute to the creation of a favorable atmosphere for the development of Anglo-Soviet relations.

Since you have raised this matter, I think it right to tell you that I see the situation in a very different light.

The Soviet Union conducts espionage against Great Britain on a large scale. Even if I were to mention only those cases which have become public knowledge during the last few years, the list would be a long one.

Many more cases, some of them very serious, are known to me and doubtless to you also. Governments which engage in intelligence activities on such a scale as this, must expect that the authorities in the countries attacked will take such precautions and countermeasures as may be open to them.

I do not accept your contention that in the interests of Anglo-Soviet relations, Her Majesty's Government should abstain from taking measures to prevent, limit or inhibit the espionage conducted by Soviet officials on such an extensive scale. It is this which places a strain upon our relations.

You are no doubt aware that the total number of Soviet officials on the staff of Soviet diplomatic, commercial and other organizations has now risen to more than 500 and you are presumably able to ascertain what proportion of these are intelligence officers. I would ask you to consider, however, how the situation must appear to the Foreign Minister of the country against which all this activity is directed. . . .

With the information at my disposal I find it hard to interpret the remarks made by Mr. Kozierev and yourself as other than a suggestion that Her Majesty's Government should allow these intelligence agents of yours to conduct their activities in the United Kingdom unhampered lest Anglo-Soviet relations should suffer. I consider this a proposition which is unreasonable for any government to make to another, whatever the state of their relations. . . .

This is not the first time that I have had occasion to bring such matters to your attention. I spoke to you on the subject during your visit to London in October, 1970. I did so in a manner which would have permitted the question to be pursued in a non-polemical way. You suggested that I should write you a letter and on December 3, 1970, I did so. To this date, to my surprise, I have received no reply, nor even an acknowledgment. Meanwhile, inadmissible Soviet activities in this country continue unabated.

I ask you to reflect upon this and to consider the extent to which these activities are obstructing the development of Anglo-Soviet relations. . . . I trust that you now will feel able to reply to my original letter and to this one, which I send in the hope that you will say that you are ready immediately to terminate such activities.

As in the case of the British foreign secretary's first letter, there was no response from the Soviet foreign minister. One of the active Russian agents to whom Sir Alec was referring was Oleg

Adolfovich Lyalin, a junior official in the Soviet trade delegation, who had been in England since 1967. Big, fair-haired with a bushy moustache, Lyalin was a bluff, hearty Russian, who spoke English without a trace of an accent and had made many friends around London. He operated mainly out of the trade delegation's Regent Street office, which was engaged in the export-import business under the name of Ranzo. Ranzo dealt with all kinds of goods, from socks to Scotch, and the bustling Lyalin gave the impression of being a capitalistic salesman, rather than a Communist functionary. In reality, however, he was neither. Oleg Adolfovich Lyalin was an active agent of the KGB. He came to his job backed by powerful family support. His uncle, Major General Serafim N. Lyalin, was chief of the KGB's Eighth Directorate, which handled code-breaking and the surveillance of communications between foreign governments and citizens of the Soviet Union.

As a member of the trade delegation, Lyalin was not restricted to the thirty-five-mile travel limit imposed on Soviet Embassy personnel. He often left his wife and young son for long periods of time, while he went on trips to take care of "business matters."

One "business matter" was his attempt to trap a Whitehall secretary, Marie Richardson, into spying for the KGB. The secretary, a Eurasian, worked in the Admiralty as personal assistant to the deputy director of the Supplies and Transport Staff. In this capacity, she had access to classified information and documents.

In 1967, Lyalin made his first approach to Marie Richardson through a civil servant, Siraj Abdoorcader, who was employed by the Greater London Council Vehicle Registration Department. Of Malayan origin, Abdoorcader hated the British. Lyalin gave him Marie Richardson's address and telephone number, as well as money for flowers and gifts, but Abdoorcader was unsuccessful in his wooing. The secretary was not interested. In the summer of 1967, she went on a cruise to Scandinavia and Leningrad. The ship's assistant purser was also working for Lyalin and he, too, tried to court Marie Richardson. He tried so hard that she became suspicious, and upon her return to England, she reported the incident to Naval Security.

Another of Lyalin's ventures proved more profitable. Between December, 1967, and November, 1968, through Abdoorcader's cooperation, Lyalin obtained from the Greater London Council Vehicle Registration Department the license numbers of all cars belonging to the British security services—useful information for any spy.

Many more of his espionage activities were revealed to British

Intelligence after he defected to the West on Sunday, September 5, 1971. Six days before his defection, Lyalin had been arrested on drunken driving charges at 1:00 A.M., as he wove along Tottenham Court Road in his Hillman. Picked up by the police, he was taken to the nearest stationhouse where he refused to take the prescribed tests. Instead, he insisted on calling his embassy, and in due course a Soviet official arrived on the scene to post £50 bail and stand security. Lyalin was instructed by the authorities to report to the Marlborough Street Courthouse on September 30 to face the charges.

By that date, the story of his defection had been made public, and his name was a household word in Great Britain.

On September 24, almost three weeks after Lyalin defected, Sir Denis Greenhill, permanent under-secretary at the Foreign Office, called on Ivan Ippolitov, Soviet chargé d'affaires, and informed him that a total of one hundred and five Soviet diplomats and their families had been declared *persona non grata* by the British government. Fifteen on the list of those to be expelled were temporarily out of the country and would not be permitted to return, nor would replacements be allowed for any of those dismissed.

In the note presented to Ippolitov, the British government pointed out: "The Soviet government can hardly fail to be conscious of the contradiction between their advocacy of a conference on European security and the scale of operations against the security of this country which Soviet officials and agents controlled by them have conducted. . . ."

One of Lyalin's accusations was that Soviet Intelligence was trying to prevent Britain's entry into the Common Market. To this end, disinformation agents had been spreading false adverse economic information to British trade union leaders, politicians, and journalists.

The most serious allegation of those released to the general public was Lyalin's charge that the Soviets were planning to infiltrate spies into England who would be under orders to commit acts of sabotage during periods of internal tension.

Lyalin was reported to be "somewhere in the south of England." British Intelligence kept him under close guard, trying to prevent a repetition of what had happened to a Russian physicist who defected to the West in 1967. The scientist, Dr. Vladimir Tkachenko, was grabbed by Soviet officials in broad daylight as he walked along the street. He was thrown into a car and taken to the Soviet Embassy. Special Branch officers, knowing Tkachenko would be flown out of the country, watched the airports and railway stations. When the Soviets attempted to fly their captive back to Moscow,

British agents took him off the plane. It was then found that the physicist had been injected with a slow-acting fatal poison. British doctors had no antidote, and, in an attempt to save his life, they returned him to the Soviet Embassy. That was the last anyone in the West heard of the unfortunate scientist.

Although the identities of the Russians sent home after Lyalin's disclosures were not made public, at least seven members of the Soviet Embassy staff were on board the Russian cruise ship, *Baltika,* when she sailed from Tilbury Dock on October 3. The ship had been diverted from its regular run to Spain and Morocco and commandeered by the Soviets to take home more than two hundred diplomats and businessmen. Never in the annals of espionage had there been such a mass exodus of spies.

The outcry in the West over Lyalin's revelations was loud and immediate. From the UN, Secretary of State Rogers warned that the scope of Soviet espionage in the West was going to be a factor in the Atlantic Alliance's decision on whether to agree to a European security conference, as desired by the Warsaw Pact countries.

Before the furor had a chance to die down, a new Soviet espionage case was blazoned in the headlines. On the very day the *Baltika* sailed, Anatoli K. Tchebotarev, a thirty-eight-year-old officer in the GRU who was attached to the Soviet trade delegation in Brussels, Belgium, fled to England and turned himself over American Intelligence. On October 7, he was flown to the United States to be interrogated by the CIA. Shortly afterward, the Belgian government received from the United States a list of thirty-two Soviet diplomats and businessmen who were engaged in espionage.

For many years, Brussels had been an active center of Soviet espionage. Belgium is the headquarters for the Common Market, the European Trade Group, the International Labor Union, and a host of other international organizations. On April 1, 1967, after Charles de Gaulle officially withdrew France from the North Atlantic Treaty Organization, Brussels also became the headquarters for NATO.

Tchebotarev's disclosures did not lead to a mass expulsion of Soviet diplomats from Brussels. Unlike the British, the Belgian authorities did not wish to publicize the spies in their midst. Anxious for more trade with the Soviet Union and eager to insure the selection of Brussels as the site for the European Security Conference, the Belgian government tried to hush up the case. Of the thirty-two Soviets named, only half were requested to leave the country.

Despite the attitude of the Belgian government, some of the acts of espionage of Soviet Intelligence in Belgium, as disclosed by

A Soviet diplomat, caught in the act of collecting intelligence material from a "dead drop" in Britain. He later was expelled with 104 other Soviet diplomatic spies.

Tchebotarev, were made public. One important result of Tchebotarev's defection was the exposure of the work of the Soviet Committee of Science and Technology (GKNT).

Long before the shift of NATO headquarters from France to Belgium, Soviet Intelligence was ready to greet the new arrivals. To aid the agents of the KGB and the GRU, a new agency, the Soviet Committee of Science and Technology (GKNT), had been set up.

The deputy chief of GKNT was Dzermanyi Gvischiani, Kosygin's son-in-law. Gvischiani's key contact in Belgium was Valentin Saitzev, a ranking KGB officer who was assigned to the Soviet trade delegation. Saitzev arranged business conferences in which prominent Belgian industrialists traveled to nearby Luxembourg to hold secret talks with Gvischiani and GKNT experts for the purpose of of negotiating mutually advantageous trade and economic deals. Out of one such arrangement, a Belgian-Soviet automobile firm called Scaldia-Volga was established. The firm installed a large service garage a mile from NATO administrative headquarters. This garage served as a GRU operational base.

The Soviet trade delegation at 31 Boulevard du Régent also served as KGB directional headquarters. Saitzev operated from this address, placing Soviet spies in universities in Belgium and France.

While Saitzev was the principal contact man for economic and scientific espionage, Anatoli G. Maschin was chief of the GRU operation against NATO. Under Maschin's direction, agents at Scaldia-Volga listened in on all calls coming out of and going into NATO administration headquarters. The sophisticated electronic equipment necessary to carry out the wiretapping had been smuggled into Belgium in the luggage of Soviet diplomats.

It was also revealed that both the KGB and the GRU made use of not only the embassy and the trade missions, but also of Aeroflot, Tass, Novosti, a firm called Belso, and other industries which had an engineer-exchange program with the Soviets, such as Agfa-Gevaert, a photographic company.

As for Anatoli Tchebotarev, the agent who exposed the Belgian network, the motivation for his actions remains unexplained, for on Sunday, December 26, 1971, he redefected, fleeing back to the Soviet Union.

According to the CIA, the GRU major had "cooperated fully at his own request" since he had arrived in October. On Tuesday, December 21, the Soviet Embassy in Washington asked that one of its officials be permitted to talk to Tchebotarev. The request was granted, and Tchebotarev met at the State Department with Minister Counselor Yuly M. Vorontsov. The official gave Tchebotarev

Soviet Base for Spying on NATO Headquarters

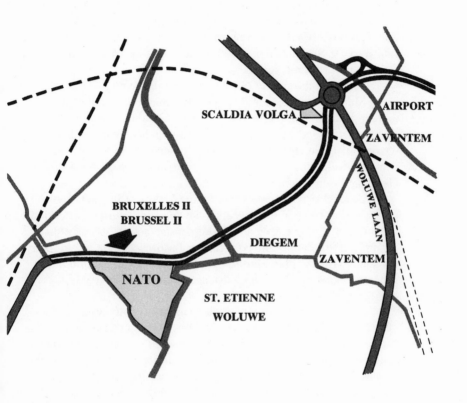

The Scaldia-Volga service garage, a Soviet espionage center, was conveniently located a short distance from its target, NATO headquarters, in Brussels, Belgium.

Source: *Dilog.*

some mail from his wife and family and was, in turn, told by the defector that he had come to the United States of his own free will and desired to remain. Two days later, he disappeared, and the State Department was informed by the Soviet Embassy that Anatoli had changed his mind and wanted to go home. Before his departure from Kennedy airport on the day after Christmas, Tchebotarev was interrogated by a U.S. immigration and naturalization officer in the company of a doctor and a State Department representative. All agreed that Tchebotarev's desire to return to Russia was genuine. After his return to the Soviet Union, nothing more was heard from him; his fate has never been revealed.

In another instance of GKNT activities, in March, 1972, GKNT agent Markarov was ordered to leave Denmark, accused of plotting to keep Scandinavia out of the Common Market. During the same month, forty-nine Soviet officials were expelled from Bolivia on charges of espionage. Many of these officials were GKNT agents who were charged with engaging in economic subversion under Gvischiani's direction.

Although Soviet Intelligence focused many of its operations on gathering information in the years following 1960, during this period the KGB was also engaged in more sinister activities. A dramatic example of the clandestine political war the Soviets were waging was revealed to the world in March, 1971, when Mexican Counterintelligence services exposed the existence of a KGB-directed plot to overthrow the Mexican government.

The plan had been years in the making. Its chief organizer was Oleg M. Netchiporenko, assigned to the Soviet Embassy in Mexico City in 1964 and considered to be the top KGB agent in Latin America. In 1968, forty-nine of the Soviet Embassy's staff of fifty-seven were KGB officers. Of this number, twenty were directed by Netchiporenko. In addition, he had carefully recruited a network of Mexicans, consisting mainly of university students belonging to the Young Communist party and the Mexican-Russian Cultural Exchange.

During this period, specially screened Mexican radicals were dispatched by Netchiporenko to study at Patrice Lumumba Friendship University in Moscow. In September, 1969, a group of these young Mexicans were secretly sent on a journey to Pyongyang, North Korea. There they put in a hard year of guerrilla training, returning to Mexico in September, 1970. The returning Mexicans had three principal assignments: to recruit guerrilla forces, to train these guerrillas, and to rob banks to get money to purchase arms. The guerrillas and the arms were to be used to launch a campaign of terror and upheaval. The opening gun, scheduled for July, 1971, was to be the

Soviet Spies Who, After Serving in the United States, Were Caught in Britain in 1971 and Deported

Boris G. Kolodyazhny, a GRU agent who was a first secretary in the Soviet Embassy in Washington, 1958-1963.

Vladimir G. Filatov, a KGB agent in the Soviet UN delegation, 1966-7.

Anatoly I. Akimov, a GRU agent in the New York Amtorg office, 1962-1966.

Sergei N. Golubev, KGB agent in the Soviet UN delegation in 1961 and also 1963-1964.

Vsevolod N. Generalov, a GRU agent who served in the Washington office of the Soviet air attaché, 1959-1961, when he was expelled for espionage.

Vyacheslav A. Yasakev, a KGB agent who attended Cornell University during the turbulent years 1965-6.

Ivan P. Azarov, a KGB agent who was a third secretary in the Washington embassy, 1951-54, and second secretary, 1961-2.

Richard K. Vaygauskas, a KGB agent attached to the UN Secretariat in New York, 1960-63.

Emilya A. Petrovicheva, a KGB agent whose husband, also employed by the KGB, served in the Washington embassy, 1962-66.

Source: *London Times.*

simultaneous bombing of fifteen hotels, airports, restaurants, and public buildings throughout Mexico. Calling themselves the *Movimiento de Acción Revolucionaria,* the guerrillas hoped to swell their ranks and multiply their acts of violent disruption, sabotage, and assassination to such a degree that the government of Luis Echeverría would fall.

Discovery of the KGB-inspired and directed plot brought the swift expulsion of Netchiporenko and four of his principal embassy lieutenants, as well as the arrest of several hundred Mexicans. President Echeverría told his intelligence chiefs, "Gentlemen, you have saved your country and our people from a terrible tragedy." [3]

One year after the KGB involvement in Mexico was brought to light, a similar plot was exposed in Bolivia. There, in March, 1972, the government of President Hugo Banzer announced that Bolivian Intelligence had uncovered a KGB-directed plan to overthrow the Banzer regime. In this instance, the KGB had been utilizing Cuban, Czech, Chilean and Brazilian terrorists, as well as Bolivians. Again, North Korea had been the training ground for the revolutionaries. Bolivian police had discovered large arms caches in La Paz, Cochabamba, and Santa Cruz. KGB-engineered plans to destroy power plants, water mains, and lines of communication were announced by the Bolivian minister of the interior. The key KGB organizer had been the Soviet Embassy's first secretary, Igor Ichalov. Many of the forty-nine Soviet officials dismissed by President Banzer were representatives of GKNT. In commenting on the attempted overthrow of his government, Bolivia's Foreign Minister Mirea Gutierrez declared that the Soviet Union offered peace and trade on the one hand, and support for guerrilla warfare on the other.

Soviet espionage in the United Nations surfaced again in 1972 when Valery Ivanovich Markelov, a Russian translator at the UN, was charged with attempting to obtain plans for the navy's new F-14A Tomcat fighter plane. On August 14, 1972, in what one observer called "a quiet concession to diplomatic relations with the Soviet Union preceding President Nixon's trip to the Soviet Union," the United States dismissed the case in a secret nighttime court session in Brooklyn. By the time the indictment was dropped, the accused spy had been out of the country for almost three months.

*   *   *   *   *

In recent years, with extraordinary developments in electronic communications, Western powers have been concentrating on technological espionage, such as the "spy in the sky" satellite, rather than on the human spy. The Soviet Union continues the full utilization of both.

This may reflect the difference, mentioned at the outset of this book, in the aim and scope of espionage as practiced by the Soviet Union and other countries. Electronic espionage may be described as defensive in character. The "spy in the sky" can report whether there are unusual troop movements or missile preparations on the territory of a potential enemy. It cannot enlist the support of a foreign national, through blackmail, bribery, or ideological persuasion, into betraying the secrets of his country. Nor can it subvert a foreign government and direct a guerrilla war. For these offensive purposes the Soviet espionage system continues to rely on human beings.

Colonel Rudolf Abel, writing in *Molodoi Kommunist* after his return to the Soviet Union, stressed the continuing importance of the individual Soviet spy. He mentioned two important points. First, the Soviet intelligence agent must be "a convinced and clearheaded Marxist." (In other words, he must be absolutely dedicated to the Communist ideology as defined by Moscow.) Second, "the conditions of work and the situation in capitalist countries require the intelligence agent to be constantly observant and to thoroughly observe the rules of conspiracy."

One of the self-evident "rules of conspiracy" is that the Soviet agent should not succumb to the temptations inevitably encountered in "capitalist countries." The most powerful temptations are those of an easier and freer way of life than can be found in the Soviet Union. The great weakness in the Soviet reliance on human spies is the risk that they will be enticed by the many attractions of the non-Communist world.

We have seen in the pages of this book how often Moscow has been betrayed by its agents. They have contributed perhaps more than any other source to the outside world's awareness of the nature and scope of Soviet intelligence operations. Without the disclosures of disillusioned Soviet spies, this book could not have been written.

APPENDIX I

Who's Who in Soviet Espionage in the United States

Soviet Officials Declared *Persona Non Grata,* Requested to Leave, or Expelled from the United States for Reasons of Espionage, 1950-1971

Name of Soviet Official	Where Official Was Assigned in U.S.	What Action Was Taken by U.S.	Date of Action
Valentin Gubitchev	UN Secretariat	Expelled	3/9/50
Yuri V. Novikov	Embassy	Declared *persona non grata*	1/14/53
Igor A. Amosov	Office of Naval Attaché	Declared *persona non grata*	2/3/54
Aleksandr P. Kovalev	UN Mission	Declared *persona non grata*	2/3/54
Leonid I. Pivnev	Office of Air Attaché	Declared *persona non grata*	5/29/54
Maksim Martynov	UN Mission	Declared *persona non grata*	2/21/55
Aleksandr K. Guryanov	UN Mission	Declared *persona non grata*	4/25/56
Boris F. Gladkov	UN Mission	Expelled	6/22/56
Ivan A. Bubchikov	Office of Military Attaché	Declared *persona non grata*	6/14/56
Rostislav E. Shapovalov	UN Mission	Declared *persona non grata*	8/20/56
Viktor I. Petrov	UN Secretariat	Dismissed	8/23/56
Konstantin P. Ekimov	UN Mission	Declared *persona non grata*	10/29/56
Yuri P. Krylov	Office of Military Attaché	Declared *persona non grata*	1/14/57
Vasily M. Molev	Embassy	Declared *persona non grata*	1/25/57
Vladimir A. Grusha	UN Mission	Declared *persona non grata*	3/25/57
Gennadi F. Mashkantsev	Embassy	Declared *persona non grata*	4/17/57
Nikolai I. Kurochkin	Embassy	Declared *persona non grata*	6/6/58
Kirill S. Doronkin	UN Secretariat	Term of employment terminated	3/3/59
Evgeni A. Zaostrovtsev	Embassy	Informal request to leave	5/13/59
Vadim A. Kirilyuk	UN Secretariat	Dismissed	1/7/60

etr Y. Ezhov	Embassy	Declared *persona non grata*	7/22/60
alentin M. Ivanov	Embassy	Declared *persona non grata*	8/13/60
gor Y. Melekh	UN Secretariat	Expelled	3/24/61
uri V. Zaitsev	UN Secretariat	Informal request to leave	8/7/62
vgeni M. Prokhorov	UN Mission	Declared *persona non grata*	9/29/62
van Y. Vyrodov	UN Mission	Declared *persona non grata*	9/29/62
iennadiy G. Sevastyanov	Embassy	Declared *persona non grata*	7/1/63
van Egorov	UN Secretariat	Expelled	10/11/63
Aleksandra Egorova		Expelled	10/11/63
ileb Pavlov	UN Mission	Declared *persona non grata*	10/30/63
uri Romashin	UN Mission	Declared *persona non grata*	10/30/63
Vladimir Olenov	UN Mission	Declared *persona non grata*	10/30/63
Vasiliy V. Zadvinskiy	Office of Military Attaché	Declared *persona non grata*	12/14/64
Aleksandr V. Udalov	Office of Air Attaché	Declared *persona non grata*	12/14/64
Vladimir P. Grechanin	Office of Military Attaché	Declared *persona non grata*	12/14/64
Boris V. Karpovich	Embassy–Counselor	Declared *persona non grata*	1/7/65
itefan M. Kirsanov	Embassy	Declared *persona non grata*	6/2/65
Vadim A. Isakov	UNICEF, UNSEC	Declared *persona non grata*	2/2/66
Valentin Revin	Embassy	Declared *persona non grata*	9/2/66
Aleksay R. Malinin	Embassy employee	Declared *persona non grata*	10/31/66
Viktor V. Kopytin	Embassy–*Tass*	Expelled	5/23/69
Valentin P. Novikov	UN Secretariat	Contract with UN not renewed	7/7/65
gor Ivanovich Andreev	SMUN, Counselor	Expelled	7/22/69
Aleksandr V. Tikhomirov	UNSEC employee	Expelled	2/17/70
Boris Mikhaylovich Orekhov	*Pravda* corres., N.Y.	Expelled	
Leonid Nikolayevich Zhegalov	*Tass* corres., Washington, D.C.	Expelled	11/8/70
Valery I. Markelov	UN Secretariat	Expelled	5/19/72

Source: Federal Bureau of Investigation.

195

APPENDIX II

Who's Who in Soviet Bloc Espionage in the United States

Soviet Bloc Officials Declared *Persona Non Grata,* Requested to Leave, or Expelled from United States for Reasons of Espionage, 1949-1971

Name of Bloc Official	Where Official Was Assigned in the U.S.	What Action Was Taken by the U.S.	Date of U.S. Action
Ervin Munk	Czech Consulate	Expelled	10/10/49
Jan Horvath	Czech Embassy	Expelled	10/24/49
Peter Varkonyi	Hungarian Legation	Declared persona non grata	7/15/51
Sandor Louis Nagy	Hungarian Legation	Declared persona non grata	7/15/51
Christache Zambeti	Rumanian Legation	Declared persona non grata	5/20/53
Karoly Meszaros	Hungarian Legation Air Attaché	Declared persona non grata	5/57
Pal Racz	UN Hungarian Mission	Declared persona non grata	5/57
Roman Skokan	Czech Embassy	Declared persona non grata	4/21/58
Miroslav Nacvalac	UN Czech Mission	Declared persona non grata	6/13/61
Kazimierz Mizior	Polish Embassy	Declared persona non grata	1/15/65
Stefan Starzewski	Polish Embassy	Declared persona non grata	5/4/66
Tadeusz Wisniewski	Office of Polish Military Attaché	Declared persona non grata	5/20/66
Jiri Opatrny	Czech Embassy	Declared persona non grata	7/13/66
Karel Simunek	Czech Embassy	Declared persona non grata	10/27/71

Source: Federal Bureau of Investigation.

APPENDIX III

How Russia Distributes Its Men Abroad

	Number of Soviet Officials Assigned to Country[1]
Great Britain	550
France	431
Belgium	81
Holland	78
West Germany	200
Italy	84
Sweden	106
Norway	25
Denmark	30
Luxembourg	30
United States	1,092[2]

1. Does not include dependents.

2. In 1972, the figure in the United States rose to 1,166. Including wives and children, the total comes to 2,593. U.S. representation in the Soviet Union is 114.

Source: *London Daily Telegraph,* 1971.

APPENDIX IV

Text of United States Memorandum
To UN On Soviet Spies

Following is the text of a letter to Secretary General Hammarskjöld from Henry Cabot Lodge, United States representative to the UN, on Soviet spies apprehended in the United States:

Enclosed herewith is a memorandum giving detailed information on the illustrative list of Soviet espionage agents apprehended in the United States since the death of Marshal Stalin to which I referred in my statement in the Security Council on May 23.

I request that this memorandum be circulated as a Security Council document.

Sincerely yours,
HENRY CABOT LODGE

Memorandum

Comdr. Igor Aleksandrovich Amosov.
Amosov entered the United States Feb. 17, 1952, as assistant Soviet naval attaché. Amosov was the Soviet principal in an intelligence operation directed by the Soviets from their naval attaché's office. He served in this capacity from June 7, 1952 until his departure in February, 1954. Targets assigned by Amosov to the recruited agent included radar developments, details of the latest cargo ships, manuals reflecting details of the latest electronic developments and bombsight data. He paid this agent a total of $2,000 for his services. Amosov was declared *persona non grata* for these activities on Feb. 3, 1954, and left the United States on Feb. 7, 1954.

Col. Ivan Aleksandrovich Bubchikov.
Bubchikov entered the United States Dec. 1, 1954, as an assistant Soviet military attaché. From July, 1955, through May, 1956, Bubchikov maintained contact with a naturalized American citizen of Russian origin who was employed as a sales engineer. In July, 1955, he appeared at the sales engineer's residence late in the evening and sought his cooperation in securing data concerning jet fuel, atomic submarines, and aeronautical developments. Bubchikov offered the engineer large sums of money. In view of these activities the Department of State on June 14, 1956, declared Bubchikov *persona non grata* for engaging "in espionage activities incompatible with his continued presence in this country." He departed the United States June 24, 1956.

Maj. Yuri Pavlovich Krylov.
Krylov entered the United States May 4, 1955, as assistant Soviet military attaché, Washington, D.C. In August of 1955, Krylov contacted an employee of the Atomic Energy Commission and attempted to obtain from him information concerning the technical aspects of nuclear power. In 1957, Krylov was declared *persona non grata* for having improperly purchased quantities of electronic equipment through American intermediaries and having attempted to purchase classified military information. He departed the United States Jan. 26, 1957.

Nikolai Ivanovich Kurochkin.
Kurochkin entered the United States April 4, 1956, as a third secretary of the Soviet Embassy, Washington, D.C. In the fall of 1956 a professional writer contacted the Soviet Embassy seeking statistics as to hosiery production in the Soviet Union. He met Kurochkin, who supplied the desired statistical data and, after a series of meetings, informed the writer that if he would obtain military information, including training and field manuals of the United States Army, to be incorporated in articles Kurochkin was writing for Russian military journals, he would share with him his proceeds from the articles. The writer obtained unclassified training and field manuals of the United States Army, which he turned over to Kurochkin, but did not deliver the classified manuals which Kurochkin had requested. He was paid approximately $450. On June 6, 1958, Kurochkin was declared *persona non grata* for engaging in activities incompatible with his diplomatic status. He departed from the United States on June 11, 1958.

Vasily Mikhailovich Molev.
From August, 1944, through January, 1957, Molev served several tours of duty in the United States, occupying positions of chauffeur and property custodian to the Soviet consulate general in New York and property custodian at the Soviet Embassy, Washington, D.C. Boris Morros, an admitted Soviet agent cooperating with the FBI was instructed by his Soviet superiors to appear in the vicinity of 58 West Fifty-eighth Street, New York City, at 3 P.M. on the first Tuesday of each month for contact by his Soviet principal. If the contact was not made, Morros was instructed by the Soviets to return the following Wednesday and Thursday. On Wednesday, Jan. 7, 1953, special agents of the Federal Bureau of Investigation observed Molev in the vicinity of 58 West Fifty-eighth Street, New York City. Morros was later instructed by his Soviet principal to meet his Soviet contact on Tuesday, March 3, 1953, on the corner of Central Park South and Avenue of the Americas, New York City. On March 3, 1953, Molev was observed by special agents of the Federal Bureau of Investigation meeting with Morros at Central Park South and Avenue of the Americas. On this occasion Morros passed to Molev a report previously obtained from Jack Soble, Morros' immediate superior, who was subsequently convicted of espionage. On Jan. 25, 1957, Jack Soble, Myra Soble, and Jacob Albam were arrested on charges of

espionage and conspiracy. Simultaneously, Molev was declared *persona non grata* because of his implication in the conspiracy. He departed the United States Jan. 28, 1957.

Aleksandr Petrovich Kovalev.

Kovalev arrived in the United States Oct. 8, 1950, as a second secretary of the Soviet delegation to the United Nations. In the course of his stay in the United States Kovalev arranged to receive undeveloped microfilms of materials of intelligence significance at a drop area in New York City. The recruited agent was told to park his car in a designated area in New York City at a designated time and to place a package wrapped in red paper therein so that it could be seen through the rear window in the event material was to be passed. An additional signal by way of marking a telephone directory in a New York restaurant was perfected to indicate to the agent that the material delivered to the dead drop was picked up. Material of intelligence significance was left by the recruited agent in the New York dead drop area and it was retrieved by Kovalev. The agent was given $500 to purchase an electronic device for delivery to the Soviets, an additional $500 in payment for delivery of a microfilm reproduction of portions of a manual dealing with an automatic steering device for ships. Kovalev was declared *persona non grata* by the Department of State for his actions in this case on Feb. 3, 1954, and he departed the United States Feb. 10, 1954.

Col. Maksim Grigorievich Martynov.

Martynov entered the United States on Nov. 3, 1954, as a member of the Soviet Representation to the United Nations Military Staff Committee. In August, 1954, a Soviet national met a U.S. Army officer in Germany. The Soviet national, aware of the officer's plan to retire from the Army, asked him to be of assistance in obtaining military manuals from the Army Command and General Staff School at Leavenworth, Kansas, when the Soviet national came to the United States. Meetings in New York City were arranged and a code phrase was established for recognition purposes. On Nov. 15, 1954, a special agent of the Federal Bureau of Investigation, made up to resemble the Army officer, was contacted at the agreed time and place in New York City by Martynov. Prearranged signals were exchanged and they talked for approximately thirty minutes. Martynov indicated he was a friend of the Soviet national who contacted the officer in Germany and he asked for the proposed assistance, paying him $250. A subsequent meeting was scheduled for Jan. 15, 1955. On that date, Martynov kept the appointment and FBI agents accosted him. Martynov identified himself and claimed diplomatic immunity. On Feb. 21, 1955, the Department of State expelled Martynov for the above activity and he departed the United States Feb. 26, 1955.

Viktor Ivanovich Petrov.
Petrov arrived in the United States Feb. 17, 1953, as a translator employed at the United Nations Secretariat, New York City. Petrov responded to an advertisement placed in a New York newspaper by an aviation draftsman for part-time work. The draftsman was an employee of one of our largest aircraft factories. At the outset, Petrov gave the draftsman insignificant drafting work, later asking him to send for various brochures on aviation. Petrov requested the draftsman to obtain information concerning United States military aircraft. The information sought was classified. It concerned the status of United States aircraft development. On Aug. 20, 1956, information concerning Petrov's activities was brought to the attention of the Secretary General of the United Nations, as a result of which Petrov's employment at the United Nations was terminated. Petrov departed the United States on Aug. 23, 1956.

Capt. Boris Fedorovich Gladkov.
Gladkov entered the United States December, 1953, as naval adviser to the Soviet representation in the Military Staff Committee of the United Nations. Gladkov met a sales engineer for a New York City marine engineering firm at a cocktail party. He cultivated the sales engineer and held a number of clandestine meetings with him. Through the engineer, Gladkov attempted to obtain information relating to United States developments and progress in the field of marine engine design and operation and informed the American citizen that he, Gladkov, had access to funds of money for the purchase of sensitive and classified information on new developments in the field of design and operation of power plants on various types of naval craft. Gladkov also sought to obtain, and offered to pay a large sum of money for, publications dealing with fleet training. During his meetings with the sales engineer, which continued on a regular basis, Gladkov furnished the engineer $1,550. On June 22, 1956, the Department of State expelled Gladkov for engaging in activities which were incompatible with his status as a member of the Soviet delegation to the United Nations. He departed July 12, 1956.

Lieut. Col. Leonid Yegorovich Pivnev.
Pivnev entered the United States on March 17, 1950, as assistant Soviet air attaché. Pivnev endeavored to utilize a Washington businessman's address as a mail drop. He explained to the businessman that he would have mail delivered to him at the businessman's address, which mail was to be addressed to a fictitious person and which, upon receipt, was to be delivered by the businessman to him.

On March 24, 1954, he inquired at a Virginia aerial photographic concern as to the possibility of purchasing aerial maps of Chicago, Ill. He instructed the firm to seek such maps and agreed to pay approximately $8,000 for them. On that date he purchased thirty-three aerial photographs of Washington, D.C., and vicinity. Pivnev, in contacting

201

this firm, identified himself as "George." On May 3, 1954, he contacted a Washington, D.C., photographer, introducing himself as a Mr. George Tinney, a representative of a private firm desirous of purchasing aerial photographs of the New York City area at a scale of 1:20,000 to 1:40,000. Photographs of this type were not commercially available. On May 13, 1954, he agreed to pay the photographer $700 to obtain the photographs. He advanced on that date the sum of $400 as partial payment. On May 20, 1954, when meeting with the photographer for the purpose of obtaining the photographs, he was accosted by special agents of the Federal Bureau of Investigation, on which occasion he identified himself. On May 29, 1954, the Department of State declared Pivnev *persona non grata* and he departed June 6, 1954.

Vadim Aleksandrovich Kirilyuk.
Kirilyuk arrived in the United States Sept. 11, 1958, as a political affairs officer employed by the Department of Trusteeship and Information of Non-Self-Governing Territories, United Nations Secretariat. In April, 1959, an American citizen contacted a Soviet official in Mexico City concerning the possibility of obtaining a Soviet university scholarship. The Soviet official obtained complete background information from the American, including the facts concerning his previous assignment in cryptographic machines and systems while serving in the United States Army. Following his return to the United States, the American was contacted by Kirilyuk, who identified himself as one "George." During the period from June through September, 1959, Kirilyuk met with the American in a clandestine manner on five occasions. On these occasions he requested data concerning cryptographic machines and instructed the American to seek employment with a vital United States government agency. Information concerning Kirilyuk's activities was brought to the attention of the Secretary General of the United Nations, whereupon Kirilyuk's employment at the United Nations was terminated. Kirilyuk and his family left the United States on Jan. 10, 1960.

Source: *New York Times*, May 23, 1960.

APPENDIX V

How Soviet Intelligence Gets Rid of Its Enemies

Partial list of terrorist actions attributed to Soviet Intelligence services between 1926 and 1960

The Victim	The Crime	The Date	The Place
Ado Birk Estonian minister.	Kidnaping, in broad daylight by OGPU.	1926	Moscow
General Simon Petlura, leader of Ukrainian Nationalist movement.	Assassination	May 25, 1926	Paris
General Alexander Kutepov, president, White Russian Federation of War Victims.	Kidnaping	January 26, 1930	Paris
George Semmelman	Murder, by a Serbian Communist, Andrei Piklovich.	July 27, 1931	
Hans Wissengir	Murder	May 22, 1932	Hamburg
Valentin Markin, chief, OGPU, in U.S.	Murder	1934	New York City
General Yevgeny Miller, president, White Russian Federation of War Victims.	Kidnaping	1936	Paris

The Victim	The Crime	The Date	The Place
International Institute of Social History	Burglary of Trotsky Archives	November 7, 1936.	Paris
Dimitri Navachine	Murder. Killed on eve of trial of Gregory Piatakov in Moscow. Had publicly announced his intention to make exposé in Paris regarding the trial.	January 21, 1937.	Paris
Juliet Stuart Poyntz had been associated with Georg Mink, (*This Is My Story*, 1947) and Ben Gitlow, (*I Confess*, 1940).	Abduction or murder	End of May/June 1937	New York City
Ignace Reiss (also known as Hans Eberhart), a GRU agent who had defected.	Murder (Killing was carried out from Paris by a surveillance execution team consisting of Roland Abbia, Rena Steiner, Etienne Martignat, and Gertrude Schildbach.)	September 5, 1937	Lausanne, Switzerland
General Eugeniy Miller president, White Russian Federation of War Veterans.	Kidnaping	September 22, 1937	Paris
Henry Moulin French Communist.	Murder	1937	Spain
Andrew Nin leader of the Workers Party of Marxist Union (POUM), Spain.	Murder, found dead on a street in Madrid.	1937	Madrid

The Victim	The Crime	The Date	The Place
Kurt Landau Austrian refugee.	Kidnaping and murder	1937	Spain
José Robles ex-professor, Spanish literature, Johns Hopkins University.	Abduction or murder, disappeared without a trace.	1937	Valencia, Spain
Marc Rein son of Menshevik exile Raphael Ambramovich.	Abduction or murder	1937	Spain
Camillo Berneri anarchist.	Murder	1937	Barcelona, Spain
Hamilton Gold British citizen.	Abduction, forcibly repatriated to USSR from Barcelona.	1937	Spain
Walter Held and wife. Trotskyites arrested in transit.	Imprisonment, (while traveling in USSR from Sweden).	1937	USSR

The Victim	The Crime	The Date	The Place
George Arutiunov (also known as Agabekov).	Murder	March, 1938	Belgium
Lt. Col. Evhen Konovalec leader of Ukrainian Nationalist movement.	Murder, killed by explosion of parcel bomb.	May, 1938	Rotterdam, Holland
Jay Lovestone papers	Burglary	July 1, 1938	New York City
Rudolf Klement (also known as Walter).	Murder	July 13, 1938	Paris
Russell Blackwell U.S. citizen.	Abduction or murder, disappeared.	August, 1938	Barcelona
Robert Sheldon Harte Trotsky bodyguard.	Abduction and murder, abducted in first abortive coup against Trotsky's villa, by David A. Siqueiros; killing attributed to Louis and Leopoldo Arenal.	May 24, 1940	Mexico
Willi Muenzenberg	Murder	June, 1940	France
Leon Trotsky	Assassination, killed with an ice-ax by Jaime Ramon del Rio Hernandez Mercador.	August 20, 1940 Died Aug. 21, 1940.	Mexico
General Walter Krivitsky NKVD officer who defected from the Soviets.	Murder	1941	Washington, D.C.

The Victim	The Crime	The Date	The Place
The Kalmuk People	Genocide Tens of thousands of peaceful Kalmuks were forcibly abducted from lands they had occupied for three hundred years, herded into unheated cattle cars in freezing weather and carted off by Soviet secret police to death or oblivion.	December, 1943	Southern Russia
Carlo Tresca U.S. writer, anti-Communist, investigating Trotsky murder.	Murder shot.	1943	New York City
Clara Herskovits	Abduction, transported with other inmates from "liberated" Nazi concentration camp; sent to USSR for slave labor.	1945	Danzig
Chief Inspector Maref police official.	Abduction or murder	1948	Vienna
Dr. Karl Sondermann	Attempted abduction	Aug. 22, 1949	Vienna (British sector)
Paul Markgraf head of police, East Berlin.	Abduction or murder	October, 1949	Disappeared in Berlin, Eastern Zone
Georgi Tregubov emigré.	Kidnaping, lured to Berlin by Soviet agent, Elizabeth Randal.	September, 1947	West Berlin
Mrs. G. S. Okolovich	Attempted kidnaping	Summer, 1950	Munich

The Victim	The Crime	The Date	The Place
G. S. Okolovich	Attempted kidnaping (failed because Okolovich was warned and informed police authorities.)	June, 1951	Munich
Bohumil Lauschman	Kidnaping	1953	Salzburg
Dr. Alexander Trushnovich head of West Berlin Russian Rescue Committee.	Kidnaping	April 13, 1954	West Berlin
Mrs. Yanina Khokhlov wife of Nikolai Khokhlov, who refused to carry out orders to assassinate Okolovich.	Seized, held as hostage	June, 1954	Moscow
Valley Tremmel NTS member.	Kidnaping	June 20, 1954	Linz, Austria (American Zone)
Abdul Fatalipeyli chief of Azerbaydzhani desk of Radio Liberation.	Murder, killed by Soviet agent, Mikhail Ismailov.	November, 1954	Munich
Nicholas Fischer former Red Army second lieutenant, scheduled to give testimony against Soviet agent.	Murder	1955	
Karl Fricke anti-Communist journalist.	Kidnaping	April 1, 1955	West Berlin
Major Sylvester Murau defector from East German Communist Police.	Kidnaping	August 6, 1955	West Berlin

The Victim	The Crime	The Date	The Place
Lisa Stein, employee of USIA-operated West Berlin radio station, RIAS.	Attempted abduction and poisoning	1955	West Berlin
Dr. V. D. Poremsky, president of NTS.	Attempted assassination	Dec. 29, 1955	Frankfurt am Main
Six hundred people	Abduction	End of World War II to 1954	West Berlin
Robert Bialek, former inspector general of East German Communist Police.	Kidnaping	February 6, 1956	Berlin, British sector
Five Russian sailors the victims had been granted political asylum in the United States.	Abduction, forcible repatriation.	April 7, 1956	New York City
Lev Rebet, Ukrainian emigré leader.	Murder, murdered by Bogdan Stashynsky, KGB agent.	October 12, 1957	Munich
Stefan Bandera, emigré OUN leader.	Murder, murdered by Bogdan Stashynsky, KGB agent.	October 14, 1959	Munich

Source: "Murder International, Inc.," Hearing before the Internal Security Subcommittee, United States Senate, March 26, 1965. "Soviet Terrorism in Free Germany," Hearings before Internal Security Subcommittee, United States Senate, September 21, 1960.

A Glossary of Espionage Terms

APPARAT. An espionage ring or cell.

APPARATCHIK. A member of an apparat.

BUNDESNACHRICHTENDIENST (BND). National Intelligence service of the Federal Republic of Germany.

CENTER. The headquarters of the KGB and the GRU.

CHUZHOI. An agent who spies for money; a Russian term.

COBBLER. A passport forger.

COMINTERN. The Third International, founded by Lenin in 1918. Its members were the Communist parties of the world; it was officially dissolved by Stalin in 1943.

CPSU. The Communist party of the Soviet Union.

DEAD DROPS. Prearranged hidden locations, selected for depositing and picking up messages and money.

DUBOK. A dead drop; a Russian term.

GLAVNI VRAG. The main enemy; a Russian term.

GKNT. Soviet Committee for Science and Technology, an agency of the KGB.

GRU. Glavnoye Razvedyvatelnoye Upravlenie—Chief Intelligence Directorate of the General Staff of the Red Army—also referred to as the Fourth Bureau.

ILLEGAL. An espionage agent who comes into a country under the guise of a false identity.

KGB. Komitat Gosudarstvennoi Bezopastnosti—Committee for State Security of the Council of Ministers of the Soviet Union. The CIA and FBI of the Soviet Union, embodied in one agency.

LEGAL. An espionage agent who comes into a country using an official job as his cover.

LEGEND. False identity, which an agent builds up through forged documents and other means such as living under the name of the person whose identity is being assumed.

MICRODOTTING. The photographic technique of reducing a page of print to the size of a period.

MI5. Formerly the fifth section of the British Military Intelligence, in charge of counterespionage, now the Directorate of Security.

MI6. Formerly the sixth section of British Military Intelligence. now the Secret Service (SIS).

MFS. Ministry of State Security of the German Democratic People's Republic (GDR). The internal and external intelligence arm of East Germany.

NKVD. Narodniy Kommissariate Vnyutrennikh Dyel—People's Commissariat for Internal Affairs. Antedated the KGB, with essentially the same functions.

NTS. National Labor Council, an anti-Communist Russian *emigré* organization.

OUN. Organization of Ukrainian Nationalists, an anti-Communist Ukrainian *emigré* organization.

PAROL. Password; a Soviet espionage term.

SAFE HOUSE. A place for a spy to hide that is not believed to be under suspicion.

SHOE. Passport; a Soviet espionage term.

SIS. British Secret Intelligence Service, also known as MI6.

SOE. British Special Operations Executive. A World War II organization which conducted espionage, sabotage and propaganda operations in the German-occupied countries of Europe.

SUYAZNYIE. A courier; a Soviet espionage term.

TREFF. Secret meeting; a Soviet espionage term.

YAVKA. Safe house; a Soviet espionage term.

Bibliography

(A) Primary Sources

International Documentation Service: Soviet Spies in the Shadow of
the UN, 1959.

Royal Canadian Commission: Report. January, 1946.

U.S. Department of Justice: The Hollow Nickel Spy Case. August, 1960.

U.S. House of Representatives: UnAmerican Activities Committee. Patterns
of Communist Espionage, 1959.

U.S. Senate Internal Security Subcommittee: Hearings on the Institute of
Pacific Relations, 1952; Soviet Terrorism in Free Germany, 1960;
Communist Forgeries, June, 1960; Exposé of Soviet Espionage, 1960;
Murder International Inc., October, 1965; Testimony of Lawrence
Britt (pseud.), May, 1971.

(B) General Works

Bernikow, Louise. *Abel.* New York: Trident Press, 1970.

Bourke, Sean. *The Springing of George Blake.* New York: The Viking
Press, 1970.

Carpozi, George, Jr. *Red Spies in Washington.* New York: Trident Press, 1968.

Chambers, Whittaker. *The Witness.* New York: Random House, 1952.

Cookridge, E. H. *The Many Sides of George Blake, Esq.* London: Vertex, 1970.

Cookridge, E. H. *Gehlen—Spy of the Century.* New York: Random House, 1971.

Copp, DeWitt S. *Incident at Boris Gleb.* New York: Doubleday, 1968.

Craig, William. *The Fall of Japan.* New York: Dell Publishing Co., 1968.

Dallin, David. *Soviet Espionage.* New Haven: Yale University Press, 1955.

Deakin, F. W.; and Storry, G. R. *The Case of Richard Sorge.* New York:
Harper & Row, 1966.

de Gramont, Sanche. *The Secret War.* New York: G. P. Putnam's Sons, 1962.

de Toledano, Ralph. *The Greatest Plot in History.* New York: Arlington
House, 1963.

de Toledano, Ralph. *Spies, Dupes and Diplomats.* New York: Arlington
House, 1967.

Donovan, James. *Strangers on a Bridge.* New York: Atheneum, 1964.

Gehlen, Gen. Reinhard. *The Service.* New York: World Publishing, 1972.

Greg, Ian. *The Assault on the West.* London: Foreign Affairs Pub. Co., 1968.

Johnson, Chalmers. *An Instance of Treason.* Stanford: Stanford University
Press, 1964.

Kravchenko, Victor. *I Chose Freedom.* New York: Scribner's, 1947.

Kubeck, Anthony. *How the Far East Was Lost*. New York: Henry Regnery, 1963.

Lewis, Flora. *The Red Pawn*. New York: Doubleday & Company, 1965.

Massing, Hede. *This Deception*. New York: Duell Sloan & Pearce, 1951.

Meissner, Hans Otto. *The Man With Three Faces*. London: Evans Bros., Ltd., 1955.

Page, Leitch, Knightly. *The Philby Conspiracy*. New York: Doubleday & Company, 1968.

Philby, Harold Kim. *My Silent War*. New York: Grove Press, 1968.

Schellenberg, Walter. *The Labyrinth*. New York: Harper Bros., 1956.

West, Dame Rebecca. *The New Meaning of Treason*. New York: The Viking Press, 1964.

Wise, David; and Ross, Thomas B. *The Espionage Establishment*. New York: Random House, 1967.

Whiting, Charles. *Gehlen—Germany's Master Spy*. New York: Ballantine Books, 1972.

Willoughby, Maj. Gen. (Ret.) Charles A. *Shanghai Conspiracy*. New York: E. P. Dutton Co., 1952.

Footnotes

Chapter One

1. Allen Dulles, *The Craft of Intelligence,* (Harper & Row, 1963), p. 86.

Chapter Two

1. General Oshima was the Japanese military attaché.

Admiral Canaris was chief of the Abwehr (German Army Intelligence Service).

Von Ribbentrop was the German foreign minister.

2. He was executed in Germany in 1945 for war crimes committed in Poland.

3. F. W. Deakin and G. R. Storry, *The Case of Richard Sorge,* (Harper & Row, 1966), p. 197.

Chapter Three

1. The ore had to be obtained from the Katangan uranium mines in the Belgian Congo, the world's principal source at the time.

2. Not until 1946, with the passage of the Atomic Energy Act, was the FBI given the security assignments for the U.S. atomic installations.

3. Igor Gouzenko, *The Iron Curtain,* (E. P. Dutton, 1948), p. 263.

4. *Ibid.,* p. 220.

5. Kudriavtzev's career in the intelligence field spans nearly forty years of espionage activity. He served under various covers as journalist, diplomat, adviser. He was ambassador to Cuba during the period leading up to the 1962 missile crisis, then ambassador to Cambodia, and most recently, in 1971, the chief of the Soviet UNESCO delegation. He served in most Western capitals and at the UN. He is reported to answer directly to the CPSU's International Section, a step above the KGB and the GRU.

6. Igor Gouzenko, *The Iron Curtain,* (E. P. Dutton, 1948), p. 240.

7. *Ibid.,* p. 266.

8. *Ibid.,* p. 275.

Chapter Four

1. "The State Security Office responsible for kidnapping and murder and assassination until Stalin's death was known as *Spetsburo* No. 1. It was organized with the approval of the Central Committee of the Soviet Communist Party. At that time the Chief of the *Spetsburo* No. 1 was Lieutenant General Sudoplatov and his deputy was Major General Eitingon. After Stalin's death the Buro was reorganized. Before, it was strictly under the Chairman of State Security; then it was put under the Foreign Intelligence Directorate of State Security and known as the Ninth Department-Otdel-, and the boss in 1953 and 1954 was Colonel Studnikov. Nowadays this Department is known as No. 13, under the Foreign Intelligence Directorate of Soviet State Security." Testimony of Peter S. Deriabin, former KGB officer, March 26, 1965, Hearing of the Subcommittee on Internal Security.

2. In March, 1954, the MGB became the KGB—*Komitat Gosudarstvennoi Bezopastnosti*—Committee for State Security, pronounced *Kah Gay Beh.*

Chapter Five

1. All of the information on Rhodes's whereabouts in the United States and the activity of his family was incorrect.

2. In 1965, Soviet writer Vadim Kozhevnikov indicated that Abel's real

name was actually Alexander Ivanovich Belov. Belov, the Soviet source said, was born in 1903, educated as an engineer, active in intelligence (Abwehr) under the name of Johann Weiss.

3. Sergeant Rhodes was later tried and found guilty by an Army court martial, dishonorably discharged, and sentenced to five years at hard labor.

4. The agreement also included the following: the release of Frederic L. Pryor, a Yale student arrested for espionage in East Berlin in August, 1961, and a Russian pledge for the early release of a University of Pennsylvania student, Marvin Makinen, who had been serving an eight-year sentence on the same charge.

5. James Donovan, *Strangers on a Bridge,* (Atheneum, 1964), p. 420.

Chapter Six

1. Allen Dulles, *Great True Spy Stories,* (Harper & Row, 1968), p. 181.

2. E. H. Cookridge, *The Many Sides of George Blake, Esq.,* (Vertex, 1970), p. 43.

3. *Ibid.,* p. 96.

4. *Ibid.,* p. 101.

5. Philip Deane, *Captive in Korea,* (Hamish Hamilton, London, 1953).

6. E. H. Cookridge, *The Many Sides of George Blake, Esq.,* (Vertex, 1970), p. 113.

7. Sean Bourke, *The Springing of George Blake,* (Viking, 1970), p. 59.

8. *Ibid.,* p. 168.

9. *Ibid.,* p. 170.

10. *Ibid.,* p. 351.

Chapter Seven

1. DeWitt S. Copp, *Incident at Boris Gleb,* (Doubleday and Co., Inc., 1968).

2. Testimony of Lawrence Britt (pseudonym), Hearings—Senate Internal Security Subcommittee, May, 1971.

3. John Barron, "The Plot to Destroy Mexico," *Reader's Digest* (November, 1971).

Index

Y
Yamasaki Yoshiko, 52, 55, 60, 61
yavka, definition, 140
Yeshukin, L. Y., 182
Yugoslavia, 16, 25

Z
Zabotin, Nikolai, 64, 65, 66, 72, 73-74, 76, 81, 85, 86
Zaitsev, Victor S., 51
Zarubin, Georgi N., 85

PHOTO CREDITS